To Ray —

Valentine's Day . . .

— Martha

EMILY DICKINSON: SELECTED LETTERS

Emily Dickinson
Selected Letters

EDITED BY THOMAS H. JOHNSON

THE BELKNAP PRESS
OF HARVARD UNIVERSITY PRESS
CAMBRIDGE, MASSACHUSETTS
1971

PUBLISHER'S NOTE

In 1958 the Belknap Press of Harvard University Press published *The Letters of Emily Dickinson*, edited by Thomas H. Johnson with Theodora Ward as Associate Editor. This three-volume collection included every letter (and prose fragment) which at that time the poet was known to have written, all carefully and thoroughly annotated. Intended as a companion to the 1955 three-volume variorum edition of *The Poems of Emily Dickinson*, edited by Thomas H. Johnson, the new publication complemented its predecessor in both arrangement and appearance.

The *Letters* were hailed by reviewers, and scholars and students alike asked when we would publish a one-volume edition of Emily Dickinson's letters. Immediate compliance was not feasible, but we liked the idea and kept it alive — until finally the time seemed opportune.

We were fortunate that Thomas H. Johnson, the foremost modern authority on the Amherst poetess, agreed to undertake the task of compressing three volumes of some 1045 letters into a book containing the most meaningful and important letters plus a representative sampling of others — without losing the spirit of Emily Dickinson. He is not only responsible for the editions of the *Poems* and *Letters*, but also the author of *Emily Dickinson: An Interpretive Biography*, a 1955 Belknap Press publication. Friendly and sympathetic to the many, sometimes divergent, interpreters, friends, and champions of Emily Dickinson and her work, he richly deserves the tribute of Robert Hillyer (*New York Times Book Review*): "There is no greater achievement of editing and research in the field of American literature."

We are grateful to Tom Johnson for undertaking this most recent assignment and proud indeed to present the result.

CONTENTS

INTRODUCTION

James Russell Lowell, himself a letter writer of distinction, most admired in that literary form the letters of Gray, Cowper, Walpole, and Lamb. "I hold that a letter which is not mainly about the writer of it lacks the prime flavor. The wine must smack a little of the cask," he said to his friend Charles Eliot Norton.[1] "Letters, so it seems to me,/ Our careless quintessence should be," he wrote. By "careless" Lowell obviously does not mean *slack* or *heedless,* or even *unpremeditated.* He has in mind what writers in the early nineteenth century meant by *genial* when they used the word in the sense of innate; and such precisely is the wine that smacks of the cask. Lowell would certainly have added Keats to his list had enough letters of Keats been published at the time for Lowell to savor them. Perhaps he would have added Emily Dickinson.

The noteworthy characteristic of the Dickinson letters, like that of the poems, is acute sensitivity. Indeed, early in the 1860's, when Emily Dickinson seems to have first gained assurance of her destiny as a poet, the letters both in style and rhythm begin to take on qualities that are so nearly the quality of her poems as on occasion to leave the reader in doubt where the letter leaves off and the poem begins. Such intensity of feeling was a handicap that she bore as one who lives with a disability, and her friends must have increased the burden by often making her aware that they felt sympathy for a pathetic situation. It left her, as those who observed her knew, though they never so phrased it, emotionally naked. In all decency, she did not dare to appear in the drawing room when guests were present. "In all the circumference of Expression," she wrote in 1884, "those guileless words of Adam and Eve never were surpassed, 'I was afraid and hid Myself.'" But the disability need not be pitied, for she knew that though she could expect no deliverance from it, she could devise compensations, and her ability to do so vests her informal correspondence

[1] *New Letters* . . . , ed. Howe, New York (1932) IV, 278.

with a charm which time does not alloy. "How frugal is the Chariot/ That bears a Human soul!" The husbandry of those whose sensibilities threaten disaster must be austere. As she herself expressed the thought in 1863, renunciation is a piercing virtue.

Letter writing became a part of Emily Dickinson's life while she was still a child. Her need of contact with those she loved led her to set whole mornings or afternoons aside to pen with intimate sprightliness missives of considerable length. Such being true of her own capabilities, she expected in return, during her adolescent years, letters of equal sociability and endurance, and repeatedly bullies or cajoles those whose replies do not measure to her expectation or are delayed longer than she feels may be a reasonable period—perhaps a day or two. She was only eleven when she wrote the earliest surviving letter, in which she expresses herself with ease and charming felicity. But it is in the letter she wrote to Abiah Root in August 1845 that one sees the culmination of her development as a child. Now fourteen, she is natural, eager, interested in people, in her studies, the world about her, and in the development of her own new dimensions as a person. This realization she unconsciously discloses by saying: "I never enjoyed myself more than I have this summer."

Yet in the same year, and but a few weeks later, her next letter to Abiah reveals how her enthusiasm for school was regarded by her parents as a sign of overstimulation, for which a term of housekeeping instruction would be a salutary remedy. "Mother thinks me not able to confine myself to school this term. She had rather I would exercise. . ." The parents had good reason to watch for signs of excitability. They had found it necessary to send her away from home for a month in the previous year after Emily had been permitted to witness for a few moments, at her own insistence, the approaching death of young Sophia Holland, a girl of her own age, and the story of that experience as Emily recounted it to Abiah in March 1846 goes far to explain the nature of the child. Emily Dickinson's quest for the unknowable began at a very early age.

The fascination of genius is in its paradox. Emily Dickinson was still a child, and on occasion of course acted childishly, but she was equipped even now with a substantial vocabulary, and had no difficulty in filling what she rightly described as a "mammoth sheet" with her thoughts and feelings. Such are discernibly the lines of force which made her the woman and poet she became. She commented to Abiah in March 1847, in a context that looks back, and also forward to the Seminary she expects to enter in the fall: "I am always in love with my teachers." The expression has that quality of candor and accurate self-evaluation which gives stature to Emily Dickinson as a person and a poet. Throughout her life she turned for leadership to a "master." After 1862 Higginson stood in that relation to her, as all her letters to him make emphatically clear. It was her feeling, certainly in part, about Dr. Wadsworth, and perhaps about others now undiscoverable. But the need for a tutor or guide, who might conduct her in the manner Dante was led through the visions of a divine comedy, is the logical extension of all sentient being, and one especially needful to poets, who seek to translate mankind to greener pastures through the symbol of language. Emily Dickinson's quest for a guide she expressed with admirable forthrightness to Higginson in August 1862. Without reticence and with clear self-appraisal she said: "I had no Monarch in my life, and cannot rule myself, and when I try to organize – my little Force explodes – and leaves me bare and charred –"

The sensitivity was present from the beginning, but the poet was as yet unborn. Her susceptibility to atmosphere invigorates the letters written in the late 1840's by pointing up the contrast of those written from home and those she wrote upon arrival at South Hadley. Before she entered the Seminary she was still writing whimsically and dwelling upon recollection of past associations which she hopes a demand visit from Abiah Root or Jane Humphrey will recapture. But the simple, factual accounts she wrote of her life at Mount Holyoke tell the inevitable story of youthful maturity. The disciplines of a good institutional experience are timeless.

Homesickness increased as the year at Mount Holyoke advanced, and the strain within was one that both parents recognized, for her father decided not to send her back for a second year, or acceded to her wish to stay home. It was typical of the Dickinson family not to accept any separation, even when it was for the good of the absent member. Such a trait shows itself in the fact that when Austin went to law school he was on the end of a tether. Home affairs, the annual and cherished Cattle Show for instance, took precedence over his occupations elsewhere. He could be sent for at any time. With the independence characteristic of the Dickinsons, who paid little heed to other people's rules, Austin was late in arriving at Cambridge for his law school classes; though he was graduated with his class, he did not bother to be present to receive his diploma, choosing instead to accompany his mother, evidently at her request, to a reunion at Monson Academy. "I think we miss each other more every day that we grow older," Emily wrote her brother on 8 April 1853, "for we're all unlike most everyone, and are therefore more dependent on each other for delight." During the same month she commented to him on some visiting cousins: "The Newmans seem very pleasant, but they are not *like us*. What makes a few of us so different from others? It's a question I often ask myself." It is a question to which she had unconsciously supplied the answer likewise during the same month: "I wish we were children now. I wish we were *always* children, how to grow up I dont know." These were the years when she was signing her letters "Emilie." To grow up meant to leave the clan. The tie with the Norcross cousins, even in later years, gave an outlet to that side of her nature which persisted in the game of "little girlhood." "Did you know there had been a fire here," she wrote them on July fourth, 1879, "and that but for a whim of the wind Austin and Vinnie and Emily would have all been homeless? . . . Vinnie came soft as a moccasin, 'Don't be afraid, Emily, it is only the fourth of July.' I did not tell that I saw it, for I thought if she felt it best to deceive, it must be that it was."

The sense of being closely knit reveals itself also in the Dickinson habit of lampooning neighbors. Though the quotations are Emily's words, the spirit is that of the clan. "'Mrs Skeeter' [perhaps Mrs. Luke Sweetser] is very feeble," she wrote Austin in March 1852, "'cant bear Allopathic treatment, cant have Homeopathic' — dont want Hydropathic — Oh what a pickle she is in — should'nt think she would deign to *live* — it is so decidedly vulgar!" As she grew older, she became more expert as a satirist. "Libbie goes to Sunderland, Wednesday," she informed the Norcross cousins in October 1863, speaking of the redoubtable aunt Elizabeth, "for a minute or two; leaves here at 6 1/2 — what a fitting hour — and will breakfast the night before; such a smart atmosphere! The trees stand right up straight when they hear her boots, and will bear crockery wares instead of fruit, I fear. She hasn't starched the geraniums yet, but will have ample time, unless she leaves before April." On occasion the witticisms became sardonic, and, as her sister's are reported to have been, they are somewhat grim. In a letter written to the Norcrosses in the same month she remarks: "No one has called so far, but one old lady to look at a house. I directed her to the cemetery to spare expense of moving."

There came a time in Emily Dickinson's life, very near her thirtieth year, when she deliberately chose never willingly to leave her home again. The decision reflects itself clearly in the letters written after 1860. Before then they are enthusiastic, sometimes ardently sentimental, and usually long. Such is especially true of the letters written in the early fifties. She easily took fright about her friendships which, because of their importance to her, seemed hazardous. Her informality has charm during these years, but the protestations of affection and the repeated concern for Austin's health as well as for her own compel the reader to traverse arid stretches. The fantastic letters in the early part of 1850 lead to the speculation that this might have been the period when she commenced in earnest to write poetry. Benjamin Newton had left Amherst, but was not married. He had sent her Emerson's poems and she was writing to him. It was in 1858 that she began to assemble her poems into the small, thread-tied manuscript "volumes" or packets, and early in 1862 she felt enough assurance in her destiny to initiate her correspondence with T. W. Higginson.

During these latter years she underwent a profound emotional change, which the letters vividly reflect. Letters now became more important to her than they ever do to most people, since they were the sole means of escape from a self-elected incarceration. They enabled her to control the time and the plane of her relationships. The degree and nature of any intimacy was hers to choose. Henceforth the letters are composed with deliberation, each with the chosen recipient in mind, and it becomes clear that a letter written to Higginson, for instance, could never have been intended for Bowles or anyone else. The letters are briefer because the thought is tersely ordered. Many, if not most of them, were now written first in rough draft and then recopied. Such is especially true of those she wrote in later years, often with cordial intimacy, to correspondents like Mrs. Todd or Professor Chickering whom she never met. And after she came to accept Higginson's verdict in 1862 that her poetry was not for publication, they served as a conveyance for her poems. They literally became her "letter to the world."

Since Emily Dickinson's full maturity as a dedicated artist occurred during the span of the Civil War, the most convulsive era of the nation's history, one of course turns to the letters of 1861–1865, and the years that follow, for her interpretation of events. But the fact is that she did not live in history and held no view of it, past or current. Walt Whitman projected himself into the world about him so intensely that not only the war but the nation itself is continuously the substance of his thought in prose and verse. The reverse was true for Dickinson, to whom the war was an annoyance, a reality only when it was mirrored to her in casualty lists. Such evidently was true in some degree for all the Dickinsons, since Austin, when drafted, exercised his privilege of paying the five-hundred-dollar fee to arrange for a substitute. Emily wrote Mrs. Bowles in the summer of 1861: "I shall have no winter this year – on account of the soldiers – Since I cannot weave Blankets, or Boots – I thought it best to omit the season." Only once again does she make any general allusion to this mighty conflict, the repercussions of which are clearly audible even after the lapse of a century. "A Soldier called –," she wrote Bowles just a year later, "a Morning ago, and asked for a Nosegay, to take to Battle. I suppose he thought we kept an Aquarium."

The attitude of mind that could prompt such shallow facetiousness can be understood in the light of her personal intent in living. Years later, on the eve of the first election of President Cleveland, she made clear to Mrs. Holland the nature and extent of her concern with social history. "Before I write to you again, we shall have had a new Czar. Is the Sister a Patriot? 'George Washington was the Father of his Country' – 'George Who?' That sums all Politics to me." The rejection of society as such thus shows itself to have been total, not only physically but psychically. It was her kind of economy, a frugality she sought in order to make the most of her world; to focus, to come to grips with those universals which increasingly concerned her.

When Emily Dickinson made use of current news in her letters, and she often did so, she employed it as part of the metaphor of her speech. In thanking Theodore Holland for a sketch he sent her in the summer of 1884, she acknowledged it with the comment: "I approve the Paint – a study of the Soudan, I take it, but the Scripture assures us our Hearts are all Dongola." She has in mind that the fate of General Gordon, whose headquarters were at Dongola in the Soudan, was in the balance, and that no man can foretell his fate. She similarly employed quotations from scripture or from Shakespeare, not as embellishment but as pointed commentary on tense situations. Taken by themselves, the words from *Coriolanus* which constitute one note to Sue in 1876 seem quite meaningless: "Doth forget that ever he heard the name of Death." But if Sue put the words in context, as she was expected to do, they constitute a tender note of apology for one whose quick tongue sometimes betrayed her stalwart heart, an apology perhaps in this case for her sister Lavinia.

It is possible in the letters to discover something about the books and authors that gave the chiefest pleasure, and something too about the way poetry is written, but on the whole the comments are desultory, often cryptic, or enthusiastic. She told Higginson in her second letter to him that among poets she admired Keats and the Brownings, among prose writers Ruskin and Sir Thomas Browne. This does not go far, and omits Shakespeare, her truest master. She singles out the book of Revelation in the Bible, yet it is but one of many books from that great repository which was her constant source of inspiration, allusion, and quotation. Whitman, an innovator of the first order himself, she told Higginson that she had read nothing of, and the statement may have remained true throughout her life. In the early years, Emerson, the Brontës, and Dickens were favorites; later she avidly awaited the appearance of a new novel by George Eliot, but she evinced no marked interest in her other contemporaries. The striking originality, and on occasion profundity, of her own verse never reveals itself in the few critical assessments scattered through her letters.

It is for a quite different reason that the letters attain stature. They are the expression of her unique personality, and of a mind which could phrase the thought, "There is always one thing to be grateful for, – that one is one's self and not somebody else." Though she never wrote about herself after adolescence, the letters nevertheless are always self-portraits, written by one who has observed herself frankly and with no self-pity or regrets. Such indeed remains true whether the letter is penned to a child or an adult, to an intimate

xv

or a casual acquaintance. They validate another statement that, like the above, she made to Higginson, one which expresses the deliberateness with which she chose her way of living. When he asked her whether, not even seeing visitors, she felt sorry not to have something to do, she answered: "I never thought of conceiving that I could ever have the slightest approach to such a want in all future time." She paused and added: "I feel that I have not expressed myself strongly enough."

T.H.J.

THE PRESENT TEXT

The text of these selections derives from *The Letters of Emily Dickinson* (The Belknap Press of Harvard University Press, 1958). The youthful letters to friends and family members have been sparsely chosen, for they frequently are long and somewhat repetitive when gathered in sequence. Letters of the later years are included even when they are very brief and seemingly trivial acknowledgments of a small gift or favor. They often are memorable for the poetic sensitivity which characterizes Emily Dickinson's way of seeing things and expressing her ideas.

All autograph letters are presented in their verbatim form.

It is to be expected that autographs privately owned will change hands. Ownership is here ascribed as it was last known.

Names of recipients are given and indexed as Emily Dickinson knew them when she was writing to them. Abiah Root and Jane Humphrey, for instance, were married after the correspondence with them had come to an end. All letters were written in Amherst except those for which the headings specify a different location.

To avoid confusion and facilitate identification the letter numbers of the 1958 edition have been retained and are used in cross references. Manuscripts referred to as "Unpublished" were of course first published in the earlier three-volume edition.

SYMBOLS USED TO IDENTIFY MANUSCRIPTS

At the present time Dickinson autograph letters are located in about fourteen institutions. Some two score individuals are known to possess one autograph or more. Individuals are named in the list of acknowledgments and identified by last name in the notes of the text. Institutions likewise are named in full in the list and briefly identified in the notes. Certain symbols are used throughout.

AAS — The American Antiquarian Society, Worcester, Massachusetts.

AC — Amherst College Library. All autograph letters, and transcripts of autograph letters, at Amherst College are in the Millicent Todd Bingham Collection, except letters to the following persons, presented by other donors: Mrs. James S. Cooper, Mr. Kendall Emerson, Mrs. Richard H. Mather, Mrs. William Henry Prince, and Mrs. Edward Tuckerman.

BPL Higg — The Thomas Wentworth Higginson papers in the Galatea Collection, Boston Public Library.

HCL — Harvard College Library. HCL ARS (letters to Abiah Root Strong); HCL B (manuscripts which had special association for Martha Dickinson Bianchi); HCL E (letters to Henry Vaughan Emmons); HCL G (letters to John L. Graves); HCL H (letters to Dr. and Mrs. Josiah Gilbert Holland); HCL JH (letters to Jane Humphrey); HCL L (letters formerly in the possession of Lavinia Norcross Dickinson or Susan Gilbert Dickinson or their heirs)

NYPL — New York Public Library.

YUL — Yale University Library.

SYMBOLS USED TO IDENTIFY PUBLICATION

AB Ancestors' Brocades: The Literary Début of Emily Dickinson. By Millicent Todd Bingham. New York: Harper, 1945.

AM The Atlantic Monthly (1875 – current).

FF Emily Dickinson Face to Face: Unpublished Letters with Notes and Reminiscences. By Martha Dickinson Bianchi. Boston: Houghton Mifflin, 1932.

FN Emily Dickinson: Friend and Neighbor. By MacGregor Jenkins. Boston: Little, Brown, 1930.

Home Emily Dickinson's Home: Letters of Edward Dickinson and His Family, with documentation and comment. Edited by Millicent Todd Bingham. New York: Harper, 1955.

L (1894) *Letters of Emily Dickinson*. Edited by Mabel Loomis Todd. 2 vols. Boston: Roberts Brothers, 1894.

L (1931) *Letters of Emily Dickinson*. New and enlarged edition. Edited by Mabel Loomis Todd. New York: Harper, 1931.

LH *Emily Dickinson's Letters to Dr. and Mrs. Josiah Gilbert Holland*. Edited by Theodora Van Wagenen Ward. Cambridge: Harvard, 1951.

LL *The Life and Letters of Emily Dickinson*. By Martha Dickinson Bianchi. Boston: Houghton Mifflin, 1924.

NEQ *The New England Quarterly* (1927 – current).

Poems (1955) *The Poems of Emily Dickinson, Including variant readings critically compared with all known manuscripts*. Edited by Thomas H. Johnson. 3 vols. Cambridge: Harvard, 1955.

Revelation *Emily Dickinson: A Revelation*. Edited by Millicent Todd Bingham. New York: Harper, 1954.

I

1842–1846

" . . . the Hens lay finely . . ."

[1842–1846]

Emily Dickinson's twelfth year brought the first interruption to the close companionship in her home, when Austin was sent away to school for a single term. His father's first letter to him said: "I sent you there to improve," and one infers that family and neighbor associations were becoming distractions not good for his studies.

The record of enrollments at Amherst Academy in the forties gives a bewildering impression of casualness in the matter of school attendance, and may reflect a similar condition elsewhere. Emily herself was in and out of school, for reasons of health, several times during her adolescent years. Some of her friends were girls sent to Amherst from other towns, to live with relatives or board in the homes of schoolmates while in residence for a term or two. Only one among the group of five who were her special friends during these years was Amherst bred.

The letters of this earliest surviving group were written to her brother and to two school friends. Her mind was developing rapidly, but she was still in the immediate world of childhood when she wrote the letters with which the series begins.

To Austin Dickinson   *18 April 1842*

My dear Brother

    As Father was going to Northampton and thought of coming over to see you I thought I would improve the opportunity and write you a few lines – We miss you very much indeed you cannot think how odd it seems without you there was always such a Hurrah wherever you was I miss My bedfellow very much for it is rare that I can get any now for Aunt Elisabeth is afraid to sleep alone and Vinnie has to sleep with her but I have the privilege of looking under the bed every night which I improve as you may suppose the Hens get along nicely the chickens grow very fast I am afraid they will be so large that you cannot perceive them with the naked Eye when you get home the yellow hen is coming off with a brood of chickens we found a hens nest with four Eggs in it I took out three and brought them in the next day I went to see if there had been any laid and there had not been any laid and the one that was there had gone so I suppose a skonk had been there or else a hen In the shape of a skonk and I dont know which – the Hens lay finely William gets two a day at his house we 5 or 6 a day here there Is one Creeper that lays on the ground the nests are so high that they cannot reach them from the ground I Expect we shall have to make some ladders for them to get up on William found the hen and Rooster after you went away that you could not find we received your letter Friday morning and very glad we were to get it you must write oftener to us the temperance dinner went off very well the other day all the Folks Except Lavinia and I there were over a Hundred there the students thought the dinner too cheap the tickets were a half a dollar a piece and so they are going to have a supper tomorrow Evening which I suppose will be very genteel Mr Jones has found in looking at his policy that his insurance is 8 thousand dollars instead of 6 which makes him feel a great deal better than he did at first Mr Wilson and his wife took tea here the other night they are going to move wednesday – they have made out to get one of the Mt Pleasant Buildings to its place of distination which is a matter of great rejoicing to the public it was really was Enough to make ones Eyes ache and I am glad it has got out of sight and hearing too— there are going to be great fixing up I expect in those buildings we are all very well and hope you are the same—we have very pleasant weather now Mr Whipple has come and we expect Miss Humphrey tomorrow—Aunt Montague—has been saying you would cry before the week was out Cousin Zebina had a fit the other day and bit his tongue into—as you say it is a rainy day and I can think of—Nothing more to say—I shall Expect an answer to my letter soon Charles Richardson has got back and is in Mr Pitkins store Sabra is not running after him at all she had not seen him when I last saw her which was Saturday I suppose she would send her *respects to you* if *she knew I was going to write* to you—I *must now close*—all send a great deal of love to you and hope you are getting along well and—Enjoy your self—

Your affectionate Sister Emily—

MANUSCRIPT: HCL (L 53). Ink. Unpublished. Addressed on the fold: Wm Austin Dickinson/Easthampton/Mass. On the date line she wrote "Amherst," and her aunt Elizabeth Dickinson added: "Mass. April 18th 1842."

A few days before his thirteenth birthday, Austin was sent to Williston Seminary, newly opened as an endowed institution at Easthampton, to attend the spring term. His father wrote to him a few days after his enrollment, and followed his letter with a visit, carrying Emily's letter with him. Sabra was the daughter of A. P. Howe, landlord of the Amherst House.

3

To Jane Humphrey   *12 May 1842*

My dear Jane

I have been looking for a letter from you this long time but not receiving any I plucked up all the remaining courage that I had left and determined to make one more effort to write you a few lines—I want to see you very much for I have got a great deal to tell you about school matters—and besides you are one of my dear friends. Sabra has had a beautiful ring given to her by Charles you know who as well as I do – the Examination at Easthampton is today – and Austin is coming home tonight. Father is sick with the Rheumatism and can not go but Mother has gone with somebody else – it is very unpleasant today – it showers most all the time – your sister is very well indeed – I believe she has gone to South hadley this afternoon – I miss you more and more every day, in my study in play at home indeed every where I miss my beloved Jane – I wish you would write to me – I should think more of it than of a mine of gold – when you write me I wish you would write me a great long letter and tell me all the news that you know of – all your friends send a great deal of love to you Austin and William Washburn send their respects to you – this Afternoon is Wednesday and so of course there was Speaking and Composition – there was one young man who read a Composition the Subject was think twice before you speak – he was describing the reasons why any one should do so – one was – if a young gentleman – offered a young lady his arm and he had a dog who had no tail and he boarded at the tavern think twice before you speak. Another is if a young gentleman knows a young lady who he thinks nature has formed to perfection let him remember that roses conceal thorns he is the sillyest creature that ever lived I think. I told him that I thought he had better think twice before he spoke – what good times we used to have jumping into bed when you slept with me. I do wish you would come to Amherst and make me a great long visit – how do you get along in Latin. I am in the class that you used to be in in Latin – besides Latin I study History and Botany I like the school very much indeed – your Sister sends a great deal of love to all your folks and to every one she knows there – My Plants grow beautifully – you know that elegant old Rooster that Austin thought so much of – the others fight him and killed him – answer this letter as soon as you can – I can think of nothing more to say now yours affectionately

Emily

MANUSCRIPT: Rosenbach 1170/17 (1). Ink. Dated: Amherst May 12 1842. Addressed on the fold: Miss Jane Humphrey/Southwick/Mass. Postmarked: Amherst Ms May 12. Written in pencil, in a different hand, is the draft of the beginning of a letter – possibly Jane's reply: "My very dear Friend/I Know you are thinking of m[e] (if thinking of me at all) as a very neg[ligent] . . ."

PUBLICATION: George Frisbie Whicher, *This Was a Poet* (1938) 43–44, in part.

Jane Humphrey had lived with the Dickinsons while she briefly attended Amherst Academy. Sabra Howe, William Washburn, and Charles Richardson were school friends. Jane's sister Helen Humphrey, was one of ED's teachers, and another sister, Mary, was a student at the Academy.

4

To Austin Dickinson   *autumn 1844*

Dear brother Austin

As Mr Baker was going directly to where you are I thought I would write a line to inform you that if it is pleasant day after tomorrow we are all coming over to see you, but you must not think too much of our coming as it may rain and spoil all our plans. however if it is not pleasant so that we do not come over father says that you may come home on Saturday, and if we do not come he will make some arrangement for you to come and write you about it.

I attend singing school. Mr Woodman has a very fine one Sunday evenings and has quite a large school. I presume you will want to go when you return home. We had a very severe frost here last night and the ground was frozen — hard. We all had our noses nipped a little. the Ladys Society meets at our house tomorrow and I expect we shall have a very pleasant meeting. If you was at home it would be perfectly sure. We wish much to hear from you, and if you have time I wish you would write a line and send by Mr Baker. Mother wishes if your stockings are any of them thin, that you should do them up in a little bundle & send them by Mr Baker. Accept much love from us all.

Your affectionate sister E

If we dont come Wednesday we may Thursday if not father will write you.

MANUSCRIPT: AC. Pencil. Dated: Monday. A.M. Addressed on the fold: William A. Dickinson, per Mr Baker.

PUBLICATION: *Home* 66–67.

Austin was a student in the Classical Department of Williston Seminary for the term ending 10 August 1842, and for the year 1844–1845. This letter was probably written in the autumn of 1844, when the early appearance of frozen ground would draw comment. Mrs. Bingham's speculation seems reasonable: "'Mr. Baker,' the bearer of the note, may have been the prosperous farmer Alfred Baker, or his brother Osmyn, a well-known lawyer who moved his office from Amherst to Northampton in 1844" (*Home* 66).

13

To Abiah Root   *Boston, 8 September 1846*

My dear friend Abiah.

It is a long – long time since I received your welcome letter & it becomes me to sue for forgiveness, which I am sure your affectionate heart will not refuse to grant. But many & unforeseen circumstances have caused my long delay. My health was very poor all the latter part of spring & continued so through the summer. As you may have heard, Dear Miss Adams is teaching in Amherst & I was very anxious to attend the Academy last term on that account & did go for 11 weeks, at the close of which I was so unwell as to be obliged to leave school. It cost me many a severe struggle to leave my studies & to be considered an invalid, but my health demanded a release from all care & I made the sacrifice. I had a severe cough for several weeks attended with a difficulty in my throat & general debility. I left school & did nothing for some time excepting to ride & roam in the fields. I have now entirely got rid of my cough & all other bad feelings & am quite well & strong. My health affected my spirits & I was quite down spirited for some time, but have with renewed health regained my usual flow of spirits. Father & Mother thought a journey would be of service to me & accordingly, I left for Boston week before last. I had a delightful ride in the cars & am now quietly settled down, if there can be such a state in the city. I am visiting in my aunt's family & am happy. Happy! Did I say? No not happy, but contented. I have been here a fortnight to day & in that time I have both seen & heard a great many wonderful things. Perhaps you might like to know how I have spent the time here. I have been to Mount Auburn, to the Chinese Museum, to

[7]

Bunker hill. I have attended 2 concerts, & 1 Horticultural exhibition. I have been upon the top of the State house & almost everywhere that you can imagine. Have you ever been to Mount Auburn? If not you can form but slight conception – of the "City of the dead." It seems as if Nature had formed the spot with a distinct idea in view of its being a resting place for her children, where wearied & dissappointed they might stretch themselves beneath the spreading cypress & close their eyes "calmly as to a nights repose or flowers at set of sun."

The Chinese Museum is a great curiosity. There are an endless variety of Wax figures made to resemble the Chinese & dressed in their costume. Also articles of chinese manufacture of an innumerable variety deck the rooms. Two of the Chinese go with this exhibition. One of them is a Professor of music in China & the other is teacher of a writing school at home. They were both wealthy & not obliged to labor but they were also Opium Eaters & fearing to continue the practice lest it destroyed their lives yet unable to break the "rigid chain of habit" in their own land They left their family's & came to this country. They have now entirely overcome the practice. There is something peculiarly interesting to me in their self *denial*. The Musician played upon two of his instruments & accompanied them with his voice. It needed great command over my risible faculty to enable me to keep sober as this amateur was performing, yet he was so very polite to give us some of his native music that we could not do otherwise than to express ourselves highly edified with his performances. The Writing Master is constantly occupied in writing the names of visitors who request it upon cards in the Chinese language – for which he charges 12½ cts. apiece. He never fails to give his card besides to the person[s] who wish it. I obtained one of his cards for Viny & myself & I consider them very precious. Are you still in Norwich & attending to music. I am not now taking lessons but I expect to when I return home.

Does it seem as though September had come? How swiftly summer has fled & what report has it borne to heaven of misspent time & wasted hours? Eternity only will answer. The ceaseless flight of the seasons is to me a very solemn thought, & yet Why do we not strive to make a better improvement of them?

With how much emphasis the poet has said, "We take no note of Time, but from its loss. T'were wise in man to give it then a tongue. Pay no moment but in just purchase of it's worth & what it's worth,

ask death beds. They can tell. Part with it as with life reluctantly."
Then we have higher authority than that of man for the improvement of our time. For God has said. "Work while the day lasts for
the night is coming in the which no man can work." Let us strive
together to part with time more reluctantly, to watch the pinions of
the fleeting moment until they are dim in the distance & the new
coming moment claims our attention. I am not unconcerned Dear A.
upon the all important subject, to which you have so frequently & so
affectionately called my attention in your letters. But I feel that I have
not yet made my peace with God. I am still a s[tran]ger – to the delightful emotions which fill your heart. I have perfect confidence in
God & his promises & yet I know not why, I feel that the world holds
a predominant place in my affections. I do not feel that I could give
up all for Christ, were I called to die. Pray for me Dear A. that I may
yet enter into the kingdom, that there may be room left for me in the
shining courts above. Why do you not come to Amherst? I long to
see you once more, to clasp you in my arms & to tell you of many
things which have transpired since we parted. Do come & make me a
long – long, visit this autumn. Will you not? There have been many
changes in Amherst since you was there. Many who were then in their
bloom have gone to their last account & "the mourners go about the
streets." Abby was in Athol when I left home on a visit to her mother
& brothers. She is very well & as lovely as ever. She will write you
soon. Abby & I talk much of the happy hours we used to spend together with yourself, Sarah & Hatty Merrill. Oh! what would I give
could we all meet again. Do write me soon Dear A & let it be a long –
long letter. Dont forget – ! ! ! ! !

Your aff. friend

Emily E. D.

Sabra Palmer was well the last time I saw her & she talked of going
to Feeding Hills. She may be there now for ought I know. Do you not
think it has been unusually hot the past summer. I have really suffered from the heat the last week. I think it remarkable that we should
have such weather in September. There were over 100 deaths in Boston
last week, a great many of them owing to the heat. Mr Taylor, Our
old Teacher, was in Amherst at Commencement time. Oh! I do love
Mr. Taylor. It seemed so like old times to meet Miss Adams & Mr

Taylor again. I could hardly refrain from singing Auld Lang Syne. It seemed so very apropos. Have you forgotten the memorable ride we all took with Mr Taylor, "Long, Long, ago."

I hear from Sarah Tracy quite often, but as to Hatty I will not ask you if you ever hear from her for it would oblige you to leave room in your next letter, to say. No, not a word. Sarah writes in very good spirits & I think she is very happy. I am so glad to think Sarah has so good a home & kind friends for she is every way worthy of them. How glad I should be to find you in A. when I return home. Dont you recollect it was the day I returned from Boston before that I first met you & introduced myself so unceremoniously?

Have you any flowers in Norwich? My garden looked finely when I left home. It is in Viny's care during my absence. Austin entered college last Commencement. Only think!!!!!! I have a brother who has the honor to be a Freshman – Will you not promise me that you will come to Commencement when he graduates? Do! Please! Viny told me if I wrote you while I was gone to give her best love to you. I have altered very much since you was here. I am now very tall & wear long dresses near[l]y. Do you beleive we shall know each other when we meet. Dont forget to write soon.

E.

MANUSCRIPT: HCL (ARS 4). Ink. Dated: Boston. Sep. 8. 1846. Addressed on the fold: Miss Abiah P. Root/Care of D. B. Tucker Esq/Norwich/Connecticut [readdressed and forwarded to: Feeding Hills/Springfield/Mass]. Postmarked: Boston Sep 10 5 cts [and] Norwich Ct. Sep 14.

PUBLISHED: L (1894) 20–23, in part; LL 120, in small part; L (1931), 16–19, in part.

The quotation from Young's *Night Thoughts* must have been from memory:

> We take no note of time
> But from its loss: to give it then a tongue
> Is wise in man.
> *Night* I, lines 54–56

II

1847–1848

"I am really at Mt Holyoke . . ."

[1 8 4 7 – 1 8 4 8]

When Emily Dickinson wrote to Abiah Root in 1846 of her happiness in the prospect of going to Mount Holyoke, she did so with the eagerness of a girl whose growth demands wider opportunities. The Seminary proved to be all that she expected, and she had no difficulties adjusting to her studies or to her newfound friends. In spite of a bronchial ailment which enforced a long absence, she completed the courses for the year satisfactorily. But, as the weeks advanced, her spirit grew less settled. The religious atmosphere of all such institutions at that time was heavily charged, and Emily was oppressed by it. Her tie to her home was strengthened rather than loosened by her absence. She returned happily to Amherst in August 1848, her formal education at an end, leaving her only record of the year in the letters she wrote to Austin and to Abiah Root while she was at South Hadley.

To Austin Dickinson   *South Hadley, 21 October 1847*

My dear Brother. Austin.

    I have not really a moment of time in which to write you & am taking time from "silent study hours," but I am determined not to break my promise again & I generally carry my resolutions into effect. I watched you until you were out of sight Saturday evening & then went to my room & looked over my treasures & surely no miser ever counted his heaps of gold, with more satisfaction than I gazed upon the presents from home.

    The cake, gingerbread, pie, & peaches are all devoured, but the – apples – chestnuts & grapes still remain & will I hope for some time. You may laugh if you want to, in view of the little time in which so many of the good things have dissappeared but you must recollect that there are *two* instead of *one* to be fed & we have keen appetites over here. I cant tell you now how much good your visit did me. My cough is almost gone & my spirits have wonderfully lightened since then. I had a great mind to be homesick after you went home, but I concluded not to, & therefore gave up all homesick feelings. Was not that a wise determination? How have you all been at home since last week? I suppose nothing of serious importance has occurred, or I should have heard of it, before this time. I received a long letter from Mary. Warner, last evening & if you see her, please give my love to her & tell her I will answer it the first moment, I have to spare from school. By the way, there has been a Menagerie, here this week. Miss. Lyon. provided, "Daddy Hawks" as a *beau,* for all the Seminary girls, who wished to see the *bears* & monkeys, & your sister not caring to go, was obliged to decline the gallantry of said gentleman, which I fear I may never have another opportunity to avail myself of. The whole company stopped in front of the Seminary & played for about a quarter of an hour, for the purpose of getting custom in the afternoon I opine. Almost all the girls went & I enjoyed the solitude finely.

    I want to know when you are coming to see me again, for I wish to see you as much as I did before. I went to see Miss Fiske. in her room yesterday & she read me, her letter from Sam & a right merry letter it was too. It sounded like him for all the world. I love Miss. Fiske. very much & think I shall love all the teachers, when I become better acquainted with them & find out their ways, which I can assure you are almost "past finding out." I had almost forgotten to tell you of a dream which I dreamed, last night & I would like to have you turn Daniel & interpret it to me, or if you dont care about going through all the perils which he did I will allow you to interpret it without, provided you will try to tell no lies about it. Well, I dreamed a dream & Lo!!! Father had failed & mother said that "our rye field which she & I planted, was mortgaged to Seth Nims." I hope it is not true but do write soon & tell me for you know "I should expire with mortification" to have our rye field mortgaged, to say nothing of it's falling into the merciless hands of a loco!!! Wont you please to tell me when you answer my letter who the candidate for President is? I have been trying to find out ever since I came here & have not yet succeeded. I dont know anything more about affairs in the world, than if I was in a trance, & you must imagine with all your "Sophomoric discernment," that it is but little & very faint. Has the Mexican war terminated yet & how? Are we beat? Do you know of any nation about to besiege South Hadley? If so, do inform me of it, for I would be glad of a chance to escape, if we are to be stormed. I suppose Miss Lyon. would furnish us all with daggers & order us to fight for our lives, in case such perils should befall us.

Tell mother, that she was very thoughtful to inquire in regard to the welfare of my shoes. Emily has a shoe brush & plenty of blacking, & I brush my shoes to my heart's content. Thank Viny 10,000. times for the beautiful ribbon & tell her to write me soon. Tell father I thank him for his letter & will try to follow its precepts. Do excuse the writing for I am in furious haste & cant write another word.

Your aff. Emily

Give much love to Father, mother, Viny, Abby, Mary, Deacon Haskell's family & all the good folks at home, whom I care anything about. I shall write Abby & Mary very soon. Do write me a long letter soon & answer all my questions, that is if you can read them. Come & see me as often as you can & bring a good load every time.

Miss Fiske. told me if I was writing to Amherst to send her love.

Not specifying to whom, you may deal it out, as your good sense & discretion prompt.

Be a good boy & mind me.

MANUSCRIPT: AC. Ink. Dated: Thursday noon. Addressed on the fold: Austin Dickinson, Esq./Amherst./Mass. Postmarked: South Hadley Mass. Oct 22.

PUBLICATION: L (1894) 65–67, in part; L (1931) 63–65, in part; *Home* 68–70, entire.

For Mary Lyon (1797–1849), founder and principal of the Seminary, this was the last full year of teaching. Her associate principal was Mary C. Whitman. Of the nine other teachers, only one is here mentioned, Rebecca W. Fiske, a recent Seminary graduate whose brother Sam was at the time a junior at Amherst College. Mary Warner and Abby Wood were Amherst friends with whom ED had grown up. The Emily who is mentioned as having the shoebrush was ED's cousin from Monson, Emily Lavinia Norcross, a senior and her roommate. ED had now been at the Seminary for three weeks.

The term "loco-foco," originally applied to any antimonopolistic wing of New York City Democrats (1835), was now used by the Whigs to describe any Democrat, and Democrats in the judgment of the Dickinsons were persons who would bear watching. Seth Nims, a Democrat, was the Amherst postmaster during the presidencies of Polk (1845–1849), Pierce, and Buchanan (1853–1861). The same tone about Nims is evident in a letter which Lavinia wrote to her brother in 1853 (*Home* 318): "Mr Nims is making awful blunders in the post office. I hope he'll be requested to retire."

18

To Abiah Root   *South Hadley, 6 November 1847*

My dear Abiah.

I am really at Mt Holyoke Seminary & this is to be my home for a long year. Your affectionate letter was joyfully received & I wish that this might make you as happy as your's did me. It has been nearly six weeks since I left home & that is a longer time, than I was ever away from home before now. I was very homesick for a few days & it seemed to me I could not live here. But I am now contented & quite happy, if I can be happy when absent from my dear home & friends. You may laugh at the idea, that I cannot be happy when away from home, but you must remember that I have a very dear home & that this is my first trial in the way of absence for any length of time in my life. As you desire it, I will give you a full account of myself since I first left the paternal roof. I came to S. Hadley six weeks ago next Thursday. I was much fatigued with the ride & had a severe cold besides, which prevented me from commencing my examinations until the next day, when I began.

I finished them in three days & found them about what I had anticipated, though the old scholars say they are more strict than they ever have been before. As you can easily imagine, I was much delighted to finish without failures & I came to the conclusion then, that I should not be at all homesick, but the reaction left me as homesick a girl as it is not usual to see. I am now quite contented & am very much occupied now in reviewing the Junior studies, as I wish to enter the middle class. The school is very large & though quite a number have left, on account of finding the examinations more difficult than they anticipated, yet there are nearly 300. now. Perhaps you know that Miss. Lyon is raising her standard of scholarship a good deal, on account of the number of applicants this year & on account of that she makes the examinations more severe than usual.

You cannot imagine how trying they are, because if we cannot go through them all in a specified time, we are sent home. I cannot be too thankful that I got through as soon as I did, & I am sure that I never would endure the suspense which I endured during those three days again for all the treasures of the world.

I room with my Cousin Emily, who is a Senior. She is an excellent room-mate & does all in her power to make me happy. You can imagine how pleasant a good room-mate is, for you have been away to school so much. Everything is pleasant & happy here & I think I could be no happier at any other school away from home. Things seem much more like home than I anticipated & the teachers are all very kind & affectionate to us. They call on us frequently & urge us to return their calls & when we do, we always receive a cordial welcome from them.

I will tell you my order of time for the day, as you were so kind as to give me your's. At 6. oclock, we all rise. We breakfast at 7. Our study hours begin at 8. At 9. we all meet in Seminary Hall, for devotions. At 10¼. I recite a review of Ancient History, in connection with which we read Goldsmith & Grimshaw. At .11. I recite a lesson in "Pope's Essay on Man" which is merely transposition. At .12. I practice Calisthenics & at 12¼ read until dinner, which is at 12½ & after dinner, from 1½ until 2 I sing in Seminary Hall. From 2¾ until 3¾. I practise upon the Piano. At 3¾ I go to Sections, where we give in all our accounts for the day, including, Absence — Tardiness — Communications — Breaking Silent Study hours — Receiving Company in our rooms & ten thousand other things, which I will not take time or place to mention. At 4½. we go into Seminary Hall, & receive advice from Miss. Lyon in the form of a lecture. We have Supper at 6. & silent-study hours from then until the retiring bell, which rings at 8¾, but the tardy bell does not ring until 9¾, so that we dont often obey the first warning to retire.

Unless we have a good & reasonable excuse for failure upon any of the items, that I mentioned above, they are recorded & a *black mark* stands against our names: As you can easily imagine, we do not like very well to get "exceptions" as they are called scientifically here. My domestic work is not difficult & consists in carrying the Knives from the 1st tier of tables at morning & noon & at night washing & wiping the same quantity of Knives. I am quite well & hope to be able to spend the year here, free from sickness. You have probably heard many reports of the food here & if so I can tell you, that I have yet seen nothing corresponding to my ideas on that point from what I have heard. Everything is wholesome & abundant & much nicer than I should imagine could be provided for almost 300. girls. We have also a great variety upon out tables & frequent changes. One thing is certain & that is, that Miss. Lyon & all the teachers, seem to consult our comfort & happiness in everything they do & you know that is pleasant. When I left home, I did not think I should find a companion or a dear friend in all the multitude. I expected to find rough & uncultivated manners, & to be sure, I have found some of that stamp, but on the whole, there is an ease & grace a desire to make one another happy, which delights & at the same time, surprises me very much. I find no Abby. or Abiah. or Mary, but I love many of the girls. Austin came to see me when I had been here about two weeks & brought Viny & Abby. I need not tell you how delighted I was to see them all, nor how happy it made me to hear them say that "they were *so lonely*." It is a sweet feeling to know that you are missed & that your memory is precious at home.

This week, on Wednesday, I was at my window, when I happened to look towards the hotel & saw Father & Mother, walking over here as dignified as you please. I need not tell you that I danced & clapped my hands, & flew to meet them for you can imagine how I felt. I will only ask you do you love your parents? They wanted to surprise me & for that reason did not let me know they were coming. I could not bear to have them go, but go they must & so I submitted in sadness. Only to think Abiah, that in 2½ weeks I shall be at my *own dear home* again. You will probably go home at Thanksgiving time & we can rejoice with each other.

You dont [know] how I laughed at your description of your introduction to Daniel Webster & I read that part of your letter to Cousin. Emily. You must feel quite proud of the acquaintance & will not I hope be vain in consequence. However you dont know Govr Briggs & I do, so you are no better off than I. I hear frequently from Abby & it is a great pleasure to receive her letters. Last eve, I had a long & very precious letter from her & she spoke of see^g a letter from you. You probably have heard of the death of *O. Coleman.* How melancholy!! Eliza. had written me a long letter giving me an account of her death, which is beautiful & affecting & which you shall see when we *meet again.*

Abiah, you must write me often & I shall write you as often as I have time. But you know I have many letters to write now I am away from home. Cousin. Emily says "Give my love to Abiah."

From your aff
Emily E. D—

MANUSCRIPT: Mount Holyoke College. Ink. Dated: Mt Holyoke. Seminary. Novr 6. 1847.

PUBLICATION: L (1894) 27–31, in part; LL 124–127, in part: *Mt. Holyoke Alumnae Quarterly* IX (1926), 153–155, entire; L (1931) 24–28, in part.

Edward Dickinson was a member of the executive council (1846–1847) of Governor George N. Briggs; both Briggs and his wife had been overnight guests in the Dickinson home. Olivia Coleman, the older sister of ED's friend Eliza, died at Princeton, New Jersey, on September 28, two days before ED had left Amherst for South Hadley. Her father Lyman Coleman, currently teaching at the College of New Jersey (Princeton), had been principal of Amherst Academy (1844–1846) when ED was a student there.

To Austin Dickinson   *South Hadley, 17 February 1848*

My dear Austin.

   You will perhaps imagine from my date, that I am quite at leisure & can do what I please even in the forenoon, but one of our teachers, who is engaged, received a visit from her intended, quite unexpectedly yesterday afternoon & she has gone to her home to show him I opine & will be absent until Saturday. As I happen to recite to her in one of my studies, her absence gives me a little time in which to write. Your *welcome* letter found me all engrossed in the history of Sulphuric Acid!!!!! I deliberated for a few moments after it's reception on the propriety of carrying it to Miss. Whitman, your friend. The result of my deliberation was a conclusion to open it with moderation, peruse it's contents with sobriety becoming my station, & if after a close investigation of it's contents I found nothing which savored of rebellion or an unsubdued will, I would lay it away in my folio & forget I had ever received it. Are you not gratified that I am so rapidly gaining correct ideas of female propriety & sedate deportment? After the proposed examination, finding it concealed no dangerous sentiments I with great gravity deposited it with my other letters & the impression that I once had such a letter is entirely obliterated by the waves of time. I have been quite lonely since I came back, but cheered by the thought that I am not to return another year I take comfort & still hope on. My visit at home was happy, very happy to me & had the idea of in so short a time returning, been constantly in my dreams, by night & day I could not have been happier. "There is no rose without a thorn" to me. Home was always dear to me & dearer still the friends around it, but never did it seem so dear as now. All, all are kind to me but their tones fall strangely on my ear & their countenances meet mine not like home faces, I can assure you, most sincerely. Then when tempted to feel sad, I think of the blazing fire, & the cheerful meal & the chair empty now I am gone. I can hear the cheerful voices & the merry laugh & a desolate feeling comes home to my heart, to think I am alone. But my good angel only waits to see the tears coming & then whispers, only this year!! Only 22. weeks more & home again you will be to stay. To you, all busy & excited, I suppose the time flies faster, but to me slowly, very slowly so that I can see his chariot wheels when they roll along & himself is often visible. But I will no longer imagine, for your brain is full of Arabian Nights fancies & it will not do to pour fuel on your already *kindled imagination.* You cant think how dissappointed I was to know that Viny was not coming until next week, for I had made all my plans to welcome her on Friday of this week instead of next. But it will be better the longer it is in coming I suppose. All the girls are waiting with impatience to see her & to about a dozen I have given her dimensions. Tell her she must look her prettiest or they will be dissappointed for I have given a glowing account of her.

I suppose you have written a few & received a quantity of Valentines this week. Every night I have looked & yet in vain for one of Cupid's messengers. Many of the girls have received very beautiful ones & I have not quite done hoping for one. Surely *my friend* THOMAS, has not lost all his former affection for me. I entreat you to tell him I am pining for a Valentine. I am sure I shall not very soon forget last Valentine week nor any the sooner, the fun I had at that time. Probably, Mary, Abby & Viny have received scores of them from the infatuated wights in the neighborhood while your *highly accomplished & gifted elder sister* is entirely overlooked. Monday afternoon, *Mistress* Lyon arose in the hall & forbade our sending "any of those foolish notes called Valentines." But those who were here last year, knowing her opinions, were sufficiently cunning to write & give them into the care of Dickinson, during the vacation, so that about 150. were despatched on Valentine morn, before orders should be put down to the contrary effect. Hearing of this act, Miss Whitman by & with the advice & consent of the other teachers, with frowning brow, sallied over to the Post office, to ascertain if possible, the number of Valentines and worse still, the names of the offenders. Nothing has yet been heard as to the amount of her information, but as Dickinson is a good hand to help the girls & no one has yet received sentence, we begin to think her mission unsuccessful. I have not written one nor do I now intend to. Your injunction to pile on the wood has not been unheeded for we have been obliged to obey it to keep from freezing up. I have had a severe cold for a few days, but think it is better now. We cannot have much more cold weather I am sure, for spring is near. Have you decided who to bring when you come? As to my opinion on that point, I confess I am in a strait betwixt two, Mary & Abby. Your better judgment will I am certain decide in the right and I will therefore leave it entirely in your hands.

Do you intend to give Miss. Whitman a ride? You had better re- sign that honor to your room-mate when he comes over again I judge. I had a note from E. Coleman, a few days since, but she said not a word of any of the family. You can probably imagine the drift of her remarks, without further information. I cannot say half that I want to for want of space.

Your affectionate Sister.

Emily.

How is Jacob. Holt now? I wish much to hear from him as not one word have I heard since I left home about him. Does your Rooster yet persist in his foolish habit of crowing under his window? I hope he has long ere this repented him of his folly. Professor. Smith. preached here last Sabbath & such sermons I never heard in my life. We were all charmed with him & dreaded to have him close. I understand the people of S. Hadley have given Mr. Belden of East-street a call to settle here. If he accepts, I hope it *will*, WILL not be until my year is out. Will you ask Viny. to get my History & Topic book, of Harriet. Parsons & bring them with her, for reviews commence very soon & I shall need them. Also will she bring a little Sweet Flag & that Comb, which I did my hair up with when I came home from Boston? Write me as long a letter as this is very soon.

Give my best love to Father, Mother, Viny, Mary, Abby, Dea. Haskell's family & all who inquire for me.

Please not to show this letter for it is strictly confidential & I should feel badly to have you show it.

MANUSCRIPT: AC. Ink. Dated: Thursday morn. Addressed on the fold: Austin. W. Dickinson./Amherst./Mass. Postmark illegible. The letter is sealed with a diamond-shaped wafer on which is printed "Believe me," followed by the first bar of the well-known musical rendering of "Believe me, if all these endearing young charms."

PUBLICATION: L (1894) 70–73, in part; LL 130–132, in part; L (1931) 69–71, in part; *Home* 78–80, entire.

As the year advanced, ED's homesickness increased. The strain must have been apparent to her family, for her father had already decided not to send her to Mount Holyoke for a second year.

The custom of exchanging valentines was not limited at this time to one day, but extended through the entire "Valentine week." The Reverend Henry B. Smith was a member of the Amherst College faculty; the Reverend Pomeroy Belden was pastor of the East Parish church in Amherst. ED's friend Thomas has not been identified.

24

To Austin Dickinson   *South Hadley, 29 May 1848*

My dear Austin.

I received a letter from home on Saturday, by Mr. Gilbert Smith and father wrote in it that he intended to send for Cousin Emily. & myself on Saturday of this week to spend the Sabbath at home. I went to Miss. Whitman, after receiving the letter & asked her if we could go if you decided to come for us. She seemed stunned by my request & could not find utterance to an answer for some time. At length, she said "did you not know it was contrary to the rules of the Seminary to ask to be absent on the Sabbath"? I told her I did not. She then took a Catalogue, from her table & showed me the law in full at the last part of it.

She closed by saying that we could not go & I returned to my room, without farther ado. So you see I shall be deprived of the pleasure of a visit home & you that of seeing me, if I may have the presumption to call it a *pleasure*!! The Teachers are not willing to let the girls go home this term as it is the last one & as I have only nine weeks more to spend here, we had better be contented to obey the commands. We shall only be the more glad to see one another after a longer absence, that will be all.

I was highly edified with your *imaginative* note to me & think your flights of fancy indeed wonderful at your age!! When are you coming to see me, or dont you intend to come at all? Viny told us, you were coming this week & it would be very pleasant to us to receive a visit from *your highness* if you can be absent from home long enough for such a purpose.

Is there anything new at home & wont you write me a long letter telling me all news? Mary. Warner. has not yet answered the note which I sent her at the commencement of the term. I cant write longer.

Your aff.

Emilie.

MANUSCRIPT: AC. Ink. Dated: Monday morn. Addressed on the fold: Austin. W. Dickinson./Amherst./Mass.

PUBLICATION: L (1894) 74-75, in part; LL 132-133, in part; L (1931) 71-72, in part; Home 81-82, entire.

The Seminary rule for that year which ED refers to reads thus: "The young ladies do not make or receive calls on the Sabbath. Neither should they spend a single Sabbath from the Seminary in term time. . . . The place of weekly labors is the most favorable spot for the scenes of the Sabbath."

26

To Abiah Root *29 October 1848*

My own dear Abiah,

For so I will still call you, though while I do it, even now I tremble at my strange audacity, and almost wish I had been a little more humble not quite so presuming.

Six long months have tried hard to make us strangers, but I love you better than ever notwithstanding the link which bound us in that golden chain is sadly dimmed, I feel more reluctant to lose you from that bright circle, whom I've called *my friends* I mailed a long letter to you the 1st of March, & patiently have I waited a reply, but none has yet cheered me.

Slowly, very slowly, I came to the conclusion that you had forgotten me, & I tried hard to forget you, but your image still haunts me, and tantalizes me with fond recollections. At our Holyoke Anniversary, I caught one glimpse of your face, & fondly anticipated an interview with you, & a reason for your silence, but when I thought to find you search was vain, for "the bird had flown." Sometimes, I think it was a fancy, think I did not *really* see my old friend, but her spirit, then your well known voice tells me it was no spirit, but yourself, living, that stood within that crowded hall & spoke to me – Why did you not come back that day, and tell me what had sealed your lips toward me? Did my letter never reach you, or did you coolly decide to love me, & write to me no more? If you love me, & never received my letter —then may you think yourself wronged, and that rightly, but if you dont want to be my friend any longer, say so, & I'll try *once* more to blot you from my memory. Tell me very soon, for suspense is intolerable. I need not tell you, this is from,

Emilie.

MANUSCRIPT: HCL (ARS 6). Ink. Unpublished. Dated: Amherst. October 29th – 1848.

The "Anniversary" at which ED caught a glimpse of Abiah was the Seminary commencement excercises, held on August 3. She was mistaken about the time that had passed since her last letter, which was written in mid-May.

III

1849–1850

"Amherst is alive with fun this winter . . ."

The years 1849–1850 were a time of expansion for Emily Dickinson. Her health was better, and new books and interests absorbed her. After her return from Mount Holyoke, she made new friends in the town and the college, and it was at this time that she enjoyed the happy companionship of Ben Newton. She afterward felt that the friendship was one of the experiences which had most enlarged her mind. None of her letters to him have survived.

In 1850, Austin was a senior at Amherst College, and some of his classmates, as well as the young tutors at the college, came frequently to the house. Lavinia was away at school, not at Mount Holyoke, but at Wheaton Seminary in Ipswich, where Mary Lyon had taught before she founded her own institution.

Among the girls at Amherst whom Emily saw most often was Susan Gilbert, who had returned in the autumn of 1848, after completing her schooling at Utica, New York. Another was Emily Fowler, whom she had not known well as a child because of a difference in age. One of the amusements of the winter season was the sending of valentines, and it is with a letter of the valentine season that this group begins.

To William Cowper Dickinson   *14 February 1849*

Cousin William,

Tis strange that a promise lives, and brightens, when the day that fashioned it, has mouldered, & stranger still, a promise looking to the day of Valentines for it's fulfillment.

Mine has been a very pleasant monitor, a friend, and kind companion, not a stern tyrant, like your own, *compelling* you to do what you would not have done, without compulsion.

Last Wednesday eve, I thought you had forgotten all about your promise, else you looked upon it as one foolish, & unworthy of fulfillment, now, I know your memory was faithful, but I sadly fear, your inclination, quarrelled with *it's* admonitions.

A little condescending, & sarcastic, your Valentine to me, I thought; a little like an Eagle, stooping to salute a Wren, & I concluded once, I dared not answer it, for it seemed to me not quite becoming — in a bird so lowly as myself — to claim admittance to an Eyrie, & conversation with it's King.

But I have changed my mind — & you are not too busy, I'll chat a while with you.

I'm a "Fenestrellan captive," if this world *be* "Fenestrella," and within my dungeon yard, up from the silent pavement stones, has come a plant, so frail, & yet so beautiful, I tremble lest it die. Tis the first living thing that has beguiled my solitude, & I take strange delight in it's society. It's a mysterious plant, & sometimes I fancy that it whispers pleasant things to me — of freedom — and the future. Cans't guess it's name? T'is "Picciola"; & to *you* Cousin William, I'm indebted for my wondrous, new, companion.

I know not how to thank you, for your kindness. Gratitude is poor as poverty itself — & the "10,000 thanks" so often cited, seem like faintest shadows, when I try to stamp them here, that I may send their impress to you. "Picciola's" first flower — I will keep for you. Had not it's gentle voice, & friendly words – assured me of a "kind remembrance" – I think I should not have presumed thus much.

The last week has been a merry one in Amherst, & notes have flown around like, snowflakes. Ancient gentlemen, & spinsters, forgetting time, & multitude of years, have doffed their wrinkles – in exchange for smiles – even this aged world of our's, has thrown away it's staff – and spectacles, & *now* declares it will be young again.

Valentine's sun is setting now however, & before tomorrow eve, old things will take their place again. Another year, a long one, & a stranger to us all – must live, & die, before it's laughing beams will fall on us again, & of "that shadowy band in the silent land" may be the present writers of these merry missives.

But I am moralizing, forgetful of you, sisterless — and for *that* reason prone to mournful reverie – perhaps. Are you happy, now that she is gone? I know you must be lonely since her leave, and when I think of you nowdays, t'is of a "melancholy gentleman, standing on the banks of river Death – sighing & beckoning Charon to convey him over."

Have I guessed right, or are you merry as a "Fine old English Gentleman – all of the Olden time"?

I'll write to Martha soon, for tis *as* desolate to be without her letters; *more* desolate than you can think. I wont forget some little pencil marks I found in reading "Picciola," for they seem to me like silent sentinels, guarding the towers of some city, in itself — too beautiful to be unguarded; I've read those passages with hightened interest on their account.

Long life to Mr Hammond, & a thousand Valentines for every year of it.

Pardon my lengthiness — if it be not unpardonable.

Sincerely, your cousin,
Emily E. Dickinson.

MANUSCRIPT: Dickinson. Ink. Dated: Valentine morn. Unpublished.
William Cowper Dickinson, valedictorian of the class of 1848, was a friend but not a close relative of ED. He returned as tutor in 1851, but this letter clearly was written before that time. Charles Hammond was principal of Monson Academy where Dickinson was teaching.
Picciola is the title of a romantic tale of Napoleonic times by X. B. Saintine (Joseph Xavier Boniface), published in 1839. In the following

decade it went through many European and American editions, the latest of which was a profusely illustrated one with decorated binding, published at Philadelphia in 1849. The story concerns a political prisoner in the stronghold of Fenestrella, whose observation of a plant growing between the stones of his prison courtyard transforms his philosophy and changes his fortunes. The Italian jailer's exclamation, "Povera picciola!" (poor little thing), provides the name which the prisoner gives the unknown flower.

29

To Joel Warren Norcross   *11 January 1850*

Dearest of all dear Uncles.

Sleep carried me away, and a dream passed along, a dream all queer, and curious – it was a dream of warning – I ought not to hide it from whom it concerns – God forbid that you trifle with vision so strange – the Spirit of love entreat you – the Spirit of warning guide – and the all helping hold – and prevent you from falling! And I dreamed – and beheld a company whom no man may number – all men in their youth – all strong and stout-hearted – nor feeling their burdens for strength – nor waxing faint – nor weary. Some tended their flocks – and some sailed on the sea – and yet others kept gay stores, and deceived the foolish who came to buy. They made life one summer day – they danced to the sound of the lute – they sang old snatches of song – and they quaffed the rosy wine – One promised to love his friend and one vowed to defraud no poor – and *one* man told a lie to his niece – they all did sinfully – and their lives were not yet taken. Soon a change came – the young men were old – the flocks had no sheperd – the boat sailed alone – and the dancing had ceased – and the wine-cup was empty – and the summer day grew cold – Oh fearful the faces then! The Merchant tore his hair – and the Sheperd gnashed his teeth – and the Sailor hid himself – and prayed to die. Some kindled the scorching fire – some opened the earthquake's mouth – the winds strode on to the sea – and serpents hissed fearfully. Oh I was very much scared and I called to see who they were – this torment waited for – I listened – and up from the pit *you* spoke! You could'nt get out you said – no help could reach so far – you had brought it upon yourself – I left you alone to die – but they told me the whole of the crime – you had broken a promise on earth – and now t'was too late to redeem it. Do you wonder at my alarm – do you blame me for running to tell you? It was'nt *all* a dream – but I know it will be fulfilled unless you stop sinning now – it is not too late to do right. Do you take any hints I wonder – can you guess the meaning of things – not yet aroused to the truth. You villain without a rival – unparraleled doer of crimes – scoundrel unheard of before – disturber of public peace – "creation's blot and blank" – state's prison filler – *magnum bonum* promise maker – harum scarum promise breaker – Oh what can I call you more? Mrs Caudle would call you "a gentleman" – that is altogether too good. Mrs Partington "a very fine fellow" – neither does this apply – I call upon all nature to lay hold of you – let fire burn – and water drown – and light put out – and tempests tear – and hungry wolves eat up – and lightning strike – and thunder stun – let friends desert – and enemies draw nigh and gibbets *shake* but never *hang* the house you walk about in! My benison not touch – my malison pursue the body that hold your spirit! Any other afflictions which now slip my mind shall be looked up and forwarded to you immediately. How will you bear them all – will they depress – and make life hang too heavily? Would that they might thus do – but I look for no such results – you will bear them like a Salamander. Old fashioned Daniel could'nt take things more coolly. Does sarcasm affect you – or the sneers of the world? "Burn flame – simmer heat – swelter toad – I have cursed thee – and thou art accursed."

Dont remember a letter I was to receive when you got back to Boston – how long and how broad – how high — or deep it should be – how many cars it should sink – or how many stages tip over – or the shaking of earth when it rested – Hav'nt the faintest recollection of the hearts to be lighter – the eyes to grow brighter and the life made longer with joy it should give – a most unfortunate mem'ry – the owner deserves our pity! Had you a pallid hand – or a blind eye – we would talk about coming to terms – but you have sent my father a letter – so there remains no more but to fight. War Sir – "my voice is for war!" Would you like to try a duel – or is that too quiet to suit you – at any rate I shall kill you – and you may dispose of your affairs with that end in view. You can take Chloroform if you like – and I will put you beyond the reach of pain in a twinkling. The last duel I fought did'nt take but five minutes in all – the "wrapping the drapery of his couch about him – and lying down to pleasant dreams" included. Lynch laws provide admirably now for wifes – and orphan children – so duels seem differently from what they formerly did to me. Uncle Loring – and Aunt Lavinia *will* miss you some to be sure – but trials *will* come in the best of families – and I think they are usually for the best – they give us new ideas – and *those* are not to be laughed at. How have you been bodily, and mentally since you were up to see us? How do you sleep *o nights* – and is your appetite waning? These are infallible symptoms, and I only thought I'd inquire – no harm done I hope. Harm is one of those things that I always mean to keep clear of – but somehow my intentions and me dont chime as they ought – and people will get hit with stones that I throw at my neighbor's dogs – not only *hit – that* is the least of the whole – but they insist upon blaming *me* instead of the *stones* – and tell me their heads ache – why it is the greatest piece of folly on record. It would do to go with a story I read – one man pointed a loaded gun at a man – and it shot him so that he died – and the people threw the owner of the gun into prison – and afterwards hung him for *murder*. Only another victim to the misunderstanding of society – such things should not be permitted – it certainly is as much as one's neck is worth to live in so stupid a world – and it makes one grow weary. Life is'nt what it purports to be. Now when I walk into your room and pluck your heart out that you die – I kill you – hang me if you like – but if I stab you while sleeping the dagger's to blame – it's no business of mine – you have no more right to accuse me of injuring you than anything else I can think of. That we understand capital punishment, and one another too I verily believe – and sincerely hope – for it's so trying to be read out of the wrong book when the right one is out of sight.

Your friends in town are comfortable – or *were* at the last accounts – tho' I hav'nt been into the Kelloggs' for several days now. Still I have seen neither Doctor, or Sexton around, and will take the fearful responsibility of assuring you that they live, and are well. You will perceive that the whole stands for a part in this place – it being one of those exceedingly *aspeny* cases that the bungling had better let alone. Have you found *Susannah* yet? "Roses will fade – time flies on – Lady of beauty," – the whole hymn is too familiar to you now for me to repeat it. Amherst is alive with fun this winter – might you be here to see! Sleigh rides are as plenty as people – which conveys to my mind the idea of very plentiful plenty. How it may seem to you I don't calculate at all – but presume you can see the likeness if you get the right light upon it. Parties cant find fun enough – because all the best ones are engaged to attend balls a week beforehand – beaus can be had for the taking – maids smile like the mornings in June – Oh a very great town is this! Chorus – a "still greater one is this." "Now for the jovial bowl," etc. You are fond of singing – I think – and by close, and assiduous practise may learn these two before I see you again. Exertion never harmed anybody – it wont begin now.

Are you all well – how are the children – please give the love of all our household to all the members of your's. Dont leave Cousin Albert out in my part! Vinnie has been to see you – she wrote what splendid times she had. We are very lonely without her – hope to linger along till she comes home. Will you write me before you go hence? Any communications will be received gratefully.

Emilie – I believe.

My kind regards to the gentlemen – White – and Leavitt. Heaven's choicest blessings attend them – and evil pass by without turning either to the right hand – or the left. Very particular indeed about the left hand – as they would be a little most likely to be there. "God bless you" to Wm Haskell – and civilized messages to all the rest of my friends.

Austin did'nt get to Boston somehow or other. He spent all but the fag end of vacation reading Hume's History – and it nearly used him up.

Had a long and very interesting letter from Emily [Norcross] a few days since. She seems contented – almost happy – says she will be glad to see us all, tho.

Manuscript: AC. Ink. Dated: Amherst New Year 11th/50.
Publication: L (1931) 57–61.
White and Leavitt were the business partners of Norcross. The character of Mrs. Caudle, a voluble scold, was created by Douglas William Jerrold for *Punch*, and *Mrs. Caudle's Curtain Lectures* was published in 1846. Mrs. Partington, a village Malaprop, was a character created by Benjamin P. Shillaber for a Boston newspaper in 1847. The first quotation in the second paragraph recalls *Paradise Lost*, II, 51: "My sentence is for open war"; the second quotation in the same paragraph, the conclusion of

Bryant's *Thanatopsis*: "Like one who wraps the drapery of his couch/ About him, and lies down to pleasant dreams."

32

To Emily Fowler (Ford)   *early 1850?*

———

I wanted to write, and just tell you that *me,* and *my spirit* were fighting this morning. It is'nt known generally, and you must'nt tell anybody.

I dreamed about you last night, and waked up putting my shawl, and hood on to go and see you, but this wicked snow-storm looked in at my window, and told me I could'nt. I hope God will forgive me, but I am very unwilling to have it storm – he is merciful to the sinning, is'nt he?

I cannot wait to be with you – Oh ugly time, and space, and uglier snow-storm than all! Were you happy in Northampton? I was very lonely without you, and wanted to write you a letter *many* times, but Kate was there too, and I was afraid you would both laugh. I should be stronger if I could see you oftener – I am very puny alone.

You make me so happy, and glad, life seems worth living for, no matter for all the trials. When I see you I shall tell you more, for I know you are busy this morning.

That is'nt an *empty* blank where I began – it is so full of affection that you cant see any – that's all. Will you love, and remember, *me* when you have time from worthier ones? God keep you till I have seen you again!

Very earnestly yrs –

Emily.

MANUSCRIPT: NYPL. Ink. Addressed on the fold: Miss Emily E Fowler./Austin. Unpublished.

This note is in the handwriting of 1850. "Kate" was very likely Catharine Hitchcock (1826–1895), daughter of Edward Hitchcock, President of Amherst College.

To William Cowper Dickinson   *about February 1850*

> "Life is but a strife –
> T'is a bubble –
> ·T'is a dream –
> And man is but a little *boat*
> Which paddles down the stream"

MANUSCRIPT: Dickinson. Ink. Addressed: Mr William C Dickinson / Amherst – / Mass –. Unpublished. The date is conjectured from the handwriting.

Although the spirit of this verse seems removed from that of the usual valentine, it seems to have been sent as such. It is illustrated with small cuts clipped from old books and papers, one cutting taken from the *New England Primer*. After line one: a man, a woman, and a boy in a doorway, beating off dogs with a broom and sticks; after line two: two boys and a girl blowing bubbles; after line three: (1) a sleeping king (from the *Primer*), and (2) a small sailboat.

To George H. Gould?   *February 1850*

Magnum bonum, "harum scarum," zounds et zounds, et war alarum, man reformam, life perfectum, mundum changum, all things flarum?

Sir, I desire an interview; meet me at sunrise, or sunset, or the new moon – the place is immaterial. In gold, or in purple, or sackcloth – I look not upon the *raiment*. With sword, or with pen, or with plough – the weapons are less than the *wielder*. In coach, or in wagon, or walking, the *equipage* far from the *man*. With soul, or spirit, or body, they are all alike to me. With host or alone, in sunshine or storm, in heaven or earth, *some* how or *no* how – I propose, sir, to see you.

And not to *see* merely, but a chat, sir, or a tete-a-tete, a confab, a mingling of opposite minds is what I propose to have. I feel sir that we shall agree. We will be David and Jonathan, or Damon and Pythias, or what is better than either, the United States of America. We will talk over what we have learned in our geographies, and listened to from the pulpit, the press and the Sabbath School.

This is strong language sir, but none the less true. So hurrah for North Carolina, since we are on this point.

Our friendship sir, shall endure till sun and moon shall wane no more, till stars shall set, and victims rise to grace the final sacrifice. We'll be instant, in season, out of season, minister, take care of, cherish, sooth, watch, wait, doubt, refrain, reform, elevate, instruct. All choice spirits however distant are ours, ours theirs; there is a thrill of sympathy — a circulation of mutuality — cognationem inter nos! I am Judith the heroine of the Apocrypha, and you the orator of Ephesus.

That's what they call a metaphor in our country. Don't be afraid of it, sir, it won't bite. If it was my *Carlo* now! The Dog is the noblest work of Art, sir. I may safely say the noblest — his mistress's rights he doth defend — although it bring him to his end — although to death it doth him send!

But the world is sleeping in ignorance and error, sir, and we must be crowing cocks, and singing larks, and a rising sun to awake her; or else we'll pull society up to the roots, and plant it in a different place. We'll build Alms-houses, and transcendental State prisons, and scaffolds — we will blow out the sun, and the moon, and encourage invention. Alpha shall kiss Omega — we will ride up the hill of glory — Hallelujah, all hail!

Yours, truly,

C.

MANUSCRIPT: missing.
PUBLICATION: *The Indicator* (Amherst College), II, 7, February 1850.

This valentine letter, dated "Valentine Eve," is typical of the nonsense ED could evoke for such occasions. Some of the expressions, such as "magnum bonum, harum scarum" she also used in her letter (no. 29) to Joel Norcross. *The Indicator* was published by a group of students among whom was George H. Gould, Austin's good friend. The preparation of the "Editor's Corner," in which the letter appears, was for this issue in the hands of Henry Shipley. It was preceded by a comment in which the editor says: "I wish I knew who the author is. I think she must have some spell, by which she quickens the imagination, and causes the high blood 'run frolic through the veins.'" On Carlo, see letter no. 314.

To Abiah Root   *7 and 17 May 1850*

Dear Remembered.

The circumstances under which I write you this morning are at once glorious, afflicting, and beneficial — glorious in *ends,* afflicting in *means,* and *beneficial* I *trust* in *both.* Twin loaves of bread have just been born into the world under my auspices — fine children – the image of their *mother* — and *here* my dear friend is the *glory.*

On the lounge asleep, lies my sick mother, suffering intensely from Acute Neuralgia — except at a moment like this, when kind sleep draws near, and beguiles her, *here* is the *affliction.*

I need not draw the *beneficial* inference — the good I myself derive, the winning the spirit of patience the genial house-keeping influence stealing over my mind, and soul, you know all these things I would say, and will seem to suppose they are *written,* when indeed they are only *thought.* On Sunday my mother was taken, had been perfectly well before, and could remember no possible imprudence which should have induced the disease, everything has been done, and tho' we think her gradually throwing it off, she still has much suffering. I have always neglected the culinary arts, but attend to them now from necessity, and from a desire to make everything pleasant for father, and Austin. Sickness makes desolation, and "the day is dark, and dreary," but health will come back I hope, and light hearts, and smiling faces. We are sick hardly ever at home, and dont know what to do when it comes, wrinkle our little brows, and stamp our little feet, and our tiny souls get angry, and command it to go away. Mrs *Brown* will be glad to see it, old-ladies *expect* to die, as for *us,* the young, and active, with all longings "for the strife," *we* to "perish by the road-side, weary with the march of life" no – no my dear "Father Mortality," get out of our way if you please, we will call if we ever want you, Good-morning Sir, ah Good-morning! When I am not at work in the kitchen, I sit by the side of mother, provide for her little wants – and try to cheer, and encourage her. I ought to be glad, and grateful that I *can* do anything now, but I do feel so very lonely, and so anxious to have her cured. I hav'nt repined but *once,* and you shall know all the why. While I washed the dishes at noon in that little "sink-room" of our's, I heard a well-known rap, and a friend I love *so* dearly came and asked me to ride in the woods, the sweet-still woods, and I wanted to exceedingly – I told him I could not go, and he said he was disappointed – he wanted me very much – then the tears came into my eyes, tho' I tried to choke them back, and he said I *could,* and *should* go, and it seemed to me unjust. Oh I struggled with great temptation, and it cost me much of denial, but I think in the end I conquered, not a glorious victory Abiah, where you hear the rolling drum, but a kind of a helpless victory, where triumph would come of itself, faintest music, weary soldiers, nor a waving flag, nor a long-loud shout. I had read of Christ's temptations, and how they were like our own, only he did'nt sin; I wondered if *one* was like mine, and whether it made him angry – I couldnt make up my mind; do you think he ever did?

I went cheerfully round my work, humming a little air till mother had gone to sleep, then cried with all my might, seemed to think I was much abused, that this wicked world was unworthy such devoted, and terrible sufferings, and came to my various senses in great dudgeon at life, and time, and love for affliction, and anguish.

What shall we do my darling, when trial grows more, and more, when the dim, lone light expires, and it's dark, so very dark, and we wander, and know not where, and cannot get out of the forest – whose is the hand to help us, and to lead, and forever guide us, they talk of a "Jesus of Nazareth," will you tell me if it be he?

I presume you have heard from Abby, and know what she now believes – she makes a sweet, girl christian, religion makes her face quite different, calmer, but full of radiance, holy, yet very joyful. She talks of herself quite freely, seems to love Lord Christ most dearly, and to wonder, and be bewildered, at the life she has always led. It all looks black, and distant, and God, and Heaven are near, she is certainly very much changed.

She has told you about things here, how the "still small voice" is calling, and how the people are listening, and believing, and truly obeying – how the place is very solemn, and sacred, and the bad ones slink away, and are sorrowful – not at their wicked lives – but at this strange time, great change. *I* am one of the lingering *bad* ones, and so do *I* slink away, and pause, and ponder, and ponder, and pause, and do work without knowing why – not surely for *this* brief world, and more sure it is not for Heaven – and I ask what this message *means* that they ask for so very eagerly, *you* know of this depth, and fulness, will you *try* to tell me about it?

It's *Friday* my dear Abiah, and that in another week, yet my mission is unfulfilled — and you so sadly neglected, and dont know the reason why. Where do you think I've strayed, and from what new errand returned? I have come from "*to* and *fro,* and walking up, and down" the same place that Satan hailed from, when God asked him where he'd been, but not to illustrate further I tell you I have been dreaming, dreaming a *golden* dream, with eyes all the while wide open, and I guess it's almost morning, and besides I have been at work, providing the "food that perisheth," scaring the timorous dust, and being obedient, and kind. *I* call it kind obedience in the books the Shadows write in, it may have another name. I am yet the Queen of the court, if regalia be dust, and dirt, have three loyal subjects, whom I'd rather releive from service. Mother is still an invalid tho' a partially restored one – Father and Austin still clamor for food, and I, like a martyr am feeding them. Would'nt you love to see me in these bonds of great despair, looking around my kitchen, and praying for kind deliverance, and declaring by "Omar's beard" I never was in such plight. *My* kitchen I think I called it, God forbid that it was, or shall be my own – God keep me from what they call *households,* except that bright one of "faith"!

Dont be afraid of my imprecations, they never did anyone harm, and they make me feel so cool, and and [*sic*] so very much more comfortable!

Where are you now Abiah, where are your thoughts, and aspirings, where are your young affections, not with the *boots,* and *whiskers;* any with *me* ungrateful, *any* tho' drooping, dying? I presume you are loving your mother, and loving the stranger, and wanderer, visiting the poor, and afflicted, and reaping whole fields of blessings. Save me a *little* sheaf – only a very little one! Remember, and care for me sometimes, and scatter a fragrant flower in this wilderness life of mine by writing me, and by not forgetting, and by lingering longer in prayer, that the Father may bless one more!

Your aff friend,
Emily.

It's a great while since I've seen your cousins, they were all very well when I did. When will you come again – Speedily, will you?

Vinnie is still at school, and I sit by my lonely window, and give bright tears to her memory. Tears are my angels now.

Do you hear from our dear Jennie Humphrey, do you know who's staying now? I feel impatiently, *very* it's so long since I've heard about her. When her father was sick she wrote me, and as soon as I could I replied; I afterwards saw his death, the day that my letter reached her. She must be bereaved indeed, and I wish I could go, and console her. She has the "Great Spirit" tho', and perhaps she does'nt need me. Do you know how she bears her trial. She is a very dear friend to me, and all of these things I think of.

What a beautiful mourner is her sister, looking so crushed, and heart-broken, yet never complaining, or murmuring, and waiting herself so patiently! She reminds me of suffering Christ, bowed down with her weight of agony, yet smiling at terrible will. "Where the weary are at rest" these mourners all make me think of — in the sweet still grave. When shall it call us?

MANUSCRIPT: HCL (ARS 8). Ink. Dated: Amherst. May 7th/50.

PUBLICATION: L (1894) 46–50, in part; LL 141–145, in part; L (1931) 40–43, in part, with part misplaced on pages 28–29.

Lavinia was still in school at Ipswich. The religious revival was of such proportions that on June 8 the *Springfield Republican* could report that it was still in progress. Edward Dickinson made confession of his faith and joined the church on 11 August. In the third paragraph ED quotes from Longfellow's "The Rainy Day," a poem to which she alludes no fewer than six times during these early years. In the eighth paragraph the quotation is from Longfellow's "Footsteps of Angels."

38

To Susan Gilbert (Dickinson)   *about December 1850*

Were it not for the *weather* Susie — *my* little, unwelcome face would come peering in today – I should steal a kiss from the sister — the darling Rover returned – Thank the wintry wind my dear one, that spares such daring intrusion! *Dear* Susie – *happy* Susie – I rejoice in all *your* joy – sustained by that dear sister you will never again be lonely. Dont forget all the little friends who have tried so hard to *be* sisters, when indeed you *were* alone!

You do not hear the wind blow on this inclement day, when the *world* is shrugging it's shoulders; your little "Columbarium is lined with warmth and softness," there is no "silence" there — so you differ from bonnie "Alice." I *miss one* angel face in the little world of sisters — dear Mary — *sainted* Mary — Remember lonely one — tho, *she* comes not to us, *we* shall return to *her*! My love to *both* your sisters — and I want so much to see Matty.

Very aff yours,

Emily

MANUSCRIPT: HCL (B 131). Ink. Dated: Thursday noon.
PUBLICATION: FF 186–187.
Susan Gilbert's sister Mary, married for less than a year to Samuel J. Learned, died on 14 July 1850. The other unmarried sister, Martha, who had been in Michigan, joined Sue in December at the home of the eldest sister Harriet (Mrs. William Cutler), in Amherst. The "Alice" here alluded to is Alice Archer in Longfellow's *Kavanagh,* whose room is described as "that columbarium lined with warmth, and softness, and silence."

IV

1851–1854

". . . we do not have much poetry,
father having made up his mind
that its pretty much all real life.*"

The close relationship between Emily Dickinson and her brother Austin is clearly shown, both in the great number of letters she wrote to him when he was away, and in the fact that he preserved so many of them. In the course of these years, while Austin was teaching in Boston and later attending Harvard Law School, the daily intimacy of home life was constantly kept before him in her frequent letters.

It was at this time, also, that Austin's courtship of Susan Gilbert was taking shape, culminating in their publicly acknowledged engagement by the end of 1853. Emily's intimacy with Sue grew with Sue's closer tie to Austin. Fond as she still was of the girls with whom she had been intimate in earlier years, Emily's feeling for Sue took precedence over other friendships, and her letters during Sue's absences were as much a part of her daily life as were those to Austin.

The letters to these two close companions dominate the correspondence of the period, but her feeling for others was not excluded. She enjoyed exchanges of books and thoughts with Henry Vaughan Emmons during his undergraduate years. And her cousin, John L. Graves, who introduced Emmons to her, she counted as a friend of her own.

40

To Emily Fowler (Ford)   *about 1851*

I'm so afraid you'll forget me dear Emily – through these cold winter days, when I cannot come to see you, that I cannot forbear writing
the least little bit of a note – to put you in mind of me; perhaps it will
make you laugh – it may be foolish in me but I love you so well sometimes – not that I do not *always* – but more dearly sometimes – and
with such a desire to see you that I find myself addressing you almost
ere I'm aware. When I am as old as you and have had so many friends,
perhaps they wont seem so precious, and then I shant write any more
little "billet doux" like these, but you will forgive me *now*, because
I cant find many so dear to me as you – then I know I cant have you
always – some day a "brave dragoon" will be stealing you away and
I will have farther to go to discover you *at all* – so I shall recollect all
these sweet opportunities and feel so sorry if I did'nt improve them.
I wish I had something new, or very happy, to tell you, which would
fill that lofty kitchen with sunshine all day long, but there *is* nothing
new – neither indeed there *can* be – for things have got so old; but
something happy there *is* if the remembrance of friends is always sweet
and joyful. Solve this little problem, dear Emily, if you possibly can:
You have "so many" friends – *you* know how *very* many – then if all
of them love you *half* so well as me, say – how much will it make?

I fancy I catch you *ciphering* on the funniest little slate, with the
airiest little pencil – I will not interrupt you –

Dear Emilie –

Goodbye!

MANUSCRIPT: NYPL. Ink. Dated: Thursday morning. Addressed on
the fold: Miss Emily E Fowler/by Vinnie.
PUBLICATION: *L* (1894) 136–137, in part; *L* (1931) 136, in part.
The date is conjectured from the handwriting. This is the second known
letter (see no. 32) written to Emily Fowler, who was one of ED's earliest
friends. ED wrote several more over the years, an especially large number

in 1853, the year of Emily Fowler's marriage. But the quality of disembodiment, uncharacteristic of most letters, is peculiarly evident in those to Emily Fowler, who was more than four years older than ED.

41

To Elbridge G. Bowdoin   *February 1851*

I weave for the Lamp of *Evening* — but fairer colors than *mine* are twined while stars are shining.

I know of a shuttle swift — I know of a fairy gift — mat for the "Lamp of *Life*" — the little Bachelor's wife!

MANUSCRIPT: AC. Ink. Dated: 1851. Addressed: Mr. Bowdoin./ Present.

PUBLICATION: *L* (1931) 138.

This valentine seems to have accompanied a lamp mat made by ED.

42

To Austin Dickinson   *8 June 1851*

It might not come amiss dear Austin to have a tiding or two concerning our state and feelings, particularly when we remember that "Jamie is gone awa."

Our state is pretty comfortable, and our feelings are *somewhat solemn* which we account for satisfactorily by calling to mind the fact that it is the "Sabbath Day." Whether a certain passenger in a certain yesterday's stage has any sombre effect on our once merry household, or the reverse "I dinna choose to tell," but be the case as it may, we are rather a crestfallen company to make the *best* of us, and what with the sighing wind, the sobbing rain, and the whining of nature *generally*, we can hardly contain ourselves, and I only hope and trust that your this evening's lot is cast in far more cheery places than the ones you leave behind.

We are enjoying this evening what is called a "northeast storm" — a little north of east, in case you are pretty definite. Father thinks "it's amazin raw," and I'm half disposed to think that he's in the right about it, tho' I keep pretty dark, and dont *say* much about it! Vinnie

[46]

is at the instrument, humming a pensive air concerning a young lady who thought she was "almost there." Vinnie seems much grieved, and I really suppose *I* ought to betake myself to weeping; I'm pretty sure that I *shall* if she dont abate her singing.

Father's just got home from meeting and Mr Boltwood's, found the last quite comfortable, and the first not quite so well.

Mother is warming her feet, which she assures me confidently are "just as cold as ice.["] I tell her I fear there is danger of icification, or ossification — I dont know certainly which! Father is reading the Bible — I take it for *consolation*, judging from outward things. He and mother take great delight in dwelling upon your character, and reviewing your many virtues, and Father's prayers for you at our morning devotions are enough to break one's heart — it is really very touching; surely "our blessings brighten" the farther off they fly! Mother wipes her eyes with the end of her linen apron, and consoles herself by thinking of several future places "where congregations ne'er break up," and Austins have no end! This being a favorite sentiment with you, I trust it will find a response in all patriotic bosoms. There has not been much stirring since when you went away — I should venture to say *prudently* that matters had come to a stand — unless something new "turns up" I cannot see anything to prevent a *quiet season*. Father takes care of the doors, and mother of the windows, and Vinnie and I are secure against all outward attacks. If we can get our *hearts "under"* I dont have much to fear — I've got all but *three* feelings down, if I can only keep them!

Tutor Howland was here *as usual*, during the afternoon — after tea I went to see Sue — had a nice little visit with her — then went to see Emily Fowler, and arrived home at 9 — found Father is great agitation at my protracted stay — and mother and Vinnie in tears, for fear that he would kill me.

Sue and Martha expressed their sorrow that you had gone away, and are going to write a postscript in the next letter I send.

Emily F[owler] talked of you with her usual deal of praise. The girls all send their love. Mother wants me to say that if you like *Aunt L's Bonnet*, and can find one for *her just like it*, that "Barkis is very willin." Vinnie sends her love, and says she is "pretty comfortable." I shall think of you tomorrow with four and twenty Irish boys — all in a row! I miss you very much. I put on my bonnet tonight, opened

[47]

the gate very desperately, and for a little while, the suspense was terrible — I think I was held in check by some invisible agent, for I returned to the house without having done any harm!

If I had'nt been afraid that you would "poke fun" at my feelings, I had written a *sincere* letter, but since the "world is hollow, and Dollie is stuffed with sawdust," I really do not think we had better expose our feelings. Write soon to *me*, they all send love to you and all the folks — love to Lizzie if there. Vinnie has commenced snoring.

Your dear Sister

Emily.

MANUSCRIPT: AC. Ink. Dated: Sunday evening.

PUBLICATION: *L* (1894) 75–76, in part; *LL* 149–151, in part; *L* (1931) 72–74, in part; *Home* 128–129, entire.

Austin left home on Saturday, 7 June 1851, to begin a year's engagement as teacher in the boys' section of the Endicott School in the North End of Boston, settled largely by Irish immigrants who had fled the potato famine of 1847. His uncle Loring Norcross was a member of the school committee. At first he lived with the Norcrosses, but shortly moved to a boarding house (see letter no. 43), though his mailing address continued to be through the Norcrosses.

The quotation "where congregations ne'er break up" is from the familiar hymn "Jerusalem! My happy home!" The William Burkitt version (1693) first introduced the word "congregations" at the end of the second stanza: "Where congregations ne'er break up,/And Sabbaths have no end."

43

To Austin Dickinson 15 June 1851

From what you say Dear Austin I am forced to conclude that you never received *my letter* which was mailed for Boston *Monday*, but *two days* after you left — I dont know where it went to, Father wrote on the outside, and to care of Uncle Loring, and waiting from day to day and receiving no reply, I naturally grew rather crusty and resolved to reserve my mss for youths more worthy of them; this will account for the fact that you heard nothing by Bowdoin. In neither of your letters, for which I heartily thank you, have you made any mention of my departed letter — Bowdoin *thinks* you told him you had not heard from home, and quite surprised at it, and grieved to have you think you were forgotten *so* quick, I will try the post again, if I cant be more successful. I'm glad you are so well pleased, I am glad you are *not* delighted, I would not that *foreign* places should wear the smile of home. We are quite alarmed for the *boys*, hope you wont *kill*, or *pack away* any of em, so near Dr. Webster's bones t'ant strange you have had temptations! You would not take it amiss if I should say we *laughed some* when each of your letters came — your respected parents were *overwhelmed* with glee, and as for the *young ladies* they gave a smile or so by way of recognizing your *descriptive* merits. Father remarks quite briefly that he "thinks they have found their master," mother bites her lips, and fears you "will be *rash* with them" and Vinnie and I say masses for poor Irish boys souls. So far as *I* am concerned I should like to have you kill some — there are so many now, there is no room for the Americans, and I cant think of a death that would be more after my mind than *scientific destruction, scholastic dissolution,* there's something lofty in it, it smacks of *going up!* Wont you please to state the *name* of the boy that turned the faintest, as I like to get such *facts* to set down in my *journal,* also anything else that's *startling* which you may chance to know — I dont think deaths or murders can ever come amiss in a young woman's journal – the country's *still* just now, and the severities alluded to will have a salutary influence in waking the people up — speaking of *getting up,* how early are *metropolitans* expected to wake up, *especially* young men — *more* especially *schoolmasters?* I miss "my department" mornings – I lay it quite to heart that I've no one to wake up. Your room looks lonely enough – I do not love to go in there — whenever I pass thro' I find I 'gin to whistle, as we read that little boys are wont to do in the graveyard. I am going to set out *Crickets* as soon as I find time that they by their shrill singing shall help disperse the gloom — will they grow if I *transplant* them?

You importune me for *news,* I am very sorry to say "Vanity of vanities" there's no such thing as news — it is almost time for the cholera, and *then* things will take a start!

We have had a man to take tea, a Mr Marsh by name — he went to school with Father.

I think him a "man of cares" tho' I know nothing concerning him —

another important item, so far as I can judge — I think he's for "law and order." Susie and Martha come often. Sue was here on Friday, for all afternoon yesterday — I gave the *manslaughter* extract to the infinite fun of Martha! They miss you very much — they send their "united loves." Vinnie rode with Howland yesterday, and Emily Fowler and [William Cowper] Dickinson also, at the same time — had a fine ride. The Reading club seems lonely — perhaps it weeps for you.

Dwight Cowan does very well — the Horse is quite "uncommon." Hunt is shingling the barn. We are going to have some new hens — a few.

I reserve the close for bad news — we cant come to hear Jennie — we are coming, but cant now. There are several reasons why — the first we are not near ready — Miss Leonard is coming this week — Grandmother is coming to see us — if we go now we cant *stay* any — we cannot come now and again — it would be all haste and confusion — we should have to hurry home, and we do not think it best. We shall come before long, when we are all prepared — "two monuments of the past" would make quite a stir in Boston! You must'nt be disappointed, nor blame the folks at all — they would be perfectly willing if we tho't best ourselves. Give our love to our friends, thank them *much* for their kindness; we *will* come and see them and you tho' now it is not convenient. All of the folks send love.

Your aff
Emily.

Mother says if there's anything more you want, if you will only write us Mrs Kimberly will make it — also if you have any things which you would like to send home Henry Kellogg is there, and you can send by him. Write as often as possible. Take care of yourself —

Special love to Emily, and the little cousins.

MANUSCRIPT: AC. Ink. Dated: Sunday Evening. Envelope addressed: Wᵐ Austin Dickinson./Care of Loring Norcross Esq./Boston./Mass. Postmarked: Amherst Ms. Jun 16.

PUBLICATION: L (1894) 80, in part; LL 154, in part; L (1931) 77–78, in part; *Home* 130–139, entire, with facsimile reproduction.
Austin wrote twice in the first week of his absence, and urged his sisters to come to Boston to hear Jenny Lind. ED cites the coming of the dressmaker as one reason for refusal. "Dr. Webster's bones" alludes to the notori-

ous murder in a Harvard laboratory of Dr. George Parkman by his colleague Dr. John W. Webster in 1849. Webster was hanged, and buried in Mount Auburn Cemetery, which ED had visited in 1846.

46

To Austin Dickinson   *6 July 1851*

I have just come in from Church very hot, and faded, having witnessed a couple of Baptisms, three admissions to church, a Supper of the Lord, and some other minor transactions time fails me to record. Knowing Rev A. M. Colton so thoroughly as you do, having received much benefit from his past ministrations, and bearing the relation of "Lamb" unto his fold, you will delight to know that he is well, and preaching, that he has preached *today* strange as it may — must seem, that just from his benediction I hurry away to you. No doubt you can call to mind his eloquent addresses, his earnest look and gesture, his calls of *now today* — no doubt you can call to mind the impetus of spirit received from this same gentleman and his enlivening preaching — therefore if you should fancy I'd looked upon the *wine* from walk or conversation a little fierce or fiery, bear all these things in mind!

Our church grows interesting, Zion lifts her head — I overhear remarks signifying Jerusalem, I do not feel at liberty to say any more today! I wanted to write you *Friday*, the night of Jennie Lind, but reaching home past midnight, and *my room* sometime after, encountering several perils starting, and on the way, among which a *kicking horse,* an inexperienced driver, a number of Jove's thunderbolts, and a very terrible rain, are worthy to have record. All of us went — just four — add an absent individual and that will make full five — the concert commenced at eight, but knowing the world was *hollow* we thought we'd start at six, and come up with everybody that meant to come up with us — we had proceeded some steps when one of the beasts showed symptoms, and just by the *blacksmith's shop* exercises commenced, consisting of kicking and plunging on the part of the horse, and whips and moral suasion from the *gentleman* who drove — the horse refused to proceed, and your respected family with much chagrin dismounted, advanced to the hotel, and for a season halted — another horse procured, we were politely invited to take our seats, and proceed, which we refused to do till the animal was warranted — about half thro' our journey thunder was said to be heard, and a suspicious *cloud* came travelling up the sky — what words express our horror when rain began to fall — in drops — sheets — cataracts — what *fancy conceive* of drippings and of drenchings which we met on the way — how the stage and its mourning captives drew up at Warner's hotel — how all of us alighted, and were conducted in, how the rain did not abate, how we walked in silence to the old Edwards Church and took our seats in the same, how Jennie came out like a child and sang and sang again, how boquets fell in showers, and the roof was rent with applause — how it thundered outside, and inside with the thunder of God and of men — judge ye which was the loudest – how we all loved Jennie Lind, but not accustomed oft to her manner of singing did'nt fancy *that* so well as we did *her* — no doubt it was very fine — but take some notes from her "Echo" — the Bird sounds from the "Bird Song" and some of her curious trills, and I'd rather have a Yankee.

Herself, and not her music, was what we seemed to love – she has an air of *exile* in her mild blue eyes, and a something sweet and touching in her native accent which charms her many friends — "Give me my thatched cottage" as she sang grew so earnest she seemed half lost in song and for a transient time I fancied she *had* found it and would be seen "na mair," and then her foreign accent made her again a wanderer — we will talk about her sometime when you come — Father sat all the evening looking *mad,* and *silly,* and yet so much amused you would have *died* a laughing — when the performers bowed, he said "Good evening Sir" — and when they retired, "very well — that will do," it was'nt *sarcasm* exactly, nor it was'nt *disdain,* it was infinitely funnier than either of those virtues, as if old Abraham had come to see the show, and thought it was all very well, but a little excess of *Monkey*! She took 4000 $ / *mistake* arithmetical/ for tickets at Northampton aside from all expenses. I'm glad you took a seat opposite Lord Mayor — if he had sat in your lap it had pleased me even better — it must seem pretty grand to be a city officer and pat the Sheriff's back, and wink to the Policemen! I'm sorry you got so tired, and would suggest respectfully a Rose in every thorn!

[52]

We are all pretty comfortable, and things get along well – Bowdoin has gone home naying – the Tutors are hanging on – Francis March is here, had not been *seen* at the latest – the Exhibition came, and *went* for all that I know – choosing not to "tend." Sanford – Valedictorian – Stebbins – Salutatorian – Carr [Karr] – Oratio Philosophico – I do not know the rest, except that Wm Washburn has a Dissertation from the delivery of which he is "respectfully excused."

About our coming to Boston – we think we shall probably *come* – we want to see our friends – yourself and Aunt L's family – we dont care a fig for the *museum,* the stillness, or Jennie Lind. We are not going to stay long – not more than a week – are sorry Emily is gone, but she shall come to see us – how long will Joel be gone – we have talked of Thursday or Friday as the earliest that we should come – perhaps not until Monday – can you write a line and send to us tomorrow, how long Joe will be gone? Give our love to our friends, and tell them we will write them and let them know our plans as soon as we hear from you – Thank them if you please for their kind invitation, and tell them we are coming not to see *sights* but *them,* and therefore all the stillness will not incommode us. I saw Martha Friday – she inquired all about you, and said she was going to write, and Susie too that I could send next time – it has rained ever since then and it is raining now, now so I disappoint you – have patience Austin, and they shall come next time. Father says your letters are altogether before Shakespeare, and he will have them published to put in our library. Emily Fowler's regards – Love from us all – dont know what I say I write in such a hurry.

Your aff Sister
Emily

MANUSCRIPT: AC. Ink. Dated: Sunday afternoon.

PUBLICATION: L (1894) 81–83, in part; L (1931) 80–83, in part; *Home* 150–153, entire.

The churches were generally the only meeting places in New England towns large enough to hold such an audience as Jenny Lind could draw. ED never heard any other singer or instrumental musician of note.

"I will never desert Micawber" however *he may* be forgetful of the "Twins" and me, I promised the Rev Sir to "cherish" Mr Micawber, and cherish him I *will*, tho Pope or Principality, endeavor to drive me from it — the "Twins" cling to him *still* — it would quite break his heart abandoned tho' he be, to hear them talk about him. Twin *Martha* broke her heart and went to the Green Mountain, from the topmost cliff of which she flings the *pieces* round. Twin *Susan* is more calm, tho' in *most deep* affliction. You'd better not come home, I say the *law* will have you, a *pupil* of the law, o'ertaken *by* the law, and brought to "condign punishment" — scene for angels and men — or rather for *Archangels* who being a little *higher* would seem to have a 'vantage so far as view's concerned! *"Are* you pretty comfortable tho," and are you deaf and dumb and gone to the asylum where such afflicted persons learn to hold their tongues?

The next time you a'nt going to write me I'd thank you to let me know — this kind of *protracted* insult is what no man can bear — fight with me like a man — let me have fair shot, and you are "caput mortuum" et "cap a pie," and that ends the business! If you really think I so deserve this silence tell me why — how — I'll be a *thorough* scamp or else I wont be *any,* just which you prefer!

[Horace] Taylor of Spencer's class went to Boston yesterday, it was in my heart to send an *apple* by him for your private use, but Father overheard some of my intentions and said they were "rather small" — whether this remark was intended for the *apple,* or for my noble self I did not think to ask him — I rather think he intended to give us *both* a cut — however, he may go!

You are coming home on Wednesday, as perhaps you know, and I am very happy in prospect of your coming, and hope you want to see us as much as we do you. Mother makes nicer pies with reference to your coming, I arrange my tho'ts in a convenient shape, Vinnie grows only *perter* and *more* pert day by day.

The Horse is looking finely, better than in his life, by which you may think him *dead* unless I add *before.* The carriage stands in state all covered in the chaise-house — we have *one foundling hen* into

whose young mind I seek to instill the fact that "Massa is a comin!"
The garden is amazing — we have beets and beans, have had *splendid
potatoes* for three weeks now. Old Amos weeds and hoes and has an
oversight of all thoughtless vegetables. The apples are fine and large
in spite of my impression that *Father* called them "small."

Yesterday there was a *fire* — at about 3. in the afternoon Mr
Kimberly's barn was discovered to be on fire — the wind was blowing
a gale directly from the west, and having had no rain, the roofs
[were] as dry as stubble. Mr Palmer's house was cleared — the *little
house* of Father's, and Mr Kimberly's also. The engine was broken
and it seemed for a little while as if the whole street must go. The
Kimberly barn was burnt down, and the house much charred and
injured, tho not at all destroyed. Mr Palmer's barn took fire and Dea
Leland's also, but were extinguished with only part burned roofs. We
all feel very thankful at such a narrow escape. Father says there was
never such imminent danger, and such miraculous escape. Father and
Mr Frink took charge of the fire, or rather of the *water,* since fire
usually takes care of *itself.* The men all worked like heroes, and after
the fire was out Father gave commands to have them march to
Howe's where an entertainment was provided for them — after the
whole was over, they gave "three cheers for Edward Dickinson, and
three more for the Insurance Company"!

On the whole it is very wonderful that we did'nt all burn up, and
we ought to hold our tongues and be very thankful. If there *must be*
a fire I'm sorry it couldnt wait until you had got home, because you
seem to enjoy such things so very much.

There is nothing of moment now which I can find to tell you
except a case of measles in Hartford. The Colemans were here last
week, passed a night here — they came to get John Emerson to travel
with Wm Flint. John went to Monson Saturday, and starts with W^m
Flint for the White Mts today.

This is one more feather in the Valedictorian's cap, I guess he
thinks he will certainly have her now — I mean will have *Eliza.* If *I*
loved a girl to disstraction, I think it would take some coaxing before
I would act as footman to her crazy friends — yet love is *pretty solemn.*
I dont know as I blame John. He is going to be Tutor next year.
Vinnie and I made Currant Wine one day last week, I think it will
suit you finely.

[55]

You remember James Kellogg's Dogs—the one they kept for a watch dog was poisoned by someone and died last week. Chauncey Russell, Frank Pierce, and George Cutler are somewhere on the coast catching fur and fishes, but principally the *former*. Perhaps they have called on you during their travels sometime tho' I dont know their route exactly. Would'nt I love to take a peep at Old Fanueil and all the little Irish, the day of the city fair?

Goodbye Sir—Fare you well, my benison to your school.

The folks all send their love. My compliments to Joel.

MANUSCRIPT: AC. Ink. Dated Sunday night. Envelope addressed: Austin Dickinson./Care of Loring Norcross Esq./Boston./Mass.

PUBLICATION: *L* (1894) 109-111, in part; *L* (1931) 104-106, in part; *Home* 157-159, entire.

The houses on the east side of the common were close together, and a fire in one endangered a large section. According to the records of the Hampshire County registry of deeds, Edward Dickinson purchased from Nathan Dickinson, 16 March 1840, a house on the east side of the common. William Flynt, a cousin from Monson, had been ill. Henry Frink was landlord of the newly opened Hygeian Hotel (American House).

50

To Abiah Root   *19 August 1851*

"Yet a little while I am with you, and again a little while and I am *not* with you" because you go to your mother! Did she not tell me saying, "yet a little while ye shall see me and again a little while and ye shall *not* see me, and I would that where I am, there *ye* may be also"—but the virtue of the text consists in *this* my dear—that "if *I go*, I *come* again, and ye shall be with me where *I am*;" that is to say, that if you come in *November* you shall be mine, and I shall be thine, and so on "vice versa" until "ad infinitum" which isn't a *great* way off! While I think of it my dear friend, and we are upon these subjects, allow me to remark that you have the funniest manner of popping into town, and the most *lamentable* manner of popping *out* again of any one I know.

It really becomes to me a matter of serious moment, this propensity of your's concerning your female friends – the "morning cloud and the early dew" are not more evanescent.

I think it was *Tuesday evening* that we were so amused by the oratorical feats of three or four young gentlemen – I remember I sat by you and took great satisfaction in such seat and society – I remember further our mutual Goodnights, our promises to meet again, to tell each other tales of our own heart and life, to seek and find each other after so long a time of distant separation – I can hardly realize Abiah that these are *recollections,* that our happy *today* joins the great band of *yesterdays* and marches on to the dead – too quickly *flown* my Bird, for me to satisfy me that you *did* sit and sing beneath my chamber window! I only went out *once* after the time I saw you – the morning of Mr Beecher, I looked for you in vain – I discovered your Palmer cousins, but if you indeed were *there* it must have been in a form to my gross sense impalpable. I was *disappointed* Abiah – I had been hoping much a little visit from you – when will the hour *be* that we shall sit together and talk of what we were, and what we *are* and may be – with the shutters *closed,* dear Abiah and the balmiest little breeze stealing in at the window? I *love* those little fancies, yet I would love them *more* were they not *quite so fanciful* as they have seemed to be – I have fancied so many times and so many times gone home to find it was *only* fancy that I am half afraid to *hope* for what I *long* for. It would seem my dear Abiah that out of all the moments crowding this little world a *few* might be vouchsafed to spend with those we love – a *separated* hour – an hour more pure and true than *ordinary* hours, when we could *pause* a moment before we journey on – we had a *pleasant* time talking the other morning – had I known it was *all my portion,* mayhap I'd *improved* it more – but it never'll come back again to try whether or no. Dont you think sometimes these brief imperfect meetings have a tale to tell – perhaps but for the sorrow which accompanies *them* we would not be reminded of brevity and change – and would build the dwelling *earthward* whose site is in the skies – perhaps the treasure *here* would be *too dear* a treasure – could'nt "the moth corrupt, and the thief break thro' and steal" – and this makes me think how I *found* a little moth in my stores the other day – a very *subtle* moth that had in ways and manners to me and mine unknown, contrived to hide itself in a favorite worsted basket – how long my little treasurehouse had furnished an arena for it's destroying labors it is not *mine* to tell – it had an *errand* there – I trust it fulfilled it's mission; it taught me dear Abiah to have no treasure *here,* or rather it tried to tell me in it's little mothy way of another *enduring* treasure, the robber cannot steal which, nor time waste away. How many a lesson learned from lips of such tiny teachers – dont it make you think of the Bible – "not many mighty – not wise"?

You met our dear Sarah Tracy after I saw you here – her sweet face is the same as in those happy school days – and in vain I search for wrinkles brought on by many cares – we all love Sarah dearly, and shall try to do all in our power to make her visit happy. Is'nt it very remarkable that in so many years Sarah has changed so little – not that she has stood still, but has made such *peaceful* progress – her thot's tho' they are *older* have all the charm of youth – have not yet lost their freshness, their innocence and peace – she seems so pure in heart – so sunny and serene, like some sweet Lark or Robin ever soaring and singing – I have not seen her much – I want to see her more – she speaks often of *you,* and with a warm affection – I hope no change or time shall *blight* these loves of ou[r]'s, I would bear them all in my arms to my home in the glorious heaven and say "here am I my Father, and those whom thou hast given me." If the life which is to come is better than dwelling *here,* and angels are there and our friends are glorified and are singing there and praising there need we fear to go – when spirits beyond *wait* for us – I was meaning to see you more and talk about such things with you – I want to know your views and your *eternal* feelings – how things *beyond* are to you – Oh there is much to speak of in meeting one you love, and it always seems to me that I might have spoken more, and I almost always think that what *was* found to say might have been left unspoken.

Shall it *always* be so Abiah – is there no *longer* day given for our communion with the spirits of our love? – writing is brief and fleeting – conversation will come again, yet if it *will,* it hastes and must be on it's way – earth is short Abiah, but Paradise is *long* there must be many moments in an eternal day – then *sometime we* shall tarry, while time and tide *roll on,* and till then Vale!

Your own dear

Emilie

MANUSCRIPT: HCL (ARS 9). Ink. Dated: Tuesday Evening.

PUBLICATION: L (1894) 53–57, in part; L (1931) 46–50, in part.
ED had seen Abiah unexpectedly during commencement activities on 12 August. Next morning Henry Ward Beecher delivered an address on "Imagination." Graduation was held on Thursday. Probably this letter was written the following Tuesday. The first quotation recalls John 16.16; the second, Matthew 6.19; the third, I Corinthians 1.26; the last, John 17.24.

52

To Austin Dickinson   *23 September 1851*

We have got home, dear Austin — it is very lonely here — I have tried to make up my mind which was better — home, and parents, and country; or city, and smoke, and dust, shared with the only being I can call my Brother — the scales dont poise very evenly, but so far as I can judge, the balance is in your favor. The folks are much more lonely than while we were away — they say they seemed to feel that we were straying together, and together would return, and the *un-attended* sisters seemed very sad to them. They had been very well indeed, and got along very nicely while we were away. When Father was gone at night, Emeline [Kellogg] stayed with mother. They have had a number of friends to call, and visit with them. Mother never was busier than while we were away — what with fruit, and plants, and chickens, and sympathizing friends, she really was so hurried she hardly knew what to do.

Vinnie and I came safely, and met with no mishap — the boquet was not withered, nor was the bottle cracked. It was fortunate for the freight car, that Vinnie and I were there, our's being the only baggage passing along the line. The folks looked very funny, who travelled with us that day — they were dim and faded like folks passed away — the conductor seemed so grand with about *half a dozen* tickets, which he dispersed, and demanded in a very small space of time — I judged that the *minority* were travelling that day, and could'nt hardly help smiling at our ticket friend, however sorry I was at the small amount of people, passing along his way. He looked as if he wanted to make an apology for not having more travellers to keep him company.

The route and the cars seemed strangely — there were no boys with fruit, there were no boys with pamphlets — one fearful little fellow

[59]

ventured into the car with what appeared to be publications and tracts — he offered them to no one, and no one inquired for them, and he seemed greatly relieved that no one wanted to buy them.

At Sunderland, we happened to think that we might find John Thompson, and find John Thompson we did, just sitting down to dinner — he seemed overjoyed to see us — wants very much to see you — asked many questions about yourself and school, all of which we answered in a most glowing manner, and John's countenance fell — we asked him if he was happy — "why, *pretty* happy" — they promised him "35." according to his own story — only 25. of whom have yet made their appearance — he thinks he will not stay more than half a term, and wonders "how in the world" you contrived to be so happy, and like Sunderland people so exceedingly well. He says he has no plan, should he not remain there — seems to be somewhat sober at the little he finds to do — studies law in his leisure. "The Elder" had gone to dinner — Mr Russell was there, seemed quite pleased to see us for our brother's sake — he asked us all about you, and expressed his sincere pleasure in your present prosperity — "wished they had had you *there*," when Thompson was not present! There has been nothing said about Mr Russell lately, as Landlord of the Hygeian — Frink is there himself, and seems to like it well, and probably will keep it, I judge from what they say. They have a great deal of company, and everything goes on well.

You wanted us to tell you about the Pelham Picnic — the folks did'nt know that there had ever been any, so I cannot give you any information there. I suspect if there *was* a party, it was composed of persons whom none of us know. Calvin Merrill is married, you *know* — he had a great wedding party at the residence of his bride, the blooming Mrs Benjamin — Tim Henderson and "suite," and Cotton Smith and suite were among the guests, and were suitably honored. Mr Merrill resides with the recent *Mrs* Merrill, alias Mrs Benjamin, *more* alias, Mrs Thompson — for the sake of the widowed lady for the third time a *bride*. I hope her buried Lords are buried very low, for if on some fine evening they should fancy to *rise* I fear their couple of angers might accompany them, and exercise themselves on grooms who erst were widowers, and widows who are brides.

Bowdoin has gone home on account of his eye — he has'nt been able to use it since we went away — the folks are afraid he will never have the use of it — he dont know when he'll come back — probably not, till it gets well, which we fear may not soon be — at present his father is sick — pretty sick with the dysentery. Howland is here with father — will stay a while I guess. They go to Northampton together, as it is court there now and seem very happy together in the law. Father likes Howland grandly, and they go along as smoothly as friendly barks at sea — or when harmonious stanzas become one melody. Howland was here last evening — is jolly and just as happy — really I cant think now what *is* so happy as he. He wants to see you, says he is going to write you. Sanford is in town, but as yet we hav'nt seen him. Nobody knows what the fellow is here for.

You remember [John] Lord the Historian who gave some lectures here — he has come round again, and is lecturing now on the "Saints and Heroes." He gives them at the chapel — I guess all of us shall go — tho' we were too tired last evening. Prof Jewett has come and is living with his wife east of Gen Mack and *his* wife. Pretty perpendicular times, I guess, in the ancient mansion. I am glad we dont come home as we used, to this old castle. I could fancy that skeleton cats ever caught spectre rats in dim old nooks and corners, and when I hear the query concerning the pilgrim fathers — and imperturbable Echo merely answers *where*, it becomes a satisfaction to know that they are there, sitting stark and stiff in Deacon Mack's mouldering arm chairs. We had'nt been home an hour, when Martha came to see us — she was here on Saturday after the stage came in, and was dreadfully disappointed because we did not come. She has'nt changed a bit, and I love her dearly. She was so indignant about her sweet boquet — she said it was kind and fragrant, and would have comforted you in the first few days of exile. I showed her all my treasures — I opened the little box containing the scented beads — I tried it on my wrist, she exclaimed it was how beautiful — then I clasped it on her own, and while she praised it's workmanship and turned it o'er and o'er, I told her it was her's, and you did send it to her — then that sweet face grew radiant, and joyful that blue eye, and Martha seemed so happy to know you'd tho't of her, it would have made you happy — *I* know! She said she should write you — if she has not, she will directly — she has had a letter from Sue — she is situated very pleasantly, and tells her sisters here that she can see no reason why she should not be happy — they are very kind to her — she loves some of her scholars. I

[61]

hav'nt seen Martha long enough to ask but a very little, but I will find out everything before I write again. It has rained very hard all day, it has been "dark and dreary" and winds "are never weary."

Mother has three shirts which she is going to send you besides the ones we bro't — also a pair of bosoms which her forgetful son failed to carry away. She will send you the whole by the first good opportunity, and we shall send some fruit as soon as we have a chance. It is beautiful — *beautiful!!* Mother sends much love and Vinnie.

Your lonely
Sister Emily

Father has just home come, having been gone today. I have therefore not till now got a glimpse of your letter. Sue's address is, Care of Mr Archer — 40. Lexington St. I will keep the note till I see, or send, to Bowdoin. I answer all the questions in your note but *one* — *that* I cannot do till they let you come home — that will be *soon,* dear Austin — do not despair — we're "with you alway, even unto the end"! Tho' absence be not for "the present, joyous, but grievous, ["] it shall work out for us a far more exceeding and "eternal weight" of *presence!*

Give our love to our Boston friends — tell them we are well and got home very nicely. Vinnie found the shawls very comfortable and thanks them much for them.

Speaking of *fireworks,* tell Joe we wont ever forget him – *forget him? – never –* "let April tree forget to bud" – etc!

Will Aunt Lavinia sometime tell Mrs Greely how beautifully the boquet came, and how much it has been admired?

You may if you would like, remember both of your sisters to Misses Knight, and French, also tell Mr Nurse we are very sorry for him!

MANUSCRIPT: AC. Ink. Dated: Tuesday Evening. Envelope addressed: Wᵐ Austin Dickinson./Care of Joel Norcross./Boston./Mass. Postmarked: Amherst Ms./Sep 24.

PUBLICATION: L (1894) 87–89, in part; LL 160–161, in part; L (1931) 86–87, in part; Home 165–168, entire.

On the journey home from Boston the girls traveled by the Vermont & Massachusetts Railroad to Grout's Corner (Miller's Falls) and then fifteen miles by stage, through Sunderland. John Thompson, whom they saw there, had taken Austin's place as teacher in the Sunderland school. To support herself, Susan Gilbert left Amherst in September against family opposition to teach at a private school in Baltimore, conducted by Robert Archer.

To Austin Dickinson   *1 October 1851*

We are just thro' dinner, Austin, I want to write so much that I omit digestion, and a *dyspepsia* will probably be the result. I want to see you more than I ever did before — I should have written again, before I got your letter, but thought there might be something which I should love to tell you, or if you should ask any questions I would want to answer those. I received what you wrote, at about 2½ oclock yesterday. Father brought home the same, and waited himself in order to have me read it — I reviewed the contents hastily — striking out all suspicious places, and then very *artlessly* and unconsciously began. My heart went "pit a pat" till I got safely by a remark concerning Martha, and my stout heart was *not* till the manuscript was over. The allusion to Dick Cowles' grapes, followed by a sarcasm on Mr Adams' tomatoes, amused father highly. He quite *laid it to heart,* he thot, it was so funny. Also the injunction concerning the college tax, father took occasion to say was "quite characteristic."

You say we must'nt trouble to send you any fruit, also your clothes must give us no uneasiness. I dont ever want to have you say any more such things. They make me feel like crying. If you'd only *teased* us for it, and declared that you *would* have it, I should'nt have cared so much that we could find no way to send you any, but you resign so cheerfully your birthright of purple grapes, and do not so much as *murmur* at the departing peaches, that I hardly can taste the one or drink the juice of the other. They are so *beautiful* Austin — we have such an *abundance* "while *you* perish with hunger."

I do hope someone will make up a mind to go before our peaches are quite gone. The world is full of people travelling *everywhere,* until it occurs to you that you will send an errand, and then by "hook or crook" you cant find any traveller, who for money or love can be induced to go and convey the opprobrious package! It's a very selfish age, that is all I can say about it! Mr storekeeper Sweetser has been "almost persuaded" to go, but I believe he has put it off "till a more convenient season," so to show my disapprobation, I shant buy any more gloves at Mr. Sweetser's store! Dont you think it will seem very cutting to see me pass by his goods, and purchase at Mr Kellogg's? I dont think I shall *retract* should he regret his course, and decide to go *tomorrow*, because it is the *"principle"* of disappointing people, which I disapprove!

You must not give it up, but that you will *yet* have some, there *may* be some good angel passing along your way, to whom we can entrust a snug little bundle — the peaches are very large — one side a *rosy* cheek, and the other a *golden,* and that peculiar coat of velvet and of down, which makes a peach so beautiful. The grapes too are fine, juicy, and *such* a purple — I fancy the robes of kings are not a *tint* more royal. The vine looks like a kingdom, with ripe round grapes for kings, and hungry mouths for subjects — the first instance on record of subjects devouring kings! You *shall* have some grapes dear Austin, if I have to come on foot in order to bring them to you.

The apples are very fine — it is'nt quite time to pick them — the cider is almost done — we shall have some I guess by Saturday, at *any rate Sunday noon!* The vegetables are not gathered, but will be before very long. The horse is doing nicely, he travels "like a bird," to use a favorite phrase of your delighted mother's. You ask about the leaves — shall I say they are falling? They had begun to fall before Vinnie and I came home, and we walked up the steps through "little brown ones rustling." Martha and I were talking of you the other night, how we wished you were here to see the autumn sun set, and walk and talk with us among the fading leaves.

Martha is very long talking of you and Susie, she seems unreconciled to letting you go away. She is down here most every day – she brings Sue's letters and reads them. It would make you laugh to hear all which she has to tell — she writes in excellent spirits, tho' Martha and I think they are *"unnatural,"* we think she is so gay because she feels so badly and fancies we shant know. Susie asks in every letter why she dont hear from you – she says "Emily and Austin were going to write *so soon,* and I'll warrant I wont hear from either of them, for *one while.*" I sent her a letter Monday — I hope if you have not written, you *will* do very soon, for Susie is so far off, and wants so much to have you. Martha wants to see you very much indeed, and sends her love to you. Emily Fowler has gone travelling somewhere with her father — New Haven and New York are to be the stopping places. Charlie has yet no school. I suspect he needs *your aid* in passing himself off somewhere. I have smiled a good many times at that fruitful ride

[64]

to Sunderland, and the blessings and favors which accompanied it, to Charles. Vinnie tells me *she* has detailed the *news* — she reserved the *deaths* for me, thinking I might fall short of my usual letter somewhere. In accordance with her wishes, I acquaint you with the decease of your aged friend — Dea Kingsbury. He had no disease that we know of, but gradually went out. Martha Kingman has been very sick, and is not yet out of danger. Jane Grout is slowly improving, tho' very feeble yet. "Elizy" has been in Boston, she came home Tuesday night. She asked her friends, and they endeavored to find you, but could not.

She says she told you when you were at home that she should go in *October*, and you were coming to see her, but as she changed her mind and went *earlier*, she did not suppose of course, that you would know she was there. She was very sorry not to be able to find you.

Father has written to Monson to have them all come up here and make us a family visit — I hardly think they will come. If they dont, sometime, next week mother means to go to Monson, and make *them* a little visit. Bowdoin's eye is better, and he has got back to the office — Howland has gone to Conway — will probably be here again in the course of two or three weeks. Did Vinnie tell you that she went with him to Ware, and how it made a hubbub in the domestic circle?

Emeline and Henry are just learning to say *"we,"* I think they do very well for such "new beginners." There was quite an excitement in the village Monday evening. We were all startled by a violent church bell ringing, and thinking of nothing but fire, rushed out in the street to see. The sky was a beautiful red, bordering on a crimson, and rays of a gold pink color were constantly shooting off from a kind of sun in the centre. People were alarmed at this beautiful Phenomenon, supposing that fires somewhere were *coloring the sky*. The exhibition lasted for nearly 15. minutes, and the streets were full of people wondering and admiring. Father happened to see it among the very first and rang the bell *himself* to call attention to it. You will have a full account from the pen of Mr Trumbell, whom I have not a doubt, was seen with a large lead pencil, a noting down the sky at the time of it's highest glory. Father will write you soon — the day that your letter came with a list of our expenses — he seemed very busy, so I did'nt read *that* part, and his hands have been so full that I have seen no time when I could show it to him — however he knows of all our

[65]

expenditures, and will make everything right when you next come home—you dont like to have us ever speak of such things, but father wrote to know, and I tho't you might think it strange he should not write about it after your letter came. You will be here now *so soon*— we are impatient for it—we want to see you, Austin, how much I cannot say here.

Your aff

Emily

Your clothes are in beautiful order, everything in waiting to have some way to send. I have heeled the lamb's wool stockings, and now and then repaired some imperfections in the destined shirts—when you *wear* them, you must'nt forget these things. You made us very happy while we were away. Love from all the folks, with a how I do want to see you!

MANUSCRIPT: AC. Ink. Dated: Wednesday noon. Envelope addressed: William Austin Dickinson./Care of Joel Norcross./Boston./Mass. Postmarked: Amherst Ms Oct 2.

PUBLICATION: L (1894) 90–93, in part; LL 162–164, in part; L (1931) 90–92, in part; Home 169–172, entire.

An account of the aurora borealis was published in the *Hampshire and Franklin Express* on 3 October. Each of the two Howland brothers, William and George, was for a time a special friend of Lavinia's. Emeline Kellogg and Henry Nash were married four years later. Samuel Kingsbury died, September 27, aged 88.

56

To Susan Gilbert (Dickinson)   *9 October 1851*

I wept a tear here, Susie, on purpose for *you*—because this "sweet silver moon" smiles in on me and Vinnie, and then it goes so far before it gets to you—and then you never told me if there *was* any moon in Baltimore—and how do *I* know Susie—that you see her sweet face at all? She looks like a fairy tonight, sailing around the sky in a little silver gondola with stars for gondoliers. I asked her to let me ride a little while ago—and told her I would *get out* when she got as far as Baltimore, but she only smiled to herself and went sailing on.

I think she was quite ungenerous — but I have learned the lesson and shant ever ask her again. To day it rained at home — sometimes it rained so hard that I fancied you could hear it's patter — patter, patter, as it fell upon the leaves — and the fancy pleased me so, that I sat and listened to it — and watched it earnestly. *Did* you hear it Susie — or was it *only* fancy? Bye and bye the sun came out — just in time to bid us goodnight, and as I told you sometime, the moon is shining now.

It is such an evening Susie, as you and I would walk and have such pleasant musings, if you were only here — perhaps we would have a "Reverie" after the form of "Ik Marvel," indeed I do not know why it would'nt be just as charming as of that lonely Bachelor, smoking his cigar — and it would be far more profitable as "Marvel" *only* marvelled, and you and I would *try* to make a little destiny to have for our own. Do you know that charming man is dreaming *again,* and will wake pretty soon — so the papers say, with *another* Reverie — more beautiful than the first?

Dont you hope he will live as long as you and I do — and keep on having dreams and writing them to us; what a charming old man he'll be, and how I envy his grandchildren, little "Bella" and "Paul"! We will be willing to die Susie — when such as *he* have gone, for there will be none to interpret these lives of our's.

Longfellow's "golden Legend" has come to town I hear — and may be seen *in state* on Mr. Adams' bookshelves. It always makes me think of "Pegasus in the pound" – when I find a gracious author sitting side by side with "Murray" and "Wells" and "Walker" in that renowned store — and like *him* I half expect to hear that they have "*flown*" some morning and in their native ether revel all the day; but for our sakes dear Susie, who please ourselves with the fancy that we are the only poets, and everyone else is *prose,* let us hope they will yet be willing to share our humble world and feed upon such aliment as *we* consent to do!

You thank me for the Rice cake — you tell me Susie, you have just been tasting it — and how happy I am to send you anything you love — how hungry you must grow before it is noon there — and then you must be faint from teaching those stupid scholars. I fancy you very often descending to the schoolroom with a plump Binomial Theorem struggling in your hand which you must dissect and exhibit to your incomprehending ones – I hope you whip them Susie – for *my* sake

– whip them *hard* whenever they dont behave just as you want to have them! I know they are very dull – sometimes – from what Mattie says – but I presume you encourage them and forgive all their mistakes. It will teach you *patience* Susie — you may be sure of that. And Mattie tells me too of your evening carousals – and the funny frights you give in personating the Master – just like you Susie – like you for all the world – how Mr .Payson would laugh if I could only tell him, and then those great dark eyes — how they would glance and sparkle! Susie – have all the fun wh' you possibly can — and laugh as often and sing, for tears are plentier than smiles in this little world of our's; only dont be so happy as to let Mattie and me grow dimmer and dimmer and finally fade away, and merrier maids than we smile in our vacant places!

Susie, *did* you think that I would never write you when you were gone away – what made you? I am sure you know my promise far too well for that – and had I never said so – I should be *constrained* to write – for what shall separate us from any whom we love – not *"hight* nor depth" . . .

MANUSCRIPT: HCL (L 5). Ink. Dated: Thursday Evening. End of letter missing.

PUBLICATION: FF 205–208.

According to ED's letter to Austin of 1 October, she had written to Sue once before, on 29 September. *Reveries of a Bachelor* (1850) by Ik Marvel (Donald G. Mitchell) was a bestseller. Longfellow's *Golden Legend* had recently been published. Lindley Murray, William Harvey Wells, and John Walker were compilers of language texts.

59

To Austin Dickinson   *25 October 1851*

Dear Austin.

I've been trying to think this morning how many weeks it was since you went away — I fail in calculations — it seems so long to me since you went back to school that I set down days for years, and weeks for a *score* of years — not reckoning time "by minutes" I dont know what to think of such great discrepancies between the *actual* hours and those which "seem to be." It may seem long to *you* since you returned to Boston – how I wish you could stay and never go back again. Everything is so still here, and the clouds are cold and gray – I think it will rain soon – Oh I am so lonely!

We had a beautiful visit, but it was all too short for we brothers and sisters, and Vinnie and I are dwelling upon the one to come. Thanksgiving is but four weeks, or a little more than four weeks and yet it seems to be a very great way off, when I look forward to it. I have thought you were very sober, since you went away, and I did when you were here, but now you are out of sight, I remember it more frequently, and wonder I did'nt ask you if anything troubled you. I hope you are better now. I waked up this morning, thinking that this was the very morning your eyes were to be well, and I really hope that oculist has'nt broken his promise. You must'nt use them much until they get very strong – you need'nt write to us except on a slip of paper, telling us how you are, and whether you are happy – and I would'nt write at all, until they were perfectly well.

You had a windy evening going back to Boston, and we thought of you many times and hoped you would not be cold. Our fire burned so cheerfully I could'nt help thinking of how many were *here* and how many were *away*, and I wished so many times during that long evening that the door would open and you come walking in. Home is a holy thing – nothing of doubt or distrust can enter it's blessed portals. I feel it more and more as the great world goes on and one and another forsake, in whom you place your trust – here seems indeed to be a bit of Eden which not the sin of *any* can utterly destroy – smaller it is indeed, and it may be less fair, but fairer it is and *brighter* than all the world beside. I hope this year in Boston will not impair your health, and I hope you will be as happy as you used to be before. I dont wonder it makes you sober to leave [this] blessed air – if it were in my power I would on every morning transmit it's purest breaths fragrant and cool to you. How I wish you could have it – a thousand little winds waft it to me this morning, fragrant with forest leaves and bright autumnal berries. I would be *willing* to give you my portion for today, and take the salt sea's breath in it's bright, bounding stead. Now Austin – you have no friend there – why not see Converse often, and laugh and talk with *him?* I think him a noble fellow – it seems to me so pleasant for you to talk with somebody, and he is much like you in many thoughts and feelings. I know he would love to have

[69]

you for a comrade and friend, and I would be with him a good deal if I were you. Mother feels quite troubled about those little boys — fears you will kill one sometime when you are punishing him — for *her sake* be careful! Emily Fowler and Mat were here all afternoon yesterday — never saw Emily F—— when she seemed more sincere — shall go and see her soon — Mat misses *you* so much, and her dear sister Susie. Henry Root was here all evening. Mother's and Vinnie's love. Remember us to Converse — take care of *yourself* —

Your aff
Emily

MANUSCRIPT: AC. Ink. Dated: Saturday noon. Addressed on the fold: For my brother Austin.

PUBLICATION: *L* (1894) 89–90, in part; *L* (1931) 87–88, in part; *Home* 193–194, entire.

Austin's visit at home lasted only two days, and he and his friend Converse left on October 23.

65

To Austin Dickinson   *15 December 1851*

Did you think I was *tardy*, Austin? For two Sunday afternoons, it has been so cold and cloudy that I did'nt feel in my very happiest mood, and so I did not write until next monday morning, determining in my heart never to write to you in any but cheerful spirits.

Even this morning Austin, I am not in merry case, for it snows slowly and solemnly, and hardly an outdoor thing can be seen a stirring — now and then a man goes by, with a large cloak wrapped around him and shivering at that, and now and then a stray kitten out on some urgent errand creeps thro' the flakes, and crawls so fast as *may* crawl half frozen away. I am glad for the sake of your body that you are not here this morning, for it is a trying time for fingers and toes, for for the heart's sake, I would verily have you *here* — you know there *are* winter mornings when the cold *without* only adds to the warm *within*, and the more it snows and the harder it blows, brighter the fires blaze, and chirps more merrily the "cricket on the hearth"; it is hardly cheery enough for such a scene this morning, and yet methinks it *would* be if you were only here. The future full of

[70]

sleighrides would chase the gloom from our minds, which only deepens and darkens with every flake that falls.

Black Fanny would "toe the mark" if you should be here tomorrow, but as the prospects are, I presume Black Fanny's hoofs will not attempt to fly. Do you have any snow in Boston? Enough for a ride, I hope, for the sake of "Auld Lang Syne." Perhaps the "Ladie" of curls, would not object to a drive. So you took Miss Mary to The Mercantile — Vinnie is quite excited about her going to Boston, and things are turning out "just as she expected." Father remarked "he was very glad of it — he thought it would please the *old folks* to have the school master pay respect to their darter." I think that "heavy cold" must be making progress as that devoted family have not yet been seen, or what is *more* suspicious, heard of.

I am glad you like Miss Nichols, it must be so pleasant for you to have somebody to care for, in such a cheerless place — dont shut yourself away from anyone whom you like, in order to keep the faith to those you leave behind! Your friends here are much happier in fancying *you* happy, than if in a pledge so stern you should refuse all friendliness. Truth to the ones you leave does not demand of you to refuse those whom you find, or who would make your exile a less desolate thing in their cheerful circles. On the contrary, Austin, I am very sure that seclusion from everyone there would make an ascetic of you, rather than restore you brighter and truer to *them*. We miss you more and more, we do not become accustomed to separation from you. I almost wish sometimes we need'nt miss you so much, since duty claims a year of you entirely to herself, and then again I think that it is pleasant to miss you if you must go away, and I would not have it otherwise, not even if I could. In every pleasure and pain you come up to our minds so wishfully, we know you'd enjoy our joy, and if you were with us Austin, we could bear little trials more cheerfully — then when we have any dainty, someone is sure to say "it is such as *Austin* loves." When I know of anything funny, I am just as apt to cry, far *more* so than to *laugh*, for I know who *loves jokes best*, and who is not here to enjoy them. We dont *have* many jokes tho' *now*, it is pretty much all sobriety, and we do not have much poetry, father having made up his mind that its pretty much all *real life*. Fathers real life and *mine* sometimes come into collision, but as yet, escape unhurt! I give all your messages to Mat — she seems to enjoy every one

[71]

more than the one before—she was here three afternoons last week, one evening she took tea here with Abby and Abiah Root, and we had such a pleasant time; how I did wish you were here, and so did all the girls—every one of them spoke of it. Did you know that Jane Humphrey's sister [Martha], that you saw at S. Hadley once was dead? They have sent for Jane to come home, I dont know whether she will, she is so far from home. I am so glad you are well, and in such happy spirits—both happy and well is a great comfort to us when you are far away.

Emilie.

Thank you for the music Austin, and thank you for the books. I have enjoyed them very much. I shall learn my part of the Duett, and try to have Vinnie her's. She is very much pleased with Charity.

She would write you now but is busy getting her lesson.

Mother is frying Doughnuts—I will give you a little platefull to have warm for your tea! *Imaginary* ones—how I'd love to send you *real* ones.

MANUSCRIPT: AC. Ink. Dated: Monday morning. Envelope addressed: Wᵐ Austin Dickinson./Boston./Mass. The letter was delivered by hand.

PUBLICATION: L (1894) 102–104, in part; LL 172–173, in part; L (1931) 100–101, in part; Home 208–210, entire, where it is dated January 12.

66

To Austin Dickinson   *24 December 1851*

Dont tell them, *will* you Austin; they are all asleep soundly and I snatch the silent night to speak a word to you. Perhaps *you* are sound asleep, and I am only chatting to the *semblance* of a man ensconced in warmest blankets and deep, downy pillows. I am afraid not, dear Austin, I'm afraid that dreadful pain will keep you wide awake all this dreary night, and *so* afraid am I, that I steal from happy dreams and come to sit with you. Since your letter came, we have thought *so* much about you, Oh more, *many* more than pen and ink can tell you —we are thinking of you *now* midst the night so wild and stormy.

Austin, I hav'nt a doubt that Vinnie and mother are dreaming *even now* of you, tho' Vinnie was *so* sleepy the last time she opened her eye, and mother has had a very fatiguing day. And you know that *I* do, *dont* you, or I should'nt incur such perils for the sake of seeing you. Hav'nt you taken cold, or exposed yourself in some way, or got too tired, teaching those useless boys? — I am so sorry for you. I do wish it was *me*, that you might be well and happy, for I have no profession, and have such a snug, warm home that I had as lief suffer some, a great deal rather than not, that by doing so, you were exempted from it. May I change places, Austin? *I* dont care how sharp the pain is, not if it dart like arrows, or pierce bone and bone like the envenomed barb, I should be twice, *thrice* happy to bear it in your place. Dont try to teach school at all, until you get thoroughly well! The committee will excuse you, I *know* they will, they *must*; tell them if they dont I will tell the Mayor of them and get them all turned out! I am glad to know you are prudent in consulting a physician; I hope he will do you good; has anyone with neuralgia, tried him, that recommended him to you? I think that warmth and rest, cold water and care, are the best medicines for it. I know you can get all these, and be your own physician, which is far the better way.

Now Austin, I cant come, I have no horse to fetch me, I can only advise you of what I think is good, and ask you if you will do it. Had I the art and skill of the greatest of all physicians, and had under my care whole hospitals of patients, I could'nt feel more anxious than in this single case; I do feel so desirous of a complete recovery!

But lest I harm my patient with too much conversation on sickness and pain, I pass to themes more cheerful and reminiscence gay. I know it would make you laugh to see Vinnie sleeping as soundly as a poker, and shovel and pair of tongs, and Cousin Emily Norcross bringing up the rear in a sleep twice as sound and full twice as sonorous, and there come snatches of music from away in mother's room, which wake a funny response in my amused being. I can think of nothing funnier than for intelligent beings to bid the world good night, and go out with their candles, and there's nothing that I enjoy more than rousing these self-same beings and witnessing their discomfiture at the *bare idea* of morning, when they're *so* sleepy yet!

Vinnie thinks me quite savage, and frequently suggests the propriety of having me transported to some barbarous country, where I may meet with those of a similar nature, and allow her to spend her days — that is, such small remainder as my inhumanity spares — in comparative ease and quietness!

She thinks ancient martyrs very trifling indeed and would *welcome* the stake in preference to the sunrise, and that shrill morning call she may be sure to hear!

A'nt you sorry for her; she thinks of your sympathies often, and thinks they would all be hers, if they were nearer home.

Father will come tomorrow, and I will take care of Mat. Had a "merry Christmas" from Sue, besides some beautiful gifts for Vinnie and me, Monday evening. We are having a cozy, rosy, posy little visit with Cousin Emily — enjoy it very much, would love to have you here, if it might be possible. I was glad you remembered Emily, it pleased her very much. Why did you apologize for any of your letters? Coming from you, Austin, they never can be otherwise than delightful to us; better than that you give us, we shall never desire.

Write to us very soon, and say how you are, and be very careful indeed, and dont write but a little, if you find it pains you. Much love.

Emily.

MANUSCRIPT: AC. Ink. Dated: Wednesday night. 12 o'clock. Envelope addressed: Wᵐ Austin Dickinson/Care of Joel Norcross. 31. Milk St./ Boston./Mass. Postmarked: Amherst Ms. Dec 25.

PUBLICATION: *Home* 204–206.

ED's Mount Holyoke roommate, Emily Norcross, was the cousin now visiting them. Edward Dickinson was in Monson, the home of the Norcross family.

72

To Austin Dickinson   *6 February 1852*

Austin.

I have never left you so long before, since you first went away, but we have had such colds that we could not use our eyes so long as to write a letter, and the privation on our part has been greater, I dare say, than it possibly could — on your's.

I have received both your letters, and enjoyed them both very much; *particularly* the notes on the agricultural convention. Miss

Kelly's part of the performance was very fine indeed, and made much fun for us. Should think you must have some *discipline* in order to write so clearly amidst so much confusion. Father seemed specially pleased with the story of the farmer. I am so glad you are better — I wish you might have been spared just for a little visit, but we will try and wait if you dont think best to come, and shall only be the gladder to see you at last. I hope you will be very careful and not get sick again, for it seems to me you've had so much miserable health since you have lived in Boston; if it dont ruin your constitution, I shall be very glad. I am very sorry to hear of the illness of the teachers; I should think you must miss them, they have been with you so long. You will tell us if they are better, when you write home again.

Since we have written you, the grand Rail Road decision is made, and there is great rejoicing throughout this town and the neighboring; that is Sunderland, Montague, and Belchertown. Every body is wide awake, every thing is stirring, the streets are full of people talking cheeringly, and you really should be here to partake of the jubilee. The event was celebrated by D. Warner, and cannon; and the silent satisfaction in the hearts of all is it's crowning attestation.

Father is realy *sober* from excessive satisfaction, and bears his honors with a most becoming air. Nobody *believes* it yet, it seems like a fairy tale, a most *miraculous* event in the lives of us all. The men begin working next week, only think of it, Austin; why I verily believe we shall fall down and worship the first "Son of Erin" that comes, and the first sod he turns will be preserved as an emblem of the struggles and victory of our heroic fathers. Such old fellows as Col' Smith *and his wife,* fold their arms complacently, and say, "well, I declare, we have got it after all" — *got it,* you good for nothings! and so we *have,* in spite of sneers and pities, and insults from all around; and we will *keep* it too, in spite of earth and heaven! How I wish you were here, it is really too bad, Austin, at such a time as now — I miss your big Hurrahs, and the famous stir you make, upon all such occasions; but it is a comfort to know that you are here — that your whole soul is here, and tho' apparently absent, yet present in the highest, and the truest sense. I have got a great deal to say, and I fancy I am saying it in rather a headlong way, but if you can read it, you will know what it means. Martha gets along nicely, was able to have her dress on, and go in the dining room for the first time yesterday. She sends you her love, and will write to you just as soon as [she] is able.

Mother has not decided yet, about going to Boston — seems to think if you are better it is hardly best to go. I will tell you more decide[d]ly when I write again — she would love to do so dearly, but it's a good deal of effort to go away from home at this season, and I hardly know what she will do. Emiline improves slowly. Tutor Howland appeared on .Wednesday, and remained in town till today — took tea here Wednesday evening — took Vinnie to ride yesterday morning, spent most of the afternoon here, and is just shutting the gate upon his last farewell, as I write this morning. I have been to ride twice since I wrote you, once with a party, manned by Root & Co. and last evening with *Sophomore Emmons*, alone; will tell you all about it when I write again, for I am in such a hurry that I cannot stop for breath. Take good care of yourself, Austin, and think much of us all, for we do so of you.

Emilie

I send you my prescription again. Will it trouble you too much to get me another bottle, of the same size as the others, namely *twice the quantity*, and send to me by the first person who comes? You are kind very, Austin, to attend to all my little wants, and I'm sure I thank you for it.

April is'nt far off, and then — and then, we are the "merrie men"!

Vinnie sends her love, and mother. Vinnie says she thinks you dont pay much attention to her.

MANUSCRIPT: AC. Ink. Dated: Friday morning. Envelope addressed: Wᵐ Austin Dickinson./Care of Joel Norcross./31 – Milk St./Boston./ Mass. Postmarked: Amherst Ms. Feb 6. The final three paragraphs are written on a separate strip of paper and on the inside of the envelope flap.

PUBLICATION: *Home* 217-218.

The *Hampshire and Franklin Express* announced on February 6 that the stock of the Amherst and Belchertown Railroad had been fully subscribed. Luke Sweetser was elected president and Edward Dickinson one of the directors.

73

To Susan Gilbert (Dickinson)   *about 6 February 1852*

Will you let me come dear Susie — looking just as I do, my dress soiled and worn, my grand old apron, and my hair — Oh Susie, time would fail me to enumerate my appearance, yet I love you just as dearly as if I was e'er so fine, so you wont care, will you? I am so glad dear Susie — that our hearts are always clean, and always neat and lovely, so not to be ashamed. I have been hard at work this morning, and I ought to be working now — but I cannot deny myself the luxury of a minute or two with you.

The dishes may wait dear Susie — and the uncleared table stand, *them* I have always with me, but you, I have "not always" — *why* Susie, Christ hath saints *manie* — and I have *few*, but thee — the angels shant have Susie — no — no no!

Vinnie is sewing away like a *fictitious* seamstress, and I half expect some knight will arrive at the door, confess himself a *nothing* in presence of her loveliness, and present his heart and hand as the only vestige of him worthy to be refused.

Vinnie and I have been talking about growing old, today. Vinnie thinks *twenty* must be a fearful position for one to occupy — I tell her I dont care if I am young or not, had as lief be thirty, and you, as most anything else. Vinnie expresses her sympathy at my "sere and yellow leaf" and resumes her work, dear Susie, tell me how *you* feel — ar'nt there days in one's life when to be old dont seem a thing so sad —

I do feel gray and grim, this morning, and I feel it would be a comfort to have a piping voice, and broken back, and scare little children. Dont *you* run, Susie dear, for I wont do any harm, and I do love you dearly tho' I do feel so frightful.

Oh my darling one, how long you wander from me, how weary I grow of waiting and looking, and calling for you; sometimes I shut my eyes, and shut my heart towards you, and try hard to forget you because you grieve me so, but you'll never go away, Oh you never will — say, Susie, promise me again, and I will smile faintly — and take up my little cross again of sad — *sad* separation. How vain it seems to *write*, when one knows how to feel — how much more near and dear to sit beside you, talk with you, hear the tones of your voice; so hard to "deny thyself, and take up thy cross, and follow me" — give me strength, Susie, write me of hope and love, and of hearts that *endured*, and great was their reward of "Our Father who art in Heaven." I dont know how I shall bear it, when the gentle spring

[77]

comes; if she should come and see me and talk to me of you, Oh it would surely kill me! While the frost clings to the windows, and the World is stern and drear; this absence is easier; the *Earth* mourns too, for all her little birds; but when they all come back again, and she sings and is so merry — pray, what will become of me? Susie, forgive me, forget all what I say, get some sweet little scholar to read a gentle hymn, about Bethleem and Mary, and you will sleep on sweetly and have as peaceful dreams, as if I had never written you all these ugly things. Never mind the letter Susie, I wont be angry with you if you dont give me any at all — for I know how busy you are, and how little of that dear strength remains when it is evening, with which to think and write. Only *want* to write me, only sometimes sigh that you are far from me, and that will do, Susie! Dont you think we are good and patient, to let you go so long; and dont we think you're a darling, a real beautiful hero, to toil for people, and teach them, and leave your own dear home? Because we pine and repine, dont think we forget the precious patriot at war in other lands! Never be mournful, Susie — be happy and have cheer, for how many of the long days have gone away since I wrote you — and it is almost noon, and soon the night will come, and then there is one less day of the long pilgrimage. Mattie is very smart, talks of you *much*, my darling; I must leave you now — "one little hour of Heaven," thank who did give it me, and will he also grant me one longer and *more* when it shall please his love — bring Susie home, ie! Love always, and ever, and true!

Emily —

MANUSCRIPT: HCL (L 10). Ink. Dated: Friday forenoon.
PUBLICATION: FF 182–184, in part.
The exact date of the letter is uncertain, but its report on Mattie's condition is similar to that of the same date in the preceding letter to Austin, and no other Friday in the month seems to apply as well.

77

To Susan Gilbert (Dickinson)   *about February 1852*

Thank the dear little snow flakes, because they fall *today* rather than some vain *weekday*, when the world and the cares of the world try so hard to keep me from my departed friend—and thank you, too, dear Susie, that you never weary of me, or never *tell* me so, and that when the world is cold, and the storm sighs e'er so piteously, I am sure of one sweet shelter, *one* covert from the storm! The bells are ringing, Susie, north, and east, and south, and *your own* village bell, and the people who love God, are expecting to go to meeting; dont *you* go Susie, not to *their* meeting, but come with me this morning to the church within our hearts, where the bells are always ringing, and the preacher whose name is Love—shall intercede there for us!

They will all go but me, to the usual meetinghouse, to hear the usual sermon; the inclemency of the storm so kindly detaining me; and as I sit here Susie, alone with the winds and you, I have the old *king feeling* even more than before, for I know not even the *cracker man* will invade *this* solitude, this sweet Sabbath of our's. And thank you for my dear letter, which came on Saturday night, when all the world was still; thank you for the love it bore me, and for it's golden thoughts, and feelings so like gems, that I was sure I *gathered* them in whole baskets of pearls! I mourn this morning, Susie, that I have no sweet sunset to gild a page for *you*, nor any bay so blue—not even a little chamber way up in the sky, as your's is, to give me thoughts of heaven, which *I* would give to you. You know how I must write you, down, down, in the terrestrial; no sunset here, no stars; not even a bit of *twilight* which I may poetize—and send you! Yet Susie, there will be romance in the letter's ride to you—think of the hills and the dales, and the rivers it will pass over, and the drivers and conductors who will hurry it on to you; and wont that make a poem such as can ne'er be written? I think of you dear Susie, *now*, I dont know how or why, but more dearly as every day goes by, and that sweet month of promise draws nearer and nearer; and I view July so differently from what I used to—once it seemed parched, and dry—and I hardly loved it *any* on account of it's heat and dust; but *now* Susie, month of all the year the best; I skip the violets—and the dew, and the early Rose and the Robins; I will exchange them *all* for that angry and hot noonday, when I can count the hours and the *minutes* before you come—Oh Susie, I often think that I will try to tell you how very dear you are, and how I'm watching for you, but the words wont come, tho' the *tears* will, and I sit down disappointed—yet darling, you know it all— then why do I seek to tell you? I do not know; in thinking of those I love, my reason is all gone from me, and I do fear sometimes that I must make a hospital for the hopelessly insane, and chain me up there such times, so I wont injure you.

Always when the sun shines, and always when it storms, and *always always*, Susie, we are remembering you, and what else besides *remembering*; I shall not *tell* you, because you know! Were it not for dear Mattie, I dont know what we would do, but she loves you so dearly, and is never tired of talking about you, and we all get together and talk it oer and oer, and it makes us more resigned, than to mourn for you *alone*. It was only yesterday, that I went to see dear Mattie, intending in my heart to stay a little while, only a *very* little one, be-cause of a good many errands which I was going to do, and will you believe it, Susie, I was there an hour — and an hour, and half an hour besides, and would'nt have supposed it had been minutes so many — and what do [you] guess we talked about, all those hours long — what would you give to know — give me one little glimpse of your sweet face, dear Susie, and I will tell you all – we did'nt talk of statesmen, and we did'nt talk of kings — but the time was *filled full*, and when the latch was lifted and the oaken door was closed, why, Susie, I real-ized as never I did before, how much a *single cottage* held that was dear to me. It is sweet — and like home, at Mattie's, but it's *sad* too — and up comes little memory and paints – and paints – and paints – and the strangest thing of all, her canvass is never full, and I find her where I left her, every time that I come — and who is she painting – Ah, Susie, "dinna choose to tell" — but it is'nt Mr Cutler, and it is'nt Daniel Boon, and I shant *tell* you any more – Susie, what will you say if I tell you that Henry Root is coming to see me, some evening of this week, and I have promised to read him some parts of all your letters; now you wont care, dear Susie, for he wants so much to hear, and I shant read him anything which I know you would not be will-ing – just some little places, which will please him so – I have seen him several times lately, and I admire him, Susie, because he talks of *you* so frequently and beautifully; and I know he is so true to you, when you are far away – We talk more of you, dear Susie, than of any other thing – he tells me how wonderful you are, and I tell him how true you are, and his big eyes beam, and he seems so delighted – I know you would'nt care, Susie, if you knew how much joy it made – As I told him the other evening of all your letters to me, he looked up *very* longingly, and I knew what he would say, were he enough acquainted — so I answered the question his heart wanted to ask, and when some pleasant evening, before this week is gone, you remember home and Amherst, then know, Loved One — that *they* are remembering *you*, and that "two or three" are gathered in your name, loving, and speaking of you — and will you be there in the midst of them? Then I've found a beautiful, new, friend, and I've told him about dear Susie, and promised to let him know you so soon as you shall come. Dear Susie, in all your letters there are things sweet and many about which I would speak, but the time says no — yet dont think I forget them — Oh no — they are safe in the little chest which tells no secrets — nor the moth, nor the rust can reach them — but when the time we dream of, comes, *then* Susie, I shall bring them, and we will spend long hours chatting and chatting of them — those precious thoughts of friends — how I loved them, and how I love them now — nothing but Susie *herself* is *half* so dear. Susie, I have not asked you if you were cheerful and well — and I cant think why, except that there's something *perrennial* in those we dearly love, immortal life and vigor; why it seems as if any sickness, or harm, would flee away, would not dare do them wrong, and Susie, while you are taken from me, I class you with the *angels*, and you know the Bible tells us — "there is no sickness there." But, dear Susie, *are* you well, and *peaceful*, for I wont make you cry by saying, are you *happy*? Dont see the *blot*, Susie. It's because I *broke the Sabbath*!

Susie, what shall I do — there is'nt room enough; not *half* enough, to hold what I was going to say. Wont you tell the man who makes sheets of paper, that I hav'nt the *slightest respect* for him!

And when shall I have a letter — when it's convenient, Susie, not when tired and faint — *ever*!

Emeline gets well so slowly; poor Henry; I guess he thinks true love's course does'nt run very smooth —

Much love from Mother and Vinnie, and then there are *some others* who do not dare to send —

Who loves you most, and loves you best, and thinks of you when others rest?

T'is Emilie —

MANUSCRIPT: HCL (L 9). Ink. Dated: Sunday morning.
PUBLICATION: FF 177–181, in part.

[81]

The beautiful new friend was probably Henry Vaughan Emmons. In a recent letter to Austin (no. 72) she spoke of having taken a ride with him alone. Henry Nash and Emeline Kellogg were married three years later (see letter no. 53).

81

To Jane Humphrey   23 March 1852

Thank you for the Catalogue, dear Jennie — why did you run away from N. England and Vinnie and me?

Jennie did'nt answer the letter I sent her a long ago, but I am not angry with her. The snows have covered Abby in her sweet church-yard rest. I was going to pick a leaf from the tree nearest her grave and send it in here, Jennie, but I thought I might disturb her — and besides the leaves are faded and would only make you cry. Your sister Helen will be very near us Jennie. I shall hope to see her sweet face when I go to Northampton with father.

Now Jennie, dont forget me and I will remember you and some sweet summer's day in the future I shall meet you — if not on earth, Jennie, I *will* somewhere else — you know where!

The folks at the West must be kind to you — tell them to be for *my* sake — they *will* not refuse me.

I send you a taste Jennie, of E. Kellogg's wedding cake — you remember her, dont you? Eat it tearfully, Jennie, for it came all the way from me!

Your aff
Emilie

Manuscript: Rosenbach 1170/17 (3). Ink. Envelope, partly torn away, addressed: Miss Jane T. H.../Wi.../La... Postmarked: Amherst Ms. Mar 24. Unpublished.

Jane Humphrey was teaching at Willoughby, Ohio. Abby Haskell died 19 April 1851. Eliza Kellogg married Hanson Read, 25 November 1851.

82

To Austin Dickinson   24 March 1852

You would'nt think it was spring, Austin, if you were at home this morning, for we had a great snow storm yesterday, and things are all white, this morning. It sounds funny enough to hear birds singing, and sleighbells, at a time. But it won't last any, so you need'nt think 'twill be winter at the time when you come home.

I waited a day or two, thinking I might hear from you, but you will be looking for me, and wondering where I am, so I shant wait any longer. We're rejoiced that you're coming home — the first thing we said to father, when he got out of the stage, was to ask if you were coming. I was sure you would all the while, for father said "of course you would," he should "consent to no other arrangement," and as you say, Austin, what father *says*, "he means." How very soon it will be now — why when I really think of it, how near, and how happy it is, my heart grows light so fast, that I could mount a grasshopper, and gallop around the *world*, and not fatigue him any! The sugar weather holds on, and I do believe it will stay until you come.

Mat came home from meeting with us last Sunday, was here Saturday afternoon when father came, and at her special request, was secreted by me in the *entry*, until he was fairly in the house, when she escaped, *unharmed*.

She inquired all about you, and is delighted enough, that you are coming home. I think Mat's got the notion that you dont care much for home or old friends, but have found their better substitutes in Boston, tho' I do my very best to undelude her. But you will be here soon, and you, of all others, know best how to convince her. I had a letter from Sue last week, at Washington — am expecting another today. Dwight Gilbert wrote Mat, that "the Pres' gave a Levee, as soon as he heard of their arrival." The "M C" remind Sue vividly of little boys at school, squabbling, and quarrelling — a very apt illustration! We had a visit from Uncle Bullard, while father was gone — he appeared Friday night, at teatime, and left us Saturday morning, had a very pleasant time. Abby Wood has got well. Emiline is able to ride out, which she did last week, with Henry, to his infinite exultation. Mat is well as ever; Jane Greely is sick with the quinzy – quite sick. Jane Gridley's husband is sick. "Mrs Skeeter" is very feeble, "cant bear Allopathic treatment, cant have Homeopathic" — dont want Hydropathic — Oh what a pickle she is in – should'nt think she would deign to *live* — it is so decidedly vulgar! They have not yet concluded where to move — *Mrs* W. will perhaps obtain board in the "celestial city," but

I'm sure I cant imagine what will become of the rest. Here comes Mattie!

She has just gone away, after staying with me two hours. We have had a beautiful time — Mat anticipates so much in seeing you. Do make the days fly, wont you? Here's her love!

Most everybody is going to move. Jane Gridley has bought the old Simeon S[t]rong place — and is going to move there soon. Frank Pierce, the Montague place, up north — Foster Cook, Mr. Harrington's house – Mr Harrington will move into the Colburn place, until his new house is done &c. This is practical enough. I never tho't I should come to it! Keep well, and happy, Austin – 13 – days, and you shall come!

Much love from us all.

Emilie.

MANUSCRIPT: AC. Ink. Dated: Wednesday morn. Envelope addressed: Wᵐ Austin Dickinson/Care of Joel Norcross./31 – Milk St./Boston/Mass. Postmarked: Amherst Ms. Mar 24.

PUBLICATION: L (1894) 106–107, in part; L (1931) 102–103, in part; Home 232–233, entire.

Jane L. Gridley (b. 1829), daughter of Dr. Timothy Gridley, married Dr. George S. Woodman, 17 September 1849.

85

To Susan Gilbert (Dickinson)   *5 April 1852*

Will you be kind to me, Susie? I am naughty and cross, this morning, and nobody loves me here; nor would *you* love me, if you should see me frown, and hear how loud the door bangs whenever I go through; and yet it is'nt anger – I dont believe it is, for when nobody sees, I brush away big tears with the corner of my apron, and then go working on — bitter tears, Susie — so hot that they burn my cheeks, and almost schorch my eyeballs, but *you* have wept much, and you know they are less of anger than *sorrow*.

And I do love to run fast — and hide away from them all; here in dear Susie's bosom, I know is love and rest, and I never would go away, did not the big world call me, and beat me for not working.

Little *Emerald Mack* is washing, I can hear the warm suds, splash. I just gave her my pocket handkerchief — so I cannot cry any more. And Vinnie sweeps — sweeps, upon the chamber stairs; and Mother is hurrying round with her hair in a silk pocket handkerchief, on account of dust. Oh Susie, it is dismal, sad and drear eno' — and the sun dont shine, and the clouds look cold and gray, and the wind dont blow, but it *pipes* the shrillest roundelay, and the birds dont sing, but twitter — and there's nobody to smile! Do I paint it *natural* — Susie, so you think how it looks? Yet dont you care — for it wont last so always, and we love you just as well — and think of you, as dearly, as if it were not so. Your precious letter, Susie, it sits here now, and smiles so kindly at me, and gives me such sweet thoughts of the dear writer. When you come home, darling, I shant have your letters, shall I, but I shall have *yourself*, which is more — Oh more, and better, than I can even think! I sit here with my little whip, cracking the time away, till not an hour is left of it — then you are here! And *Joy* is here — joy now and forevermore!

Tis only a few days, Susie, it will soon go away, yet I say, go now, this very moment, for I need her — I must have her, Oh give her to me!

Mattie is dear and true, I love her very dearly — and Emily Fowler, too, is very dear to me — and Tempe — and Abby, and Eme', I am sure — I love them all — and I hope they love me, but, Susie, there's a great corner still; I fill it with that is gone, I hover round and round it, and call it darling names, and bid it speak to me, and ask it if it's Susie, and it answers, Nay, Ladie, Susie is stolen away!

Do I repine, is it all murmuring, or am I sad and lone, and cannot, cannot help it? Sometimes when I do feel so, I think it may be wrong, and that God will punish me by taking you away; for he is very kind to let me write to you, and to give me your sweet letters, but my heart wants *more*.

Have you ever thought of it Susie, and yet I know you have, how much these hearts claim; why I dont believe in the whole, wide world, are such hard little creditors — such real little *misers*, as you and I carry with us, in our bosoms every day. I cant help thinking sometimes, when I hear about the ungenerous, Heart, keep very still — or someone will find you out!

I am going out on the doorstep, to get you some new — green grass — I shall pick it down in the corner, where you and I used to sit, and have long fancies. And perhaps the dear little grasses were growing all the while — and perhaps they heard what we said, but they cant *tell!* I have come in now, dear Susie, and here is what I found — not quite so glad and green as when we used to sit there, but a sad and pensive grassie — mourning o'er hopes. No doubt some spruce, young *Plantain. leaf* won its young heart away, and then proved false — and dont you wish *none* proved so, but little Plantains?

I do think it's wonderful, Susie, that our hearts dont break, *every day*, when I think of all the whiskers, and all the gallant men, but I guess I'm made with nothing but a hard heart of stone, for it dont break any, and dear Susie, if mine is stony, your's is stone, upon stone, for you never yield *any*, where *I* seem quite beflown. Are we going to *ossify* always, say, Susie — how will it be? When I see the Popes and the Polloks, and the John-Milton Browns, I think we are *liable*, but I dont know! I am glad there's a big *future* waiting for me and you. You would love to know what I read – I hardly know what to tell you, my catalogue is so small.

I have just read three little books, not great, not thrilling — but sweet and true. "The Light in the Valley," "Only," and A "House upon a Rock" – I know you would love them all — yet they dont *bewitch* me any. There are no walks in the wood — no low and earnest voices, no moonlight, nor stolen love, but pure little lives, loving God, and their parents, and obeying the laws of the land; yet read, if you meet them, Susie, for they will do one good.

I have the promise of "Alton Lock" — a certain book, called "Olive," and the "Head of a Family," which was what Mattie named to you. Vinnie and I had "Bleak House" sent to us the other day — it is like him who wrote it — that is all I can say. Dear Susie, you were so happy when you wrote to me last – I am so glad, and you will be happy *now*, for *all* my sadness, *wont* you? I cant forgive me ever, if I have made you sad, or dimmed your eye for me. I write from the Land of Violets, and from the Land of Spring, and it would ill become me to carry you nought but sorrows. I remember you, Susie, *always* – I keep you ever here, and when *you* are gone, then I'm gone — and we're 'neath one willow tree. I can only thank "the Father" for giving me such as you, I can only pray unceasingly, that he will bless my Loved One, and bring her back to me, to "go no more out forever." "Herein is Love."

But *that* was Heaven — *this* is but *Earth*, yet Earth so *like* to heaven, that I would hesitate, should the true one call away.

Dear Susie — adieu!

Emilie —

Father's sister is dead, and Mother wears black on her bonnet, and has a collar of crape. A great deal of love from Vinnie, and she wants that *little note*. Austin comes home on Wednesday, but he'll only stay two days, so I fancy we shant go sugaring, as "we did last year." *Last year is gone*, Susie, did you ever think of *that*? Joseph [Lyman] is out south somewhere, a very great way off, yet we hear from him —

MANUSCRIPT: HCL (L 13). Ink. Dated: Monday morning.
PUBLICATION: FF 197–200, in part.

"Emerald" was used to distinguish Mrs. Mack, the Irish washerwoman, from members of the family of Deacon David Mack. In "the Popes and the Polloks and the John-Milton Browns" ED is characterizing the young men of her acquaintance. The works of Alexander Pope were studied in schools as models of English verse; Robert Pollock, a Scottish poet, wrote *The Course of Time* (1827), which had great contemporary reputation. Perhaps she intends the ambiguity of "John-Milton Brown." Of the several John Browns known at the time, the best known was the Scottish divine (1784–1858), who wrote voluminously on religious subjects.

The books mentioned are as follows: *The Light in the Valley*, a memorial of Mary Elizabeth Stirling, who died at Haddonfield, New Jersey, 30 January 1852 (Philadelphia, American Baptist Publication Society, 1852); *Only*, by Matilda Anne Mackarness (Boston & Cambridge, J. Monroe, 1850); *idem, A House upon a Rock* (1852); *Alton Locke*, by Charles Kingsley (1850); *Olive*, by Dinah Maria Craik (Miss Mulock) (1850); *idem, Head of a Family* (1851). Dickens' *Bleak House* was published in monthly parts in 1852–1853.

Edward Dickinson's sister Mary (Mrs. Mark Newman) died 30 March 1852.

93

To Susan Gilbert (Dickinson) *early June 1852*

They are cleaning house today, Susie, and I've made a flying retreat to my own little chamber, where with affection, and you, I will spend this my precious hour, most precious of all the hours which dot my flying days, and the one so dear, that for it I barter everything, and as soon as it is gone, I am sighing for it again.

I cannot believe, dear Susie, that I have stayed without you almost a whole year long; sometimes the time seems short, and the thought of you as warm as if you had gone but yesterday, and again if years and years had trod their silent pathway, the time would seem less long. And now how soon I shall have you, shall hold you in my arms; you will forgive the tears, Susie, they are so glad to come that it. is not in my heart to reprove them and send them home. I dont know why it is — but there's something in your name, now you are taken from me, which fills my heart so full, and my eye, too. It is not that the mention *grieves* me, no, Susie, but I think of each "sunnyside" where we have sat together, and lest there be no more, I guess is what makes the tears come. Mattie was here last evening, and we sat on the front door stone, and talked about life and love, and whispered our childish fancies about such blissful things — the evening was gone so soon, and I walked home with Mattie beneath the silent moon, and wished for you, and Heaven. You did not come, Darling, but a bit of Heaven did, or so it *seemed* to us, as we walked side by side and wondered if that great blessedness which may be our's sometime, is granted now, to some. Those unions, my dear Susie, by which two lives are one, this sweet and strange adoption wherein we can but look, and are not yet admitted, how it can fill the heart, and make it gang wildly beating, how it will take *us* one day, and make us all it's own, and we shall not run away from it, but lie still and be happy!

You and I have been strangely silent upon this subject, Susie, we have often touched upon it, and as quickly fled away, as children shut their eyes when the sun is too bright for them. I have always hoped to know if you had no dear fancy, illumining all your life, no one of whom you murmured in the faithful ear of night — and at whose side in fancy, you walked the livelong day; and when you come home, Susie, we must speak of these things. How dull our lives must seem to the bride, and the plighted maiden, whose days are fed with gold, and who gathers pearls every evening; but to the *wife*, Susie, sometimes the *wife forgotten*, our lives perhaps seem dearer than all others in the world; you have seen flowers at morning, *satisfied* with

[88]

the dew, and those same sweet flowers at noon with their heads bowed in anguish before the mighty sun; think you these thirsty blossoms will *now* need naught but – *dew*? No, they will cry for sunlight, and pine for the burning noon, tho' it scorches them, scathes them; they have got through with peace – they know that the man of noon, is *mightier* than the morning and their life is henceforth to him. Oh, Susie, it is dangerous, and it is all too dear, these simple trusting spirits, and the spirits mightier, which we cannot resist! It does so rend me, Susie, the thought of it when it comes, that I tremble lest at sometime I, too, am yielded up. Susie, you will forgive me my amatory strain — it has been a very long one, and if this saucy page did not here bind and fetter me, I might have had no end.

I have got the letter, Susie, dear little bud, and all – and the tears came again, that alone in this big world, I am not *quite* alone. Such tears are showers – friend, thro' which when smiles appear, the angels call them rainbows, and mimic them in Heaven.

And now in four weeks more – you are mine, *all* mine, except I *lend* you a little occasionally to Hattie and Mattie, if they promise not to lose you, and to bring you back very soon. I shall not count the days. I shall not fill my cups with this expected happiness, for perhaps if I do, the angels, being thirsty, will drink them up – I shall only *hope*, my Susie, and *that* tremblingly, for hav'nt barques the fullest, stranded upon the shore?

God is good, Susie, I trust he will save you, I pray that in his good time we once more meet each other, but if this life holds not another meeting for us, remember also, Susie, that it had no *parting* more, wherever that hour finds us, for which we have hoped so long, we shall not be separated, neither death, nor the grave can part us, so that we only *love*!

Your Emilie –

Austin has come and gone; life is so still again; why must the storm have calms? I hav'nt seen Root this term, I guess Mattie and I, are not sufficient for him! When will you come again, in a week? Let it be a *swift* week!

Vinnie sends much love, and Mother; and might I be so bold as to enclose a *remembrance*?

MANUSCRIPT: HLC (L 20). Ink. Dated: Friday morning.

PUBLICATION: *LL* 43, in part.
Sue returned home early in July.

94

To Susan Gilbert (Dickinson)   *11 June 1852*

I have but one thought, Susie, this afternoon of June, and *that* of you, and I have one prayer, only; dear Susie, *that* is *for* you. That you and I in *hand* as we e'en *do* in heart, might ramble away as children, among the woods and fields, and forget these many years, and these sorrowing cares, and each become a child again – I would it were so, Susie, and when I look around me and find myself alone, I sigh for you again; little sigh, and vain sigh, which will not bring you home.

I need you more and more, and the great world grows wider, and dear ones fewer and fewer, every day that you stay away – I miss my biggest heart; my own goes wandering round, and calls for Susie – Friends are too dear to sunder, Oh they are far too few, and how soon they will go away where you and I cannot find them, *dont* let us forget these things, for their remembrance *now* will save us many an anguish when it is *too late* to love them! Susie, forgive me Darling, for every word I say — my heart is full of you, none other than you in my thoughts, yet when I seek to say to you something not for the world, words fail me. If you were here — and Oh that you were, my Susie, we need not talk at all, our eyes would whisper for us, and your hand fast in mine, we would not ask for language – I try to bring you nearer, I chase the weeks away till they are quite departed, and fancy you have come, and I am on my way through the green lane to meet you, and my heart goes scampering so, that I have much ado to bring it back again, and learn it to be patient, till that dear Susie comes. Three weeks — they cant last always, for surely they must go with their little brothers and sisters to their long home in the west!

I shall grow more and more impatient until that dear day comes, for till now, I have only *mourned* for you; now I begin to *hope* for you.

Dear Susie, I have tried hard to think what you would love, of something I might send you – I at last saw my little Violets, they begged me to let *them* go, so here they are — and with them as Instructor, a bit of knightly grass, who also begged the favor to accompany them — they are but small, Susie, and I fear not fragrant now, but they will speak to you of warm hearts at home, and of the something faithful which "never slumbers nor sleeps" — Keep them 'neath your pillow, Susie, they will make you dream of blue-skies, and home, and the "blessed countrie"! You and I will have an hour with "Edward" and "Ellen Middleton", sometime when you get home — we must find out if some things contained therein are true, and if they are, what you and me are coming to!

Now, farewell, Susie, and Vinnie sends her love, and mother her's, and I add a kiss, shyly, lest there is somebody there! Dont let them see, *will* you Susie?

Emilie —

Why cant *I* be a Delegate to the great Whig Convention? — dont I know all about Daniel Webster, and the Tariff, and the Law? Then, Susie I could see you, during a pause in the session — but I dont like this country at all, and I shant stay here any longer! "Delenda est" America, Massachusetts and all!

open me carefully

MANUSCRIPT: HCL (L 2). Ink. Dated: Friday afternoon. Addressed on the fold: Miss Susan H. Gilbert./40–Lexington St./Baltimore./Md–
PUBLICATION: FF 215–217, in part.

Edward Dickinson was a delegate to the national Whig convention, which met in Baltimore on 16 June 1852. He delivered the letter.

95

To Austin Dickinson   *20 June 1852*

Your last letter to us, Austin, was very short and very unsatisfying — we do not feel this week that we have heard anything from you for a very great while, and father's absence, besides, makes us all very lonely.

I infer from what you said, that my last letter did'nt suit you, and you tried to write as bad a one as you possibly could, to pay me for it; but before I began to write, Vinnie said *she* was going to, and I must'nt write any news, as she was depending upon it to make her letter of, so I merely talked away as I should if we'd been together, leaving all the matter o'fact to our practical sister Vinnie — well, we had calls Sunday evening, until too late to write, and Vinnie was sound asleep when the mail went out in the morning. I was determined to send you *my* letter, that very day, so Vinnie's note of news, for which I had starved my own, is as yet unwritten. We have looked every day for a long letter from you, and really felt sadly enough when Saturday came without it. I should have written you sooner, but we have had Miss Bangs cutting dresses for us this week, and have been very busy, so I could'nt possibly write, but we have all *thought* of you, and *that* is better than writing. Father has not got home, and we dont know when to expect him. We had a letter from him yesterday, but he did'nt say when he should come. He writes that he "should think the whole world was there, and some from other worlds" — he says he meets a great many old friends and acquaintances, and forms a great many new ones — he writes in very fine spirits, and says he enjoys himself very much. I think it will do him the very most good of anything in the world, and I do feel happy to have father at last, among men who sympathize with him, and know what he really is. I wish you could have gone with him, you would have enjoyed it so, but I did'nt much suppose that selfish old school would let you. Father writes that he's called on Sue, twice, and found her very glad to see him. She will be home in a fortnight — only think of that!

Mattie gets along nicely — she sends her love to you — she is down here most every day. Abby Wood had a little party, week before last — a very pleasant one. Last week, the Senior Levee came off at the President's. Vinnie went to the Levee, and I went to walk with Emmons. Vinnie had a nice time — said everything went off pleasantly, and very much as usual. I believe Prof. Haven is to give one soon — and there is to be a Reception at Prof. Tyler's, next Tuesday evening, which I shall attend. You see Amherst is growing lively, and by the time you come, everything will be in a buzz.

Uncle Samuel's family are here, boarding at Mr Palmer's. Uncle Samuel was here himself, about a week, and is now in New York. Arthur, the oldest one, is going to work on a farm this summer, so as to grow stout and strong, before entering college. Porter Cowles is going to take him. Mr Bowdoin is here still — comes round with the news every day — he has formed quite a fancy for Mat, since Mary became so feeble — has called on her two or three times, been to walk with her once, and walked home with her from the President's. Mat smiles and looks very peculiarly when we mention Mr Bowdoin. I hav'nt seen Mary Warner since you went away — the last time I *heard* of her, she had Thurston and Benjamin, *weeding her flower garden.* *That's* romantic, is'nt it — she better have her heart wed, before she weeds her garden!

As father has'nt come, Mother cant say certainly how soon you will see her in Boston; just as soon as he comes, she will go, tho, and we shall let you know. She has got her new teeth in, and I think they look very nicely. We all send you our love.

Emilie.

I hope you will write me a letter as soon as you possibly can.

MANUSCRIPT: AC. Ink. Dated: Sunday morning. Envelope addressed: Wᵐ Austin Dickinson/Care of Joel Norcross./31 – Milk St./Boston. Postmarked: Amherst Ms. Jun 21.

PUBLICATION: L (1894) 108, in part; L (1931) 104, in part; *Home* 246–247, entire.

The *Hampshire and Franklin Express,* 10 September 1852, reported that Edward Dickinson "had the honor to represent the old Sixth District in the National nominating Convention. To that convention he carried a firm and unwavering friendship to Daniel Webster, which led him to stand by the great statesman through the fifty-five ballots of that body."

97

To Susan Gilbert (Dickinson)   *early December 1852*

Dear Friend.

I regret to inform you that at 3. oclock yesterday, my mind came to a stand, and has since then been stationary.

Ere this intelligence reaches you, I shall probably be a snail. By this untoward providence a mental and moral being has been swept ruthlessly from her sphere. Yet we should not repine — "God moves in a mysterious way, his wonders to perform, he plants his foot upon the sea, and rides upon the storm," and if it be his will that I become a *bear* and bite my fellow men, it will be for the highest good of this fallen and perishing world. If the gentleman in the air, will please to stop throwing snowballs, I may meet you again, otherwise it is uncertain. My parents are pretty well—Gen Wolf is here—we're looking for Major Pitcairn in the afternoon stage.

We were much afflicted yesterday, by the supposed removal of *our Cat* from time to Eternity.

She returned, however, last evening, having been detained by the storm, beyond her expectations.

I see by the Boston papers that Giddings is up again—hope you'll arrange with Corwin, and have the North all straight.

Fine weather for sledding—have spoken for 52 cord black walnut. We need some paths our way, shant you come out with the team?

Yours till death—

Judah

Manuscript: HCL (B 176). Ink. Dated: Friday noon.

Publication: LL 55, in part, and altered.

Sue was in Amherst. In the autumn of 1852, Edward Dickinson was the Whig candidate for Congress from the tenth district, and was elected in December. The gentlemen identified with the historic figures General Wolfe (who died victorious at Quebec) and Major Pitcairn (fatally wounded at Bunker Hill) were probably political visitors, calling on Edward Dickinson. Joshua Reed Giddings broke with the Whig party in 1848. Thomas Corwin, Fillmore's Secretary of the Treasury, had also opposed the Fugitive Slave Law endorsed by the Whig convention. The quotation from William Cowper's "Light Shining out of Darkness," with which ED would be especially familiar from its hymn setting, seems to have been from memory, since it alters the third line, which reads: "He plants his footsteps in the sea." The historical associations with the name Judah are so many that the private association for which ED uses it as a signature makes any conjecture about its intent in this letter, largely a *jeu d'esprit*, pure guesswork.

98

To Emily Fowler (Ford)   *about 13 January 1853*

Dear Emily—

I fear you will be lonely this dark and stormy day, and I send this little messenger to say you must not be.

[94]

The day is long to me, because I have no Vinnie, and I think of those today who never had a Vinnie, and I'm afraid they are lone. I have wanted to come and see you – I have tried earnestly to come, but always have been detained by some ungenerous care, and now this falling snow, sternly, and silently, lifts up its hand between.

How glad I am affection can always leave and go – How glad that the drifts of snow pause at the outer door, and go no farther, and it is as warm within as if no winter came! Dear Emily, do not sorrow, upon this stormy day — "into each life some *'flakes'* must fall, some days must be dark and dreary." Let us think of the pleasant summer whose gardens are far away, and whose Robins are singing always!

If it were not for blossoms we know that we shall see, and for that brighter sunshine above – beyond – away – these days were dark indeed, but I try to keep recollecting that we are away from home — and have many brothers and sisters who are expecting us. Dear Emilie — dont weep, for you will both be so happy, where "sorrow cannot come."

Vinnie left her Testament on a little stand in our room, and it made me think of her, so I thought I w'd open it, and the first words I read were in those sweetest verses — "Blessed are the poor – Blessed are they that mourn – Blessed are they that weep, for they shall be comforted." Dear Emily, I thought of you, and I hasted away to send this message to you.

Emilie –

MANUSCRIPT: NYPL. Ink. Dated: Thursday evening.
PUBLICATION: L (1894) 134–135, in part; L (1931) 134, in part.
The year is conjectured from the handwriting. There was a heavy snowstorm on January 13. Professor Fowler was still in Europe. Lavinia was presumably making one of her customary visits to Boston. The quoted lines in the third paragraph paraphrase Longfellow's "The Rainy Day" (see letter no. 36).

99

To Emily Fowler (Ford)   *early 1853?*

Dear Emily,

I said when the Barber came, I would save you a little ringlet, and fulfilling my promise, I send you one today. I shall never give you anything again that will be half so full of sunshine as this wee lock of hair, but I wish no hue more sombre might ever fall to you.

All your gifts should be rainbows, if I owned *half* the skies, and but a bit of sea to furnish raindrops for me. Dear Emily—this is all—It will serve to make you remember me when locks are crisp and gray, and the quiet cap, and the spectacles, and "John Anderson my Joe" are all that is left of me.

I must have one of yours–Please spare me a little lock sometime when you have your scissors, and there is one to spare.

Your very aff

Emilie–

MANUSCRIPT: NYPL. Pencil. Addressed on the outer fold: Emilie.
PUBLICATION: L (1894) 133; L (1931) 132–133.

ED was wearing her hair short at the time. In the late summer of 1852 Lavinia wrote to Austin: "Emilie's hair is cut off & shes very pretty." (*Home* 248). Mrs. Ford's collection of her friends' hair is in NYPL, but ED's ringlet is missing.

100

To John L. Graves   *about February* 1853

Cousin John.

I thought perhaps you and your friend would come in to drink *wine* this evening, as I asked you to do, after Vinnie got home, but I want to tell you something.

Vinnie and I are asked out this evening, and Vinnie's obliged to go. It will not be as pleasant when she is absent from home, and now I want to know if you will be busy *next* week, and if not, wont you save an evening, or an hour of one, when you will come and see us, and taste the currant wine?

Please tell your friend—Mr Emmons, and invite him to come with you upon another evening.

Vinnie and I are sorry, but fortune is unkind.

Your Cousin Emily.

MANUSCRIPT: HCL (G 5). Ink. Dated: Friday afternoon.

PUBLICATION: *Home* 224–225.
John Graves, now a sophomore at Amherst College, had introduced his friend Henry Vaughan Emmons to the Dickinson girls a year earlier. ED counted Graves as her friend, yet the formal address was customary. Vinnie had been away in January.

101

To John L. Graves   *about February 1853*

I wonder if Cousin John has a lesson to learn this evening?

Emilie—

MANUSCRIPT: HCL (G 9). Pencil. Addressed: Cousin John. Unpublished.

ED here suggests that John might call this evening, if he is free to do so.

107

To Susan Gilbert (Dickinson)   *12 March 1853*

Dear Susie—

I'm so amused at my own ubiquity that I hardly know what to say, or how to relate the story of the wonderful correspondent. First, I arrive from Amherst, then comes a ponderous tome from the learned Halls of Cambridge, and again by strange metamorphosis I'm just from Michigan, and am Mattie and Minnie and Lizzie in one wondering breath—Why, dear Susie, it must'nt scare you if I loom up from Hindoostan, or drop from an Appenine, or peer at you suddenly from the hollow of a tree, calling myself King Charles, Sancho Panza, or Herod, King of the Jews—I suppose it is all the same.

"Miss Mills," that is, Miss Julia, never *dreamed* of the depths of *my clandestiny*, and if *I* stopped to think of the figure I was cutting, it would be the last of me, and you'd never hear again from you poor Jeremy Bentham—

But I say to my mind, "tut, tut," "Rock a bye baby" conscience, and so I keep them still!

And as for the pulling of wool over the eyes of Manchester, I

[97]

trust to the courtesy of the Recording Angel, to say nothing of *that*. One thing is true, Darling, the world will be none the wiser, for Emilie's omnipresence, and two big hearts will beat stouter, as tidings from *me* come in. I love the opportunity to serve those who are mine, and to soften the least asperity in the path which ne'er "ran smooth," is a delight to me. So Susie, I set the trap and catch the little mouse, and love to catch him dearly, for I think of you and Austin—and know it pleases you to have my tiny services. Dear Susie, you are gone —One would hardly think I had lost you to hear this revelry, but your absence insanes me so—I do not feel so peaceful, when you are gone from me—All life looks differently, and the faces of my fellows are not the same they wear when you are with me. I think it is this, dear Susie; you sketch my pictures for me, and 'tis at their sweet colorings, rather than this dim real that I am used, so you see when you go away, the world looks staringly, and I find I need more vail— Frank Peirce thinks I mean *berage* vail, and makes a sprightly plan to import the "article," but dear Susie knows what I mean. Do you ever look homeward, Susie, and count the lonely hours Vinnie and I are spending, because that you are gone?

Yes, Susie, very lonely, and yet is it very sweet too to know that you are happy, and to think of you in the morning, and at eventide, and noon, and always as smiling and looking up for joy—I could not spare you *else*, dear Sister, but to be sure your life is warm with such a sunshine, helps me to chase the shadows fast stealing upon mine— I *knew* you would be happy, and you know now of something I had told you.

There *are* lives, sometimes, Susie—Bless God that we catch faint glimpses of his brighter Paradise from *occasional* Heavens *here*!

Stay, Susie; yet *not* stay! I cannot spare your sweet face another hour more, and yet I want to have you gather more sheaves of joy— for bleak, and waste, and barren, are most of the fields found here, and I want you to *fill* the *garner*. *Then* you may come, dear Susie, and from our silent home, Vinnie and I shall meet you. There is much to tell you, Susie, but I cannot bring the deeds of the rough and jostling world into that sweet inclosure; they are fitter *fonder, here*— but Susie, I do bring you a Sister's fondest love—and gentlest tenderness; little indeed, but "a'," and I know you will not refuse them. Please remember me to your friend, and write soon to

your lonely
Emilie –
Vinnie sends you her love – She would write, but has hurt her hand –
Mother's love too – Oh Susie!

MANUSCRIPT: HCL (L 4). Ink. Dated: Saturday noon.
PUBLICATION: *FF* 190–192, in part.
In the first paragraph ED alludes to the various envelopes addressed in
her hand: first her own letters to Sue; then Austin's, in the envelopes she
addressed for him; and finally those sent in her care and forwarded to Sue
from her relatives in Michigan, her sister Martha and the two sisters-in-law.
Julia Mills, in *David Copperfield*, was the bosom friend of Dora Spenlow,
and described as "interested in others' loves, herself withdrawn." It is Austin
who is identified with the philosopher and jurist Bentham.

109

To Austin Dickinson   24 March 1853

Dear Austin.

How much I miss you, how lonely it is this morning — how I wish
you were here, and how very much I thank you for sending me that
long letter, which I got Monday evening, and have read a great many
times, and presume I shall again, unless I soon have another.

I find life not so bright without Sue and you, or Martha, and for
a little while I hav'nt cared much about it. How glad I was to know
that you had'nt forgotten us, and looked forward to home, and the
rustic seat, and summer, with so much happiness. You wonder if we
think of you as much as you of us – I guess so, Austin — it's a great
deal anyhow, and to look at the empty nails, and the empty chairs in
the kitchen almost obscures my sight, if I were used to tears. But *I*
think of the rustic seat, and I think of the July evening just as the
day is done, and I read of the one come back, worth all the "ninety
and nine" who have not gone from home, and these things strengthen
me for many a day to come.

I'm so glad you are cheerful at Cambridge, for cheerful indeed
one must be to write such a comic affair as your last letter to me. I

believe the message to Bowdoin, w'd have killed father outright if he had'nt just fortified nature with two or three cups of tea. I could hardly contain myself sufficiently to read a thing so grotesque, but it did me good indeed, and when I had finished reading it, I said with a pleasant smile, "then there is something left"! I have been disgusted, ever since you went away, and have concluded several times that it's of no use minding it, as it is only a puff ball. But your letter so raised me up, that I look round again, and notice my fellow men.

I think you far exceed Punch — much funnier — much funnier, cant keep up with you at all!

I suppose the young lady will be getting home today — how often I thought of you yesterday afternoon and evening. I did "drop in at the Revere" a great many times yesterday. I hope you have been made happy. If so I am satisfied. I shall know when you get home.

I have been to see Mrs Cutler several times since Sue has been gone. *Mr Cutler* has missed her dreadfully, which has gratified me much. What I was going to tell you was that Mr Cutler's folks had written Sue to meet *Mr Sweetser* in Boston last week, and come to Amherst with him. I knew she would'nt come, and I couldnt help laughing to think of him returning to town alone — that's all! Sue's outwitted them all — ha-ha! just imagine me giving three cheers for American Independence!

I did get that little box, and do with it as you told me. I wrote you so at the time, but you must have forgotten it. Write again soon, Austin, for this is a lonely house, when we are not all here.

Emilie.

Mother says "tell Austin I think perhaps I shall write him a letter myself."

Mother sends her love, and is very much obliged to you for the message to her, and also for the comb, which you told us was coming. She wants you to send your clothes home just as soon as you can, for she thinks you must certainly need some by this time. We hav'nt had much maple sugar yet, but I shall send you some when Mr Green goes back. We have had some maple molasses. I know you would love some, if you were here — how I do wish you were here! I read the proclamation, and liked it very much. I had a letter from Mat, last night — she said a great deal of Sue and you, and *so* affectionately. If

Sue thinks Mat would be willing, I will send the letter to you, the next time I write.

MANUSCRIPT: AC. Pencil. Dated: Thursday morning. Postmarked: Mar 24. An attempt has been made throughout to erase Sue's name.
PUBLICATION: *Home* 269–270.

According to a carefully contrived plan between Austin and Sue, the latter returned from Manchester by way of Boston. The correspondence that follows indicates that they became engaged at this time. Sue arrived in Amherst on March 24. Lavinia's hand had recovered sufficiently for her to write a note to Austin that was enclosed with Emily's.

110

To Austin Dickinson   27 March 1853

Oh my dear "Oliver," how chipper you must be since any of us have seen you? How thankful we should be that you have been brought to Greenville, and a suitable frame of mind! I really had my doubts about your reaching Canaan, but you relieve my mind, and set me at rest completely. How long it is since you've been in this state of complacence towards God and your fellow men? I think it must be sudden, hope you are not deceived, would recommend "Pilgrim's Progress," and "Baxter upon the will." Hope you have enjoyed the Sabbath, and sanctuary privileges — it is'nt *all* young men that have the preached word.

Trust you enjoy your closet, and meditate profoundly upon the Daily Food! I shall send you Village Hymns, by earliest opportunity.

I was just this moment thinking of a favorite stanza of your's, "where congregations ne'er break up, and Sabbaths have no end."

That must be a delightful situation, certainly, quite worth the scrambling for!

Quite likely you have *tickets* for your particular friends – hope I should be included, in memory of "old clothes."

And Austin is a Poet, Austin writes a psalm. Out of the way, Pegasus, Olympus enough "to him," and just say to those "nine muses" that we have done with them!

Raised a living muse ourselves, worth the whole nine of them. Up, off, tramp!

Now Brother Pegasus, I'll tell you what it is—I've been in the habit *myself* of writing some few things, and it rather appears to me that you're getting away my patent, so you'd better be somewhat careful, or I'll call the police! Well Austin, if you've stumbled through these two pages of folly, without losing your hat or getting lost in the mud, I will try to be sensible, as suddenly as I can, before you are quite disgusted. *Mademoiselle* has come, quite to the surprise of us all. I concluded you had concluded to sail for Australia. Sue's very sober yet, she thinks it's pretty desolate without old Mr Brown.

She seems to be absent, sometimes, on account of the "old un," and I think you're a villainous rascal to entrap a young woman's "phelinks" in such an awful way.

You deserve, let me see; you deserve hot irons, and Chinese Tartary; and if I were Mary Jane, I would give you one such "mitten" Sir. as you never had before! I declare, I have half a mind to *throw a stone* as it is, and kill five barn door fowls, but I wont, I'll be considerate! Miss Susie was here on Friday, was here on Saturday, and Miss Emilie, there, on Thursday. I suppose you will go to the "*Hygeum*" as usual, this evening. Think it a dreadful thing for a young man under influences to frequent a hotel, evenings! Am glad our Pilgrim Fathers got safely out of the way, before such shocking times! Are you getting on well with "the work," and have you engaged the Harpers? Shall bring in a bill for my Lead Pencils, 17, in number, disbursed at times to you, as soon as the publishment. Also, two envelopes daily, during *despatch of proofs*, also Johnnie Beston, also David Smith, and services from same!

Dear Austin, I am keen, but you are a good deal keener, I am *something* of a fox, but you are more of a hound! I guess we are very good friends tho', and I guess we both love Sue just as well as we can.

You need'nt laugh at my letter—it's a few *Variations* of *Greenville* I thought I would send to you.

Affy
Emilie.

Love from us all. Monday noon. Oh Austin, Newton is dead. The first of my own friends. Pace.

MANUSCRIPT: AC. Ink. Dated: Sabbath evening. Postmarked: Amherst Ms Mar 28. An attempt has been made to erase "Sue" in the second paragraph above the signature.

PUBLICATION: L (1931) 109–110, in part; Home 271–273, entire.

The salutation "Oliver" may be an oblique congratulation on Austin's recent and still secret engagement to Sue, suggested by Oliver's comment on his love for Celia (*As You Like It*, V, ii): ". . . my sudden wooing . . . her sudden consenting." Benjamin Newton died at Worcester, 24 March 1853 (see letter no. 153). Johnnie Beston was a youthful handyman; so probably was David Smith.

119

To Henry V. Emmons   *spring 1853*

Mr Emmons –

Since receiving your beautiful writing I have often desired to thank you thro' a few of my flowers, and arranged the fairest for you a little while ago, but heard you were away –

I have very few today, and they compare but slightly with the immortal blossoms you kindly gathered me, but will you please accept them — the "Lily of the field" for the blossoms of Paradise, and if 'tis ever mine to gather those which fade not, from the garden we have not seen, you shall have a brighter one than I can find today.

Emilie E. Dickinson

MANUSCRIPT: HCL (E 1). Pencil.
PUBLICATION: NEQ XVI (1943) 366–367.

Although the nature of Emmons's "beautiful writing" is not specified, it is possible he had lent ED a copy of his dissertation "Sympathy in Action," presented at the Spring Exhibition on April 19.

120

To Henry V. Emmons   *spring 1853*

Ungentle "Atropos"! And yet I dare not chide her, for fear those saucy fingers will ply the shears again.

Perhaps she suspects the *wine*! Please tell her it's only *Currant* Wine, and would she be so kind as to lend me her shears a little, that I might cut a thread?

Vinnie and I wait patiently the coming of our friends, and trust a brighter evening will soon reward us all for the long expectation.

Your friends,
Emilie & Vinnie Dickinson –

MANUSCRIPT: HCL (E 6). Ink.
PUBLICATION: *NEQ* XVI (1943) 370.
The friend included in the invitation is John Graves.

124

To Emily Fowler (Ford)   *about June 1853*

The Buds are small, dear Emily, but will you please accept one for your Cousin and yourself? I quite forgot the *Rosebugs* when I spoke of the buds, last evening, and I found a family of them taking an early breakfast on my most precious bud, with a smart little worm for Land-lady, so the sweetest are gone, but accept my love with the smallest, and I'm

Lovingly,
Emilie.

MANUSCRIPT: NYPL. Pencil.
PUBLICATION: *L* (1894) 133; *L* (1931) 133.
The cousin was Julia Jones of Bridgeport, Connecticut.

125

To Austin Dickinson   *5 June 1853*

Dear Austin.

It is Sunday, and I am here alone. The rest have gone to meeting, to hear Rev Martin Leland. I listened to him this forenoon in a state of mind very near frenzy, and feared the effect too much to go out this afternoon. The morning exercises were perfectly ridiculous, and we spent the intermission in mimicking the Preacher, and reciting extracts from his most memorable sermon. I never heard father so funny. How I did wish you were here. I know you'd have died laughing. Father said he didn't dare look at Sue — he said he saw her bonnet coming round our way, and he looked "straight ahead" — he said he ran out of meeting for fear somebody would ask him what he tho't of the preaching. He says if anyone asks him, he shall put his hand to his mouth, and his mouth in the dust, and cry, Unclean — Unclean!! But I hav'nt time to say more of Martin Leland, but I wish you were here today, Austin, and could hear father talk, and you would laugh so loud they would hear you way down in Cambridge. Vinnie and I got your letters just about bedtime last evening. I had been at Sue's all the evening and communicated to her the fact that they had not come. She had felt all the time she said, perfectly sure that [*remainder of letter missing, Postscript on first page*]: All send love to you Austin — write us again very soon – I am glad for "The Honeysuckle."

MANUSCRIPT: AC. Pencil. Dated: Sunday afternoon. Envelope franked and addressed by Edward Dickinson. Postmarked: Amherst Ms Jun 6. The letter has been torn in half, and an attempt has been made throughout to erase or alter the name "Sue."

PUBLICATION: *Home* 292.

131

To Austin Dickinson   8 *July 1853*

Dear Austin –

I must write you a little before the cars leave this noon — just to tell you that we got your letter last evening, and were rejoiced to hear from you after so long a time, and that we want to see you, and long to have you come, much more than I can tell you—

We did'nt know what to make of it that we did'nt hear from you, but owed it to the post masters on the way, and not to you, but now we know you've had company, you are rather more excusable –

Susie was here last night, saying she'd had a letter, and that we should have one at home before bedtime, which we did about 10 – o'clock, when father came home from the office. Now Austin — we hav'nt written you oftener, because we've had so much company, and so many things to do. We want to get all our work done before you come home, so as not to be busy sewing when we want to see you; that's why we dont write oftener. You dont know how much we think of you, or how much we say, or how wish you were here every hour in the day, but we have to work very hard, and cannot write half as often as we want to to you. We think you dont write to us any, and we must all be patient until you get home, and then I rather think we shall wipe out old scores in a great many good talks. You say it is hot and dry. It is very dry here, tho' now for two or three days the air is fine and cool – Everything is so beautiful, it's a real Eden here; how happy we shall be roaming round it together! The trees are getting over the effect of the Canker worm, and we hope we may have some apples yet, tho' we cant tell now — but we feel very thankful that the leaves are not all gone, and there's a few green things which hav'nt been carried away – Mother expects to go to Monson tomorrow afternoon, to spend the Sabbath – They want very much to have her, and we think she had better go – She will come home Monday afternoon –

Vinnie will write what she thinks about Mary Nichols' coming in her next. What would please you about it? I want you should all do what will make you the happiest — after that I dont care.

I am glad you have enjoyed seeing Gould – About something for Mother – I think it would please her very much if you should bring her something, tho' she would'nt wish you to get anything very expensive –

Vinnie and I will think of something and write you *what* next time – I hope to send father's Daguerreotype before you come, and will if I can get any safe opportunity. We shall write you again in a day or two, and all send our love –

Your aff sister

Emilie –

Manuscript: AC. Pencil. Dated: Friday noon. The envelope, not franked, is addressed by ED: Wm Austin Dickinson./Law School./Cambridge./Mass. Postmarked: Amherst Ms Jul 9.
Publication: *Home* 305–306.
Mary Nichols was a Boston friend of Austin's. The daguerreotype of Edward Dickinson is not now known to be in existence.

To Dr. and Mrs. J. G. Holland   *autumn 1853*

Dear Dr. and Mrs Holland — dear Minnie — it is cold tonight, but the thought of you so warm, that I sit by it as a fireside, and am never cold any more. I love to write to you — it gives my heart a holiday and sets the bells to ringing. If prayers had any answers to them, you were all here to-night, but I seek and I don't find, and knock and it is not opened. Wonder if God is just — presume he is, however, and t'was only a blunder of Matthew's.

I think mine is the case, where when they ask an egg, they get a scorpion, for I keep wishing for you, keep shutting up my eyes and looking toward the sky, asking with all my might for you, and yet you do not come. I wrote to you last week, but thought you would laugh at me, and call me sentimental, so I kept my lofty letter for "Adolphus Hawkins, Esq."

If it wasn't for broad daylight, and cooking-stoves, and roosters, I'm afraid you would have occasion to smile at my letters often, but so sure as "this mortal" essays immortality, a crow from a neighboring farm-yard dissipates the illusion, and I am here again.

And what I mean is this — that I thought of you all last week, until the world grew rounder than it sometimes is, and I broke several dishes.

Monday, I solemnly resolved I would be *sensible*, so I wore thick shoes, and thought of Dr Humphrey, and the Moral Law. One glimpse of *The Republican* makes me break things again — I read in it every night.

Who writes those funny accidents, where railroads meet each other unexpectedly, and gentlemen in factories get their heads cut off quite informally? The author, too, relates them in such a sprightly way, that they are quite attractive. Vinnie was disappointed to-night, that there were not more accidents — I read the news aloud, while Vinnie was sewing. *The Republican* seems to us like a letter from you, and we break the seal and read it eagerly. . . .

Vinnie and I talked of you as we sewed, this afternoon. I said — "how far they seem from us," but Vinnie answered me "only a little way" . . . I'd love to be a bird or bee, that whether hum or sing, still might be near you.

Heaven is large — is it not? Life is short too, isn't it? Then when one is done, is there not another, and — and — then if God is willing, we are neighbors then. Vinnie and mother send their love. Mine too is here. My letter as a bee, goes laden. Please love us and remember us. Please write us very soon, and tell us how you are. . . .

Affy,

Emilie.

MANUSCRIPT: missing. The text is from *Letters* (1894), which reproduces in facsimile the first paragraph (showing the letter to be dated: Tuesday Evening), and the signature: Affy, Emilie.

PUBLICATION: *L* (1894) 157–158; *LL* 185–186; *L* (1931) 156–157; *LH* 32–34.

Emily and Vinnie visited the Hollands in September, pursuant to plans made in July. Mrs. Holland's sister Amelia (Minnie) Chapin lived with the Hollands until her marriage in 1856. Dr. Heman Humphrey, president of Amherst College from 1823 until 1845, had taught moral philosophy. Adolphus Hawkins, in Longefellow's prose romance *Kavanagh*, is a character whose writings satirize the effusions of the village poet. The scripture paraphrase in the first paragraph is from Matthew 7. 7–8; that in the second, from Luke 11. 12: "Or if he shall ask an egg, will he offer him a scorpion?"; that in the third, from I Corinthians 15. 53.

136

To Henry V. Emmons   *autumn 1853*

I send you the book with pleasure, for it has given me happiness, and I love to have it busy, imparting delight to others.

Thank you for the beautiful note — It is too full of poesy for a Saturday morning's reply, but I will not forget it, nor shall it fade as the leaves, tho' like them gold and crimson —

I send a note for your friend — Please remember me to her, with a sincere affection —

I am happy that she is with you — I have not read the book of which you speak — I will be happy to whenever agreable [sic] to you — and please give me an opportunity to see you "sirrah" very soon —

Your friend

Emily E. Dickinson

MANUSCRIPT: HCL (E 3). Pencil. Dated: Saturday morn.
PUBLICATION: *NEQ* XVI (1943) 368.
The friend here mentioned is not Susan Phelps, to whom Emmons became engaged in the following year (see letter no. 169). ED had not yet
met her. The person referred to is probably Eliza Judkins, formerly a
teacher at Amherst Academy.

137

To John L. Graves   *late 1853*

In memory of Æolus.

Cousin John – ,

I made these little Wristlets. Please wear them for me. Perhaps
they will keep you warm.

Emilie.

MANUSCRIPT: HCL (G 6). Pencil. Addressed on the fold: Mr John L
Graves/Present. Unpublished.
At the top ED sketched a grave, with head and foot stones. The wristlets were sent as a gift in return for an aeolian harp which Graves had
made and presented ED in April.

146

To Emily Fowler Ford   *21 December 1853*

Dear Emily,

Are you there, and shall you always stay there, and is it not dear
Emily any more, but Mrs. Ford of Connecticut, and must we stay
alone, and will you not come back with the birds and the butterflies,
when the days grow long and warm?

Dear Emily, we are lonely here. I know Col. S[mith] is left, and
Mr. and Mrs. K[ellogg], but pussy has run away, and you do not come
back again, and the world has grown so long! I knew you would go
away, for I know the roses are gathered, but I guessed not yet, not
till by expectation we had become resigned. Dear Emily, when it came,
and hidden by your veil you stood before us all and made those prom-

ises, and when we kissed you, all, and went back to our homes, it seemed to me translation, not any earthly thing, and if a little after you'd ridden on the wind, it would not have surprised me.

And now five days have gone, Emily, and long and silent, and I begin to know that you will not come back again. There's a verse in the Bible, Emily, I don't know where it is, nor just how it goes can I remember, but it's a little like this — "I can go to her, but she cannot come back to me." I guess that isn't right, but my eyes are full of tears, and I'm sure I do not care if I make mistakes or not. Is it happy there, dear Emily, and is the fireside warm, and have you a little cricket to chirp upon the hearth?

How much we think of you — how dearly love you — how often hope for you that it may all be happy.

Sunday evening your father came in — he stayed a little while. I thought he looked solitary. I thought he had grown old. How lonely he must be — I'm sorry for him.

Mother and Vinnie send their love, and hope you are so happy. Austin has gone away. Father comes home to-morrow. I know father will miss you. He loved to meet you here.

> "So fades a summer cloud away,
> So smiles the gale when storms are o'er
> So gently shuts the eye of day,
> So dies a wave along the shore."

Kiss me, dear Emily, and remember me if you will, with much respect, to your husband. Will you write me sometime?

Affectionately,

Emily.

MANUSCRIPT: missing.

PUBLICATION: L (1894) 145–146; L (1931) 143–144, dated (presumably by ED): Wednesday Eve.

Emily Fowler married Gordon L. Ford, 16 December 1853. The stanza quoted is from the Barbauld hymn beginning "How blest the righteous when he dies," but it is evidently quoted from memory, since the second word of the second line actually is *sinks*.

To Henry V. Emmons   *early January 1854*

I will be quite happy to ride tomorrow, as you so kindly propose, tho' I regret sincerely not to see you this evening –

Thank you for remembering Father. He seems much better this morning, and I trust will soon be well. I will ride with much pleasure tomorrow, at any hour in the afternoon most pleasant to yourself – Please recollect if you will two little volumes of mine which I thought Emily lent you –

Your friend
E. E. D –

MANUSCRIPT: HCL (E 4). Pencil.
PUBLICATION: *NEQ* XVI (1943) 368–369.
On his return from Boston on 29 December 1853, Edward Dickinson was in a train that was stalled by heavy snow for twenty hours near Framingham.

To Henry V. Emmons   *early January 1854*

Cousin John & Mr Emmons please not regret the little mishap of last evening, for Vinnie and I quite forgot Mr Saxe, in our delightful ride, and were only disappointed lest you should *think* us so.

Will you please receive these blossoms – I would love to make *two garlands* for certain friends of mine, if the summer were here, and till she comes, perhaps one little cluster will express the wish to both. Please share it together, and come in for an evening as soon as college duties are willing you should do.

Your friends, Emilie
and Vinnie –

MANUSCRIPT: HCL (E 5). Ink. Dated: Wednesday morn.
PUBLICATION: *NEQ* XVI (1943) 369–370.
The letter was sent to both Emmons and John Graves. The currently

popular poet John Godfrey Saxe lectured at Easthampton on Tuesday, January 2. There is no record of an engagement in Amherst at the time, yet he seems to have been speaking somewhere within easy reach.

153

To Edward Everett Hale   *13 January 1854*

Rev Mr Hale –

Pardon the liberty Sir, which a stranger takes in addressing you, but I think you may be familiar with the last hours of a Friend, and I therefore transgress a courtesy, which in another circumstance, I should seek to observe. I think, Sir, you were the Pastor of Mr B. F. Newton, who died sometime since in Worcester, and I often have hoped to know if his last hours were cheerful, and if he was willing to die. Had I his wife's acquaintance, I w'd not trouble you Sir, but I have never met her, and do not know where she resides, nor have I a friend in Worcester who could satisfy my inquiries. You may think my desire strange, Sir, but the Dead was dear to me, and I would love to know that he sleeps peacefully.

Mr Newton was with my Father two years, before going to Worcester – in pursuing his studies, and was much in our family.

I was then but a child, yet I was old enough to admire the strength, and grace, of an intellect far surpassing my own, and it taught me many lessons, for which I thank it humbly, now that it is gone. Mr Newton became to me a gentle, yet grave Preceptor, teaching me what to read, what authors to admire, what was most grand or beautiful in nature, and that sublimer lesson, a faith in things unseen, and in a life again, nobler, and much more blessed –

Of all these things he spoke – he taught me of them all, earnestly, tenderly, and when he went from us, it was as an elder brother, loved indeed very much, and mourned, and remembered. During his life in Worcester, he often wrote to me, and I replied to his letters – I always asked for his health, and he answered so cheerfully, that while I knew he was ill, his death indeed surprised me. He often talked of God, but I do not know certainly if he was his Father in Heaven – Please Sir, to tell me if he was willing to die, and if you think him at Home, I should love so much to know certainly, that he was today in Heaven.

Once more, Sir, please forgive the audacities of a Stranger, and a few lines, Sir, from you, at a convenient hour, will be received with gratitude, most happy to requite you, sh'd it have opportunity.

Yours very respectfully,

Emily E. Dickinson

P.S. Please address your reply to Emily E. Dickinson –
Amherst – Mass –

MANUSCRIPT: Lilly. Ink. Dated: Amherst. Jan 13th.

PUBLICATION: T. F. Madigan's catalog, *The Autograph Album* I (1933) 50, in part; *American Literature* VI (1935) 5, entire; G. F. Whicher, *This Was a Poet* (1938), 84–85, in part.

Hale's reply is not known to survive. ED referred to Newton on at least four other occasions. Her earliest comment is in a letter written to Austin on 27 March 1853, three days after Newton's death (no. 110): "Oh Austin, Newton is dead. The first of my own friends. Pace." Three later allusions, almost certainly to Newton, are in letters to Higginson. The first, in a letter written in 1862 (no. 261), says: "When a little Girl, I had a friend, who taught me Immortality – but venturing too near, himself – he never returned." The second, written in the same year (no. 265), comments: "My dying Tutor told me that he would like to live till I had been a poet. . ." The third, written fourteen years later (no. 457), indicates how vivid the memory of Newton continued to remain: "My earliest friend wrote me the week before he died 'If I live, I will go to Amherst – if I die, I certainly will.'"

None of the correspondence between ED and Newton has ever been found, and the assumption therefore is that important letters revealing the development of Emily Dickinson as a poet have long since been destroyed.

158

To Austin Dickinson   *19, 21 March 1854*

I have just come from meeting, Austin – Mr Luke Sweetser presided, and young Mr Hallock made a prayer which I dont doubt you heard in Cambridge – It was really very audible – Mr Dwight was not there – Sue did not go – Tempe Linnell sat by me – I asked her if she was engaged to Sam Fiske, and she said *no*, so you can tell Mrs Jones she was slightly mistaken. Have you had a pleasant day, Austin? Have you been to meeting today? We have had a lovely Sunday, and have thought of you very much. Mr Dwight preached all day. Mr Williston and [William S.] Clark were at our church this morning – There was a letter read from the Congregational c'h in Washington – D C, requesting the company of the Pastor and a Delegate, at the ordination of that Rev Mr Duncan, who was so much admired by Father when he was at home before – Father was chosen Delegate, but whether Mr Dwight will go or not, I dont know –

Tuesday morning –

Austin – I had'nt time to finish my note Sunday night – I shall do so now – Received your note last evening, and laughed all night till now – You must not be so facetious – It will never do. Susie was here when the note arrived, and we just sat and screamed. I shall keep the letter always. Marcia is here this morning – the work goes briskly on –

We are almost beside ourselves with business, and company – "Lysander" has not yet called – Emmons spent Friday evening here. I went with Cousin John last evening to call on Sue – stayed till most 11 – and had a splendid time – Sue seemed her very finest – She sends this little note.

Was at Mr Dwight's yesterday – they had a great deal to say about you and Susie and how happy Vinnie and I must be to have such a beau[tiful sister?]

We had two letters from Father last night – one to mother and one to me – I shall telegraph to him soon! Charlie sings every day – Everybody admires him – You must tell Aunt Lavinia –

How did Mr Bourne bear the announcement that both the black eyes were disposed of? It must have been quite a shock to him. Mrs Noyes has gone home – Helped us a great deal – Cenith has just arrived, so between her and "Judah" and Marcia and Miss Cooly, I guess the folks will go – Cousin John is going to stay here at night when they are away, and wants to know quite eagerly "when it is to come off." I am glad you have got settled and are not afraid of ghosts. You must have pleasant times with Clark.

We all send our love to you – Wont you write soon about John White – He is anxious to know, and Mrs Mack wants very much to have him come in there. Good bye Austin – Great hurrah – Remember us always to Clark –

Emily –

MANUSCRIPT: AC. Pencil. Dated: Sunday Evening. Envelope addressed (in ink): Wm Austin Dickinson./Law School./Cambridge./Mass. Postmarked: Amherst Ms Mar 22.

PUBLICATION: *Home* 346–351, with facsimile 347–350.

An attempt has been made to alter every reference to Sue. The women named in the paragraph next to the last evidently were seamstresses and other helpers called in to assist Mrs. Dickinson and Lavinia to prepare for their impending trip to Washington.

160

To John L. Graves   *spring 1854?*

> Dear John –
>
> Be happy –
> Emily –
> Early Monday morning –

MANUSCRIPT: HCL (G 7). Pencil. Addressed: Cousin John.
PUBLICATION: *Home* 400.

See letter no. 170.

161

To Emily Fowler Ford   *spring 1854*

I have just come home from meeting, where I have been all day, and it makes me so happy to think of writing you that I forget the sermon and minister and all, and think of none but you. . . . I miss you always, dear Emily, and I think now and then that I can't stay without you, and half make up my mind to make a little bundle of all my earthly things, bid my blossoms and home good-by, and set out on foot to find you. But we have so much matter of fact here that I don't dare to go, so I keep on sighing, and wishing you were here.

I know you would be happier amid this darling spring than in ever so kind a city, and you would get well much faster drinking our morning dew — and the world here is so beautiful, and things so sweet and fair, that your heart would be soothed and comforted.

[115]

I would tell you about the spring if I thought it might persuade you even now to return, but every bud and bird would only afflict you and make you sad where you are, so not one word of the robins, and not one word of the bloom, lest it make the city darker, and your own home more dear.

But nothing forgets you, Emily, not a blossom, not a bee; for in the merriest flower there is a pensive air, and in the bonniest bee a sorrow — they know that you are gone, they know how well you loved them, and in their little faces is sadness, and in their mild eyes, tears. But another spring, dear friend, you must and shall be here, and nobody can take you away, for I will hide you and keep you — and who would think of taking you if I hold you tight in my arms?

Your home looks very silent — I try to think of things funny, and turn the other way when I am passing near, for sure I am that looking would make my heart too heavy, and make my eyes so dim. How I do long once more to hear the household voices, and see you there at twilight sitting in the door — and I shall when the leaves fall, sha'n't I, and the crickets begin to sing?

You must not think sad thoughts, dear Emily. I fear you are doing so, from your sweet note to me, and it almost breaks my heart to have you so far away, where I cannot comfort you.

All will be well, I know, and I know all will be happy, and I so wish I was near to convince my dear friend so. I want very much to hear how Mr. Ford is now. I hope you will tell me, for it's a good many weeks since I have known anything of him. You and he may come this way any summer; and how I hope he may — and I shall pray for him, and for you, and for your home on earth, which will be next the one in heaven.

Your very affectionate,
Emilie.

I thank you for writing me, one precious little "forget-me-not" to bloom along my way. But one little one is lonely — pray send it a blue-eyed mate, that it be not alone. Here is love from mother and father and Vinnie and me. . . .

MANUSCRIPT: missing.
PUBLICATION: *L* (1894) 142–144; *L* (1931) 141–143, dated (presumably by ED): Sunday Afternoon.

Before moving to Brooklyn, New York, where they permanently resided, the Gordon Lester Fords lived briefly in New London, Connecticut.

162

To Henry V. Emmons   *about 1854*

Friend.

I look in my casket and miss a pearl – I fear you intend to defraud me.

Please not forget your promise to pay "mine own, with usury."

I thank you for Hypatia, and ask you what it means?

Have you heard from your friend, Miss Judkins, recently? I desire to write to her, but have not her address, and will you please tell Johnny if a little note to her would make your next too heavy.

Your Friend
Emilie –

MANUSCRIPT: HCL (E 12). Pencil. Dated: Tuesday morn.
PUBLICATION: *NEQ* XVI (1943) 372.

Kingsley's *Hypatia* was published in 1853. Eliza Maria Judkins had taught drawing, painting, and penmanship at Amherst Academy in 1841–1842, and had probably been one of ED's teachers. The first sentence of the letter may be a reminder that Emmons still has not returned the book which ED had lent him (see letter no. 150). Johnny Beston was a youthful handyman.

166

To Abiah Root   *about 25 July 1854*

My dear Child.

Thank you for that sweet note, which came so long ago, and thank you for asking me to come and visit you, and thank you for loving me, long ago, and today, and too for all the sweetness, and all the gentleness, and all the tenderness with which you remember me — your quaint, old fashioned friend.

I wanted very much to write you sooner, and I tried frequently, but till now in vain, and as I write tonight, it is with haste, and fear lest something still detain me. You know my dear Abiah, that the summer has been warm, that we have not a girl, that at this pleasant season, we have much company—that this irresolute body refuses to serve sometimes, and the indignant tenant can only hold it's peace— all this you know, for I have often told you, and yet I say it again, if mayhap it persuade you that I do love you indeed, and have not done neglectfully. Then Susie, our dear friend, has been very ill for several weeks, and every hour possible I have taken away to her, which has made even smaller my "inch or two, of time." Susie is better now, but has been suffering much within the last few weeks, from a Nervous Fever, which has taken her strength very fast. She has had an excellent Nurse, a faithful Physician, and her sister has been unwearied in her watchfulness, and last of all, *God* has been loving and kind, so to reward them all, poor Susie just begins to trudge around a little—went as far as her garden, Saturday, and picked a few flowers, so when I called to see her, Lo a bright boquet, sitting upon the mantel, and Susie in the easy-chair, quite faint from the effort of arranging them–I make my story long, but I knew you loved Susie– Abiah, and I thought her mishaps, quite as well as her brighter fortunes, would interest you.

I think it was in June, that your note reached here, and I did snatch a moment to call upon your friend. Yet I went in the dusk, and it was Saturday evening, so even then, Abiah, you see how cares pursued me–I found her very lovely in what she said to me, and I fancied in her face so, although the gentle dusk would draw her curtain close, and I did'nt see her clearly. We talked the most of you—a theme we surely loved, or we had not discussed it in preference to all. I would love to meet her again—and love to see her longer.

Please give my love to her, for your sake. You asked me to come and see you—I must speak of that. I thank you Abiah, but I dont go from home, unless emergency leads me by the hand, and then I do it obstinately, and draw back if I can. Should I ever leave home, which is improbable, I will with much delight, accept your invitation; till then, my dear Abiah, my warmest thanks are your's, but dont expect me. I'm so old fashioned, Darling, that all your friends would stare. I should have to bring my work bag, and my big spectacles, and I half forgot my grandchildren, my pin-cushion, and Puss—Why think of it seriously, Abiah—*do* you think it my *duty* to leave? Will you write me again? Mother and Vinnie send their love, and here's a kiss from me—

> Good Night, from Emily—

MANUSCRIPT: HCL (ARS 10). Ink. Dated: Tuesday Evening.
PUBLICATION: *L* (1894) 63–64, in part; *L* (1931) 55–56, in part.
On August 4, Susan Gilbert went to Geneva. This is ED's last known letter to Abiah, who married the Reverend Samuel W. Strong later in the year. There is a finality to the last paragraph which suggests that this letter terminated the correspondence between them.

169

To Henry V. Emmons   *August 1854*

My heart is full of joy, Friend—Were not my parlor full, I'd bid you come this morning, but the hour must be *stiller* in which we speak of *her*. Yet must I see you, and I will love most dearly, if quite convenient to you, to ride a little while this afternoon—Do not come if it's not so, and please tell little Pat when you will like to go, if you still find it possible—Of her I cannot write, yet do I thank the Father who's given her to you, and wait impatiently to speak with you—Please not regard the ride, unless it be most convenient—

My hand trembles—

> Truly and warmly,
>
> Emily—

MANUSCRIPT: HCL (E 14). Pencil.
PUBLICATION: *NEQ* XVI (1943) 374.
ED met Susan Phelps sometime before Emmons left Amherst during the week after commencement. This note seems to have been written the morning after the meeting.

170

To John L. Graves   *15 August 1854*

Dear John—

Are you very happy? Why did'nt you tell me so before you went away? And why too, did'nt I ask you that pleasant evening long, when we sat and talked together?

I have wanted to ask you many times, and I thought you would tell me, but someone would come in, and something else would happen and put me all to flight — but tonight, John, so still is it, and the moon so mild, I'm sure that you would tell me, were you sitting here. You know what I mean, dont you, and if you are so happy, I kneel and thank God for it, before I go to sleep.

Then you and your former College friend are reconciled again — he told me all about it, and tears of happiness came shining in my eyes. Forgiving one another as Jesus — us.

I have hoped for this very often, John, when you were fast asleep, and my eyes will shut much sooner, now all is peace. I loved to have you both my friends, and friends to one another, and it grieved me very often that you were enemies — now all is safe. It is lonely without you John — we miss you very much, and I'm thinking we'll miss you more when a year from now comes, and the crickets sing.

Quite sad it is when friends go, and sad when all are gone, to sit by pensive window, and recollect them, but I would not forget them – Please not forget us John, in your long vacation – We'll often think of you, and wish that we could see you. Mary is with us yet. Eliza went yesterday morning. I miss her thoughtful eyes, and did not Mary's merry ones linger with us still, the day would be too long; but Mary strokes the sunshine and coaxes it along, and drives the shadows home — much like a "honie bee" she seems, among more antique insects! She wants me to give you her compliments, and say to you beside, that she thanks you sincerely for the "social capacity,["] which she forgot to do, there were so many in. Good night, and gentle dreams, John — my pen is very bad. I write not any more. Vinnie sends her love.

Mine if you will to Hattie, and for your mother too. Had you been here tonight, John, I should have talked with you – You are not, and I write – I "wish you a merry Christmas," and a vacation as good as summer days are long –

Affy,
Emilie –

MANUSCRIPT: HCL (G 3). Ink. Dated: Tuesday Evening.
PUBLICATION: *Home* 399–400.

[120]

Since there is no other allusion to the misunderstanding and recon-
ciliation between John Graves and his friend, the natural inference that
Henry Emmons was the friend cannot be verified (but see letter no. 160).
The identity of "Mary" is also uncertain. She and Eliza Coleman seem to
have been among the Dickinson commencement guests of whom ED had
written in her letter to Emmons of August 8. A year earlier there had been
some correspondence between Lavinia and Austin about inviting a Mary
Nichols to visit them (*Home* 307). Another Boston girl, Mary Lyman,
may have been the one. "Hattie" was John Graves's younger sister. He
had gone home for the summer vacation before starting his senior year
at Amherst.

171

To Henry V. Emmons   *18 August 1854*

I find it Friend – I read it – I stop to thank you for it, just as the
world is still – I thank you for them all — the pearl, and then the onyx,
and then the emerald stone.

My crown, indeed! I do not fear the king, attired in this grandeur.

Please send me gems again – I have a flower. It looks like them,
and for it's bright resemblances, receive it.

A pleasant journey to you, both in the pathway home, and in the
longer way – *Then* "golden morning's open flowings, *shall* sway the
trees to murmurous bowings, in metric chant of blessed poems" –

Have I convinced you Friend?

Pleasantly,
Emily.

MANUSCRIPT: HCL (E 8). Pencil. Dated: Friday Evening.
PUBLICATION: *NEQ* XVI (1943) 371.

Before leaving Amherst, Emmons sent a farewell gift to ED, probably
a book of poems. An interpretation is offered by Aurelia G. Scott in *NEQ*
XVI (December 1943) 627–628, in which the writer points out that the
initial letters of pearl, onyx, and emerald spell "Poe." The lines at the end
form the conclusion of an essay by Emmons published in the *Amherst
Collegiate Magazine* for July 1854, entitled "The Words of Rock Rim-
mon": "And I arose and looked forth upon the broad plain with a strange
earnestness thrilling in my heart.

> The golden morning's open flowings,
> Did sway the trees in murmurous bowings,
> In metric chant of blessed poems."

To Susan Gilbert (Dickinson)   *about 1854*

Sue – you can go or stay – There is but one alternative – We differ often lately, and this must be the last.

You need not fear to leave me lest I should be alone, for I often part with things I fancy I have loved, — sometimes to the grave, and sometimes to an oblivion rather bitterer that death — thus my heart bleeds so frequently that I shant mind the hemorrhage, and I only add an agony to several previous ones, and at the end of day remark — a bubble burst!

Such incidents would grieve me when I was but a child, and perhaps I could have wept when little feet hard by mine, stood still in the coffin, but eyes grow dry sometimes, and hearts get crisp and cinder, and had as lief burn.

Sue — I have lived by this. It is the lingering emblem of the Heaven I once dreamed, and though if this is taken, I shall remain alone, and though in that last day, the Jesus Christ you love, remark he does not know me — there is a darker spirit will not disown it's child.

Few have been given me, and if I love them so, that for *idolatry*, they are removed from me — I simply murmur *gone*, and the billow dies away into the boundless blue, and no one knows but me, that one went down today. We have walked very pleasantly — Perhaps this is the point at which our paths diverge — then pass on singing Sue, and up the distant hill I journey on.

> I have a Bird in spring
> Which for myself doth sing –
> The spring decoys.
> And as the summer nears –
> And as the Rose appears,
> Robin is gone.
>
> Yet do I not repine
> Knowing that Bird of mine
> Though flown –

Learneth beyond the sea
Melody new for me
And will return.

Fast in a safer hand
Held in a truer Land
Are mine –
And though they now depart,
Tell I my doubting heart
They're thine.

In a serener Bright,
In a more golden light
I see
Each little doubt and fear,
Each little discord here
Removed.

Then will I not repine,
Knowing that Bird of mine
Though flown
Shall in a distant tree
Bright melody for me
Return.

E–

MANUSCRIPT: HCL (L 17). Ink. Dated: Tuesday morning.

PUBLICATION: The letter is unpublished. The poem is in *FF* 181–182;
Poems (1955) 7–8.

There is nothing in other letters to indicate a rift between the girls at
this time. The draft of a letter (HCL-Dickinson collection) from Austin
to Susan, 23 September 1851, alludes to some differences between the girls
about which he refuses to take sides, but this letter is in the handwriting of
1854. It is placed here to follow the emotional tone of the letter to Susan
of late August, though the disagreement on spiritual matters that seems to
lie behind it may have no connection with the feeling of neglect shown
in the earlier one.

To Dr. and Mrs. J. G. Holland   *about 26 November 1854*

Dear Friends,

I thought I would write again. I write you many letters with pens which are not seen. Do you receive them?

I think of you all today, and dreamed of you last night.

When father rapped on my door to wake me this morning, I was walking with you in the most wonderful garden, and helping you pick — roses, and though we gathered with all our might, the basket was never full. And so all day I pray that I may walk with you, and gather roses again, and as night draws on, it pleases me, and I count impatiently the hours 'tween me and the darkness, and the dream of you and the roses, and the basket never full.

God grant the basket fill not, till, with hands purer and whiter, we gather flowers of gold in baskets made of pearl; higher — higher! It seems long since we heard from you — long, since how little Annie was, or any one of you — so long since Cattle Show, when Dr. Holland was with us. Oh, it always seems a long while from our seeing you, and even when at your house, the nights seemed much more long than they're wont to do, because separated from you. I want so much to know if the friends are all well in that dear cot in Springfield — and if well whether happy, and happy — *how* happy, and why, and what bestows the joy? And then those other questions, asked again and again, whose answers are so sweet, do they love — remember us — wish sometimes we were there? Ah, friends — dear friends — perhaps my queries tire you, but I so long to know.

The minister to-day, not our own minister, preached about death and judgment, and what would become of those, meaning Austin and me, who behaved improperly — and somehow the sermon scared me, and father and Vinnie looked very solemn as if the whole was true, and I would not for worlds have them know that it troubled me, but I longed to come to you, and tell you all about it, and learn how to be better. He preached such an awful sermon though, that I didn't much think I should ever see you again until the Judgment Day, and then you would not speak to me, according to his story. The subject of perdition seemed to please him, somehow. It seems very solemn to me. I'll tell you all about it, when I see you again.

I wonder what you are doing today — if you have been to meeting? Today has been a fair day, very still and blue. Tonight the crimson children are playing in the west, and tomorrow will be colder. How sweet if I could see you, and talk of all these things! Please write us very soon. The days with you last September seem a great way off, and to meet you again, delightful. I'm sure it won't be long before we sit together.

Then will I not repine, knowing that bird of mine, though flown -- learneth beyond the sea, melody new for me, and will return.

Affectionately,

Emily.

MANUSCRIPT: missing.

PUBLICATION: *L* (1894) 160–162; *L* (1931) 157–159; *LH* 37–38, dated (presumably by ED): Sabbath Afternoon.

The letter is placed here because the phrasing of the reference to the weather exactly parallels that in the letter which follows, written to Susan Gilbert on November 27; and because the conclusion echoes lines from the poem sent to Susan in September (letter no. 173).

176

To Susan Gilbert (Dickinson)   27 November–3 December 1854

Susie — it is a little thing to say how lone it is — anyone can do it, but to wear the loneness next your heart for weeks, when you sleep, and when you wake, ever missing something, *this*, all cannot say, and it baffles me. I would paint a portrait which would bring the tears, had I canvass for it, and the scene should be — *solitude*, and the figures — solitude — and the lights and shades, each a solitude. I could fill a chamber with landscapes so lone, men should pause and weep there; then haste grateful home, for a loved one left. Today has been a fair day, very still and blue. Tonight, the crimson children are playing in the West, and tomorrow will be colder. In all I number you. I want to think of you each hour in the day. What you are saying — doing — I want to walk with you, as seeing yet unseen. You say you walk and sew alone. *I* walk and sew alone. I dont see much of Vinnie — she's mostly dusting stairs!

We go out very little — once in a month or two, we both set sail in silks — touch at the principal points, and then put into port again — Vinnie cruises about some to transact the commerce, but coming to anchor, is most that I can do. Mr and Mrs Dwight are a sunlight to me, which no night can shade, and I still perform weekly journeys there, much to Austin's dudgeon, and my sister's rage.

I have heard it said "persecution kindles" — think it kindled me! They are sweet and loving, and one thing, dear Susie, always ask for you. Sunday Afternoon. I left you a long while Susie, that is, in pen and ink — my heart kept on. I was called down from you to entertain some company — went with a sorry grace, I fear, and trust I acted with one. There is a tall — pale snow storm stalking through the fields, and bowing here, at my window — shant let the fellow in!

I went to church all day in second dress, and boots. We had such precious sermons from Mr Dwight. One about unbelief, and another Esau. Sermons on unbelief ever did attract me. Thanksgiving was observed throughout the state last week! Believe we had a Turkey, and two kinds of Pie. Otherwise, no change. Father went Thanksgiving night. Austin goes tomorrow, unless kept by storm. He will see you, Darling! What I cannot do. Oh *could* I! We did not attend the Thanksgiving "Soiree" — owing to our sadness at just parting with father. Your sister will give particulars. Abby is much better — rode horseback every day until the snow came, and goes down street now just like other girls — Abby seems more gentle, more affectionate, than she has.

Eme Kellogg wonders she does not hear from you. I gave your message to her, and bring you back the same. Eme is still with Henry, tho' no outward bond has as yet encircled them. Edward Hitchcock and baby, and Mary, spent Thanksgiving here. I called upon Mary — she appears very sweetly, and the baby is quite becoming to her. They all adore the baby. Mary inquired for you with a good deal of warmth, and wanted to send her love when I wrote. Susie — had that been you — well — well! I must stop, *Sister*. Things *have* wagged, dear Susie, and they're wagging still. "Little Children, love one another." Not all of life to live, is it, nor all of death to die.

Susie — we all love you — Mother — Vinnie — me. *Dearly!* Your Sister Harriet is our most intimate friend. The last night of the term, John sent his love to you. I have not heard from Mat for months.

"They say that absence conquers." It has vanquished me. Mother and Vinnie send their love. Austin must carry his.

MANUSCRIPT: HCL (L 9). Ink. Dated: Monday Evening.
PUBLICATION: FF 211–213, in part.

The letter, begun on Monday, November 27, was concluded on the following Sunday. Austin and Susan were expecting to be married in the autumn of 1855. For some time Austin had been planning a trip to Chicago, to size up his prospects for establishing a good law practice there. He left Amherst on December 4, and returned early in January, after a visit to the Gilberts in Grand Haven, Michigan. Edward Dickinson returned to Washington on November 30 for the second session of the Thirty-third Congress, which convened about December first.

The conclusion of the next to the last paragraph is a paraphrase of the two lines concluding the second stanza of James Montgomery's hymn, beginning: "O where shall rest be found:"

> The world can never give
> The bliss for which we sigh;
> 'Tis not the *whole* of life to live;
> Nor *all* of death to die.

V

1855–1857

"To live, and die, and mount
again in triumphant body . . .
is no schoolboy's theme!"

[1855–1857]

The substantial exchange of letters between Austin and Emily Dickinson came abruptly to an end when he returned to Amherst from law school and settled into the practice of law there for the rest of his life. Her correspondence with Susan Gilbert necessarily altered its character after Susan's marriage to Austin in July 1856.

The most important event in these years for the family occurred when, after Deacon David Mack died in September 1854, the Dickinson homestead on Main Street came onto the market. Mack had purchased it in 1833, and Edward Dickinson bought it back in April 1855. The family moved into it in November. The other event in that year of particular significance to Emily was her trip to Washington and her return stopover in Philadelphia, where probably she met the Reverend Charles Wadsworth, though the import of the meeting came later.

The few surviving letters of 1855 and 1856 merely hint at the changes taking place within her. No poem or letter can certainly be placed in the year 1857, and one trivial event only can be associated with it. In October 1856 she had won second prize at the Cattle Show for her rye and indian bread, and the Hampshire and Franklin Express, on 27 August 1857, announced her name as one of the members of the Cattle Show committee for that year who would act as judges of the Rye and Indian Bread display.

Perhaps in a desultory manner she was trying to write poetry. Whatever was happening, the inner forces shaping her destiny are hinted at in her recurrently expressed speculations on the theme of immortality.

178

To Susan Gilbert (Dickinson)   *Washington, 28 February 1855*

Sweet and soft as summer, Darlings, maple trees in bloom and grass green in the sunny places — hardly seems it possible this is winter still; and it makes the grass spring in this heart of mine and each linnet sing, to think that you have come.

Dear Children — Mattie — Sue — for one look at you, for your gentle voices, I'd exchange it all. The pomp — the court - the etiquette — they are of the earth — will not enter Heaven.

Will you write to me — why hav'nt you before? I feel so tired looking for you, and still you do not come. And you love me, come soon — this is *not* forever, you know, this mortal life of our's. Which had you rather I wrote you — what I am doing here, or who I am loving *there*?

Perhaps I'll tell you both, but the "last shall be first, and the first last." I'm loving you at home — I'm coming every hour to your chamber door. I'm thinking when awake, how sweet if you were with me, and to talk with you as I fall asleep, would be sweeter still.

I think I cannot wait, when I remember you, and that is *always*, Children. I shall love you more for this sacrifice.

Last night I heard from Austin — and I think he fancies we are losing sight of the things at home - Tell him "not so," Children — Austin is mistaken. He says we forget "the Horse, the Cats, and the geraniums" — have not remembered Pat — proposes to sell the farm and move west with mother — to make boquets of my plants, and send them to his friends — to come to Washington in his Dressing gown and mortify me and Vinnie. Should be delighted to see him, even in "dishabille," and will promise to *notice* him whenever he will come. The *cats* I will confess, have not so absorbed my attention as they are apt at home, yet do I still remember them with tender emotion; and as for my sweet flowers, I shall know each leaf and every bud that bursts, while I am from home. Tell Austin, never fear! My thoughts are far from idle, concerning e'en the *trifles* of the world at home, but all is jostle, here — scramble and confusion, and sometimes in writing home I cant stop for detail, much as I would love. Vinnie met the other evening, in the parlor here a certain Mr Saxton, who inquired of her for his Amherst cousins. Vinnie told him joyfully, all she knew of you, and another evening, took me down to him. We walked in the hall a long while, talking of you, my Children, vieing with each other in compliment to those we loved so well. I told him of you both, he seemed very happy to hear so much of you. He left Washington yesterday morning. I have not been well since I came here, and that has excused me from some gaieties, tho' at that, I'm gayer than I was before. Vinnie is asleep this morning — she has been out walking with some ladies here and is very tired. She says much of you — wants so much to see you. Give my love to your sister — Kiss Dwightie for me — my love for Abbie and Eme, when you see them, and for dear Mr & Mrs Dwight — Tell Mother and Austin they need'nt flatter themselves we are forgetting them — they'll find themselves much mistaken before long. We think we shall go to Philadelphia next week, tho' father has'nt decided. Eliza writes most every day, and seems impatient for us. I dont know how long we shall stay there, nor how long in New York. Father has not de[ci]ded. Shant you write, when this gets to you?

Affy — E —

MANUSCRIPT: HCL (L 14). Ink. Dated: Wednesday morning. Envelope addressed: Miss Susan H. Gilbert./Amherst./Mass. Franked: Edw. Dickinson M.C.

PUBLICATION: *FF* 202–205, in part.
The sisters stayed in Washington with their father from the middle of February until early March, and visited the Colemans in Philadelphia on the way home. Aside from this letter and the one that follows, hitherto associated with the spring of 1854, the only record of the weeks spent in Washington is the inscription in Elizabeth Stuart Phelps, *The Last Leaf from Sunnyside*, given to the girls by Mrs. James Brown, and dated "February 19, 1855, Washington." The book is in the Jones Library, Amherst, Massachusetts. "J. Brown & Lady" from Alabama are recorded as arrivals at Willard's Hotel on February 5. Susan and Martha Gilbert arrived at Amherst on February 10. "Little Dwightie" was the youngest child of their sister Harriet, Mrs. William Cutler, with whom they now lived. See Appendix: Eastman.

To Mrs. J. G. Holland *Philadelphia, 18 March 1855*

Dear Mrs. Holland and Minnie, and Dr. Holland too — I have stolen away from company to write a note to you; and to say that I love you still.

I am not at home — I have been away just five weeks today, and shall not go quite yet back to Massachusetts. Vinnie is with me here, and we have wandered together into many new ways.

We were three weeks in Washington, while father was there, and have been two in Philadelphia. We have had many pleasant times, and seen much that is fair, and heard much that is wonderful — many sweet ladies and noble gentlemen have taken us by the hand and smiled upon us pleasantly — and the sun shines brighter for our way thus far.

I will not tell you what I saw — the elegance, the grandeur; you will not care to know the value of the diamonds my Lord and Lady wore, but if you haven't been to the sweet Mount Vernon, then I *will* tell you how on one soft spring day we glided down the Potomac in a painted boat, and jumped upon the shore — how hand in hand we stole along up a tangled pathway till we reached the tomb of General George Washington, how we paused beside it, and no one spoke a word, then hand in hand, walked on again, not less wise or sad for that marble story; how we went within the door — raised the latch he lifted when he last went home — thank the Ones in Light that he's since passed in through a brighter wicket! Oh, I could spend a long day, if it did not weary you, telling of Mount Vernon — and I will sometime if we live and meet again, and God grant we shall!

I wonder if you have all forgotten us, we have stayed away so long. I hope you haven't — I tried to write so hard before I went from home, but the moments were so busy, and then they *flew* so. I was sure when days *did* come in which I was less busy, I should seek your forgiveness, and it did not occur to me that you might not forgive me. Am I too late today? Even if you are angry, I shall keep praying you, till from very weariness, you will take me in. It seems to me many a day since we were in Springfield, and Minnie and the *dumb-bells* seem as vague — as vague; and sometimes I wonder if I ever dreamed —

then if I'm dreaming now, then if I *always* dreamed, and there is not a world, and not these darling friends, for whom I would not count my life too great a sacrifice. Thank God there is a world, and that the friends we love dwell forever and ever in a house above. I fear I grow incongruous, but to meet my friends does delight me so that I quite forget time and sense and so forth.

Now, my precious friends, if you won't forget me until I get home, and become more sensible, I will write again, and more properly. Why didn't I ask before, if you were well and happy?

Forgetful

Emilie.

MANUSCRIPT: missing.

PUBLICATION: L (1894) 162–164; LL 190–191; L (1931) 160–161; LH 40–42, dated (presumably by ED): Philadelphia.

Congress adjourned on Sunday, March 4, and Edward Dickinson arrived home presumably on Wednesday. (On Tuesday, March 6, Susan Gilbert wrote her brother Dwight, mentioning Mr. Dickinson and saying: "I suppose he will be home Wednesday." HCL – Dickinson collection). One conjectures that the girls left Washington with their father, who saw them met in Philadelphia, then continued on home. They remained as guests in Philadelphia of Mr. and Mrs. Coleman and their daughter Eliza, an early friend of ED's. The Colemans were members of the Arch Street Presbyterian Church, of which the Reverend Charles Wadsworth was the pastor.

184

To John L. Graves   *late April 1856*

It is Sunday – now – John – and all have gone to church – the wagons have done passing, and I have come out in the new grass to listen to the anthems.

Three or four Hens have followed me, and we sit side by side – and while they crow and whisper, I'll tell you what I see today, and what I would that you saw –

You remember the crumbling wall that divides us from Mr Sweetser – and the crumbling elms and evergreens – and *other* crumbling things – that spring, and fade, and cast their bloom within a simple twelvemonth – well – *they* are *here*, and skies on me fairer far than

Italy, in blue eye look down – up – see! – away – a league from here, on the way to Heaven! And here are Robins – just got home – and giddy Crows – and Jays – and will you trust me – as I live, here's a *bumblebee* – not such as *summer* brings – John – earnest, manly bees, but a kind of a Cockney, dressed in jaunty clothes. Much that is gay – have I to show, if you were with me, John, upon this April grass – then there are *sadder* features – here and there, *wings* half gone to dust, that fluttered so, last year – a mouldering plume, an empty house, in which a bird resided. Where last year's flies, their errand ran, and last year's *crickets fell!* We, too, are flying – fading, John – and the song "here lies," soon upon lips that love us now – will have hummed and ended.

To live, and die, and mount again in triumphant body, and *next* time, try the upper air – is no schoolboy's theme!

It is a jolly thought to think that we can be Eternal — when air and earth are *full* of lives that are gone – and done – and a conceited thing indeed, this promised Resurrection! *Congratulate* me – John – Lad – and "here's a health to *you*" — that we have each a *pair* of lives, and need not chary be, of the one "that *now* is" –

Ha – ha – if any can afford – 'tis *us* a roundelay!

Thank you for your letter, John – Glad I was, to get it – and gladder had I got them *both*, and glad indeed to see – if in your heart, *another* lies, bound one day to me – Mid your momentous cares, pleasant to know that "Lang Syne" has it's own place – that nook and cranny still retain their accustomed guest. And when busier cares, and dustier days, and cobwebs, less unfrequent – shut what *was* away, still, as a ballad hummed, and lost, remember early friend, and drop a tear, if a *troubadour* that strain may chance to sing.

I am glad you have a school to teach – and happy that it is pleasant – amused at the *Clerical Civility* – of your new friends – and shall feel – I know, delight and pride, always, when you succeed. I play the old, odd tunes yet, which used to flit about your head after honest hours – and wake dear Sue, and madden me, with their grief and fun — How far from us, that spring seems – and those triumphant days – Our April got to Heaven *first* – Grant we may meet her there – at the "right hand of the Father." Remember, tho' you rove – John – and those who do *not* ramble will remember you. Susie's, and Mattie's compliments, and Vinnie's just here, and write again if you will –

[135]

MANUSCRIPT: HCL (G 4). Ink.
PUBLICATION: *Home* 401–402.

John Graves had graduated in the previous August and was now serving as principal of Orford Academy, Orford, New Hampshire. He had recently become engaged to Fanny Britton, daughter of one of the founders of the school. The allusion to "our April" is probably in recollection of the time, two years before, when John stayed with Emily and Susan Gilbert at the Dickinson house, while the family was in Washington.

185

To Mrs. J. G. Holland   *early August 1856?*

Don't tell, dear Mrs. Holland, but wicked as I am, I read my Bible sometimes, and in it as I read today, I found a verse like this, where friends should "go no more out"; and there were "no tears," and I wished as I sat down to-night that we were *there* — not *here* — and that wonderful world had commenced, which makes such promises, and rather than to write you, I were by your side, and the "hundred and forty and four thousand" were chatting pleasantly, yet not disturbing us. And I'm half tempted to take my seat in that Paradise of which the good man writes, and begin forever and ever *now*, so wondrous does it seem. My only sketch, profile, of Heaven is a large, blue sky, bluer and larger than the *biggest* I have seen in June, and in it are my friends — all of them — every one of them — those who are with me now, and those who were "parted" as we walked, and "snatched up to Heaven."

If roses had not faded, and frosts had never come, and one had not fallen here and there whom I could not waken, there were no need of other Heaven than the one below — and if God had been here this summer, and seen the things that *I* have seen — I guess that He would think His Paradise superfluous. Don't tell Him, for the world, though, for after all He's said about it, I should like to see what He *was* building for us, with no hammer, and no stone, and no journeyman either. Dear Mrs. Holland, I love, to-night — love you and Dr. Holland, and "time and sense" — and fading things, and things that do *not* fade.

I'm so glad you are not a blossom, for those in my garden fade, and then a "reaper whose name is Death" has come to get a few to help him make a bouquet for himself, so I'm glad you are not a rose — and I'm glad you are not a bee, for where they go when summer's done, only the thyme knows, and even were you a robin, when the west winds came, you would coolly wink at me, and away, some morning!

As "little Mrs. Holland," then, I think I love you most, and trust that tiny lady will dwell below while we dwell, and when with many a wonder we seek the new Land, *her* wistful face, *with* ours, shall look the last upon the hills, and first upon — well, *Home!*

Pardon my sanity, Mrs. Holland, in a world *in*sane, and love me if you will, for I had rather *be* loved than to be called a king in earth, or a lord in Heaven.

Thank you for your sweet note — the clergy are very well. Will bring such fragments from them as shall seem me good. I kiss my paper here for you and Dr. Holland — would it were cheeks instead.

Dearly,

Emilie.

P.S. The bobolinks have gone.

MANUSCRIPT: missing.

PUBLICATION: *L* (1894) 169–170; *LL* 199–200; *L* (1931) 164–165; *LH* 48–50, dated (presumably by ED): Sabbath Night.

Since the manuscript is missing, and the contents do not indicate the time of writing, the date given by Mrs. Todd — 1856 — has been retained. The departure of the bobolinks sets the season as early August. Several phrases in the first paragraph are taken from Revelation, where they are found in 3.12; 21.4; and 14.3. The final sentence in the paragraph is suggested by Luke 24.51. The quoted phrase in the third paragraph is the opening line of Longfellow's "The Reaper and the Flowers."

VI

1858–1861

"Much has occurred . . .
so much – that I stagger as I write,
in its sharp remembrance."

The number of letters surviving in each of the years that follow is materially larger than it was in the years just preceding. Of special importance is the year 1858, for sometime then Emily Dickinson became seriously interested in writing poetry, and began to fashion her packets —the slim manuscript volumes that she continued to assemble for another decade or so. It is also the year when she began her correspondence with Samuel Bowles and his wife, an association that became intimate for all members of the Dickinson family.

There is no certainty when she first wrote the Reverend Charles Wadsworth, but he paid a call upon her early in 1860. Whether he or another is the one she addresses as "Dear Master" in the draft of the letter with which this group opens, may never be surely known. At present one conjectures no other whom she might thus have designated.

In 1861 the first child of Austin and Susan Dickinson was born, an event that engrossed Sue's attention. The continued exchange of notes with Sue thereafter is warm but never urgent.

This too is the period when she began to correspond with her younger cousins, Louise and Frances Norcross. At a domestic level it continued until her death, with an intimacy she shared with no others except Mrs. Holland.

It is, finally, the period when she was beginning to think of herself as one who might write for posterity. The letter exchange with Sue about the "Alabaster" poem, which occurred in the middle or late summer of 1861, seems to have been her first effort at consultation about her way of poetry. Her next and last takes place in April 1862, when she initiated a correspondence with T. W. Higginson. The years 1858 to 1861 are a period when her forces were gathering. The flood of her talent is rising.

To recipient unknown   *about 1858*

Dear Master

I am ill, but grieving more that you are ill, I make my stronger hand work long eno' to tell you. I thought perhaps you were in Heaven, and when you spoke again, it seemed quite sweet, and wonderful, and surprised me so – I wish that you were well.

I would that all I love, should be weak no more. The Violets are by my side, the Robin very near, and "Spring" – they say, Who is she – going by the door –

Indeed it is God's house – and these are gates of Heaven, and to and fro, the angels go, with their sweet postillions – I wish that I were great, like Mr. Michael Angelo, and could paint for you. You ask me what my flowers said – then they were disobedient – I gave them messages. They said what the lips in the West, say, when the sun goes down, and so says the Dawn.

Listen again, Master. I did not tell you that today had been the Sabbath Day.

Each Sabbath on the Sea, makes me count the Sabbaths, till we meet on shore – and (will the) whether the hills will look as blue as the sailors say. I cannot talk any more (stay any longer) tonight (now), for this pain denies me.

How strong when weak to recollect, and easy, quite, to love. Will you tell me, please to tell me, soon as you are well.

MANUSCRIPT: AC. Ink.
PUBLICATION: *Home* 431–432.
This draft was left among ED's own papers, and no one knows whether a fair copy was made or sent to the person addressed. That it was meant as a reply to one from him is shown by the allusion to his question. She may have had the Reverend Charles Wadsworth in mind as "Master."

To Mr. and Mrs. Samuel Bowles   *about June 1858*

Dear Friends.

I am sorry you came, because you went away.

Hereafter, I will pick no Rose, lest it fade or prick me.

I would like to have you dwell here. Though it is almost nine o'clock, the skies are gay and yellow, and there's a purple craft or so, in which a friend could sail. Tonight looks like "Jerusalem." I think Jerusalem must be like Sue's Drawing Room, when we are talking and laughing there, and you and Mrs Bowles are by. I hope we may all behave so as to reach Jerusalem. How are your Hearts today? Ours are pretty well. I hope your tour was bright, and gladdened Mrs Bowles. Perhaps the Retrospect will call you back some morning.

You shall find us all at the gate, if you come in a hundred years, just as we stood that day.

If it become of "Jasper," previously, you will not object, so that we lean there still, looking after you.

I rode with Austin this morning.

He showed me mountains that touched the sky, and brooks that sang like Bobolinks. Was he not very kind? I will give them to you, for they are mine and "all things are mine" excepting "Cephas and Apollos," for whom I have no taste.

Vinnie's love brims mine.

Take   Emilie.

MANUSCRIPT: AC. Ink.

PUBLICATION: *L* (1894) 212–213; *LL* 245–246; *L* (1931) 187–188, in part.

The extensive collection of the letters of Samuel Bowles to Austin and Susan Dickinson (HCL) shows that their friendship began to develop about 1858. At that time a letter written in friendly but not intimate terms speaks of Mrs. Bowles's sorrow at the birth of a stillborn child. ED's hope that their trip had "gladdened Mrs. Bowles" suggests that the visit to Amherst had been made for Mrs. Bowles's sake. The time of the year is indicated by the nine o'clock sunset. The concluding biblical allusion is to 1

Corinthians 3.21–22: "Therefore let no man glory in men. For all things are yours."

This is the only letter written jointly to Mr. and Mrs. Bowles.

190

To Joseph A. Sweetser   *early summer 1858*

Much has occurred, dear Uncle, since my writing you – so much – that I stagger as I write, in its sharp remembrance. Summers of bloom – and months of frost, and days of jingling bells, yet all the while this hand upon our fireside. Today has been so glad without, and yet so grieved within – so jolly, shone the sun – and now the moon comes stealing, and yet it makes none glad. I cannot always see the light – please tell me if it shines.

I hope you are well, these many days, and have much joy.

There is a smiling summer here, which causes birds to sing, and sets the bees in motion.

Strange blooms arise on many stalks, and trees receive their tenants.

I would you saw what I can see, and imbibed this music. The day went down, long time ago, and still a simple choir bear the canto on.

I dont know who it is, that sings, nor *did* I, would I tell!

God gives us many cups. Perhaps you will come to Amherst, before the wassail's done. Our man has mown today, and as he plied his scythe, I thought of *other* mowings, and garners far from here.

I wonder how long we shall wonder; how early we shall *know*.

Your brother kindly brought me a Tulip Tree this morning. A blossom from his tree.

I find them very thoughtful friends, and love them much. It seems very pleasant that other ones will so soon be near.

We formed Aunt Kate's acquaintance, for the first – last spring, and had a few sweet hours, as do new found *girls*.

I meet some octogenarians – but men and women seldomer, and at *longer* intervals – "little children," of whom is the "Kingdom of Heaven." How tiny some will have to grow, to gain admission there! I hardly know what I have said – my words put all their feathers on – and fluttered here and there. Please give my warmest love to my aunts

[143]

and cousins – and write me, should you please, some summer's evening.

Affy,

Emilie.

MANUSCRIPT: Jones Library. Ink. Dated: Friday night.
PUBLICATION: L (1931) 397–398.
After the Dickinsons moved back to Main Street, the Luke Sweetsers were their closest neighbors. ED here anticipates a visit at the home of the latter of some members of the Joseph Sweetser family. In a letter to Mrs. Joseph Sweetser, which she wrote many years later, ED alludes to her childhood memories of her Aunt Kate, possibly in the period of 1840–1842, when, as Mrs. Bingham suggests (*Home* 506), the family was probably living in Amherst. The visit of the previous spring, here mentioned, may have been ED's first opportunity as an adult to know her aunt. In "this hand upon our fireside," ED alludes probably to the continued poor health of her mother.

The date is conjectured from the handwriting.

193

To Samuel Bowles   *late August 1858?*

Dear Mr Bowles.

I got the little pamphlet. I think you sent it to me, though unfamiliar with your hand – I may mistake.

Thank you if I am right. Thank you, if not, since here I find bright pretext to ask you how you are tonight, and for the health of four more, Elder and Minor "Mary," Sallie and Sam, tenderly to inquire. I hope your cups are full. I hope your vintage is untouched. In such a porcelain life, one likes to be *sure* that all is well, lest one stumble upon one's hopes in a pile of broken crockery.

My friends are my "estate." Forgive me then the avarice to hoard them! They tell me those were poor early, have different views of gold. I dont know how that is. God is not so wary as we, else he would give us no friends, lest we forget him! The Charms of the Heaven in the bush are superceded I fear, by the Heaven in the hand, occasionally. Summer stopped since you were here. Nobody noticed her – that is, no men and women. Doubtless, the fields are rent by petite anguish, and "mourners go about" the Woods. But this is not for us. Business enough indeed, our stately Resurrection! A special Courtesy, I judge, from what the Clergy say! To the "natural man," Bumblebees would seem an improvement, and a spicing of Birds, but far be it from me, to impugn such majestic tastes. Our Pastor says we are a "Worm." How is that reconciled? "Vain – sinful Worm" is possibly of another species.

Do you think we shall "see God"? Think of "Abraham" strolling with him in genial promenade!

The men are mowing the second Hay. The cocks are smaller than the first, and spicier.

I would distill a cup, and bear to all my friends, drinking to her no more astir, by beck, or burn, or moor!

Good night, Mr Bowles! This is what they say who come back in the morning, also the closing paragraph on repealed lips. Confidence in Daybreak modifies Dusk.

Blessings for Mrs Bowles, and kisses for the bairns' lips. We want to see you, Mr Bowles, but spare you the rehearsal of "familiar truths."

Good Night,

Emily.

MANUSCRIPT: AC. Ink. Dated: Amherst.
PUBLICATION: L (1894) 190–192; LL 202–203; L (1931) 182–183.
No information has been found on the nature of the "little pamphlet" that Bowles had sent. At this time there were three young children in the Bowles family: Sarah Augusta (Sallie), born in 1850; Samuel, born in 1851; and Mary (Mamie), born in 1854.

195

To Dr. and Mrs. J. G. Holland   *about 6 November 1858*

Dear Hollands,

Good-night! I can't stay any longer in a world of death. Austin is ill of fever. I buried my garden last week — our man, Dick, lost a little girl through the scarlet fever. I thought perhaps that *you* were dead, and not knowing the sexton's address, interrogate the daisies. Ah!

dainty—dainty Death! Ah! democratic Death! Grasping the proudest zinnia from my purple garden,—then deep to his bosom calling the serf's child!

Say, is he everywhere? Where shall I hide my things? Who is alive? The woods are dead. Is Mrs. H. alive? Annie and Katie—are they below, or received to nowhere?

I shall not tell how short time is, for I was told by lips which sealed as soon as it was said, and the open revere the shut. You were not here in summer. *Summer?* My memory flutters—had I—was there a summer? You should have seen the fields go—gay little entomology! Swift little ornithology! Dancer, and floor, and cadence quite gathered away, and I, a phantom, to you a phantom, rehearse the story! An orator of feather unto an audience of fuzz,—and pantomimic plaudits. "Quite as good as a play," indeed!

Tell Mrs. Holland she is mine. Ask her if *vice versa?* Mine is but just the thief's request—"Remember me to-day." Such are the bright chirographies of the "Lamb's Book." Goodnight! My ships are in!—My window overlooks the wharf! One yacht, and a man-of-war; two brigs and a schooner! "Down with the topmast! Lay her a' hold, a' hold!"

Manuscript: missing.

Publication: L (1894) 179–180; LL 307–308; L (1931) 173–174; LH 51–52: dated (presumably by ED): Saturday Eve.

In October 1858, Austin Dickinson was taken ill with typhoid fever. Harriet Matthews, the eight-year-old daughter of Richard Matthews, the Dickinson stableman, died of scarlet fever on November 1.

196

To Mrs. Samuel Bowles　　　　　　　　　　　　*about December 1858*

Dear Mrs Bowles.

Since I have no sweet flower to send you, I enclose my heart; a little one, sunburnt, half broken sometimes, yet close as the spaniel, to it's friends. Your flowers came from Heaven, to which if I should ever go, I will pluck you palms.

My words are far away when I attempt to thank you, so take the silver tear instead, from my full eye. You have often remembered me.

I have little dominion — Are there not wiser than I, who with curious treasure, could requite your gift. Angels fill the hand that loaded

Emily's!

MANUSCRIPT: AC. Ink. Undated.
PUBLICATION: L (1894) 213; LL 246; L (1931) 201.

The date is conjectured from the handwriting. The gift which this letter acknowledges may have been a birthday remembrance. There was hardly another month when ED could have said: "I have no sweet flower to send you."

199

To Louise Norcross   *about 4 January 1859*

Since it snows this morning, dear Loo, too fast for interruption, put your brown curls in a basket, and come and sit with me.

I am sewing for Vinnie, and Vinnie is flying through the flakes to buy herself a little hood. It's quite a fairy morning, and I often lay down my needle, and "build a castle in the air" which seriously impedes the sewing project. What if I pause a little longer, and write a note to you! Who will be the wiser? I have known little of you, since the October morning when our families went out driving, and you and I in the dining-room decided to be distinguished. It's a great thing to be "great," Loo, and you and I might tug for a life, and never accomplish it, but no one can stop our looking on, and you know some cannot sing, but the orchard is full of birds, and we all can listen. What if we learn, ourselves, some day! Who indeed knows? [?] said you had many little cares; I hope they do not fatigue you. I would not like to think of Loo as weary, now and then. Sometimes *I* get tired, and I would rather none I love would understand the word. . . .

Do you still attend Fanny Kemble? "Aaron Burr" and father think her an "animal," but I fear zoölogy has few such instances. I have heard many notedly *bad* readers, and a fine one would be almost a fairy surprise. When will you come again, Loo? For you remember, dear, you are one of the ones from whom I do not run away! I keep an ottoman in my heart exclusively for you. My love for your father and Fanny.

Emily.

MANUSCRIPT: destroyed.

PUBLICATION: L (1894) 229–230; LL 207–208; L (1931) 215–216, dated January, 1859.

A three-day snowstorm commenced on 4 January 1859. The Norcross and Dickinson families had been together during the previous October. Fanny Kemble gave public readings from Shakespeare after her retirement from the stage in 1849. This is perhaps ED's first letter to Louise Norcross, who was but sixteen at the time.

200

To Mrs. Joseph Haven   *13 February 1859*

Dear Mrs Haven.

Your remembrance surprises me. I hardly feel entitled to it. A most sweet surprise, which can hardly be affirmed of all our surprises. I grieve that I cannot claim it in a larger degree. Perhaps tho', sweeter as it is – *unmerited* remembrance – "Grace" – the saints would call it. Careless girls like me, cannot testify. Thank you for this, and your warm note.

We have hardly recovered laughing from Mr Haven's jolly one. I insist to this day, that I have received internal injuries. Could Mr H. be responsible for an early grave? The Coat is still in the dark, but the mirth to which it has given rise, will gleam when coats and rascals have passed into tradition.

The letters of suspected gentlemen form quite a valuable addition to our family library, and father pursues the search with a mixture of fun and perseverence, which is quite diabolical! I will give you the earliest intelligence of the arrest of our friend, who for the mirth he has afforded, surely merits *triumph*, more than transportation.

Father is in New York, just now, and Vinnie in Boston – while Mother and I for greater celebrity, are remaining at home.

My mother's only sister has had an invalid winter, and Vinnie has gone to enliven the house, and make the days shorter to my sick aunt. I would like more sisters, that the taking out of one, might not leave such stillness. Vinnie has been all, so long, I feel the oddest fright at parting with her for an hour, lest a storm arise, and I go unsheltered.

She talked of you before she went – often said she missed you, would add a couplet of her own, were she but at home. I hope you are well as I write, and that the far city seems to you like home. I do not know your successors. Father has called upon Mr S[eelye] but I am waiting for Vinnie to help me do my courtesies. Mr S. preached in our church last Sabbath upon "predestination," but I do not respect "doctrines," and did not listen to him, so I can neither praise, nor blame. Your house has much of pathos, to those that pass who loved you.

I miss the geranium at the window, and the hand that tended the geranium.

I shall miss the clustering frocks at the door, bye and bye when summer comes, unless myself in a *new* frock, am too far to see.

How short, dear Mrs Haven!

> A darting fear – a pomp – a tear –
> A waking on a morn
> to find that what one waked for,
> inhales the different dawn.

Receive much love from

Emilie –

MANUSCRIPT: HCL (Haven 3). Ink. Dated: Sabbath Eve.

PUBLICATION: *Indiana Quarterly for Bookmen* I (1945) 117–118; *Home* 404–405. The concluding quatrain is in *Poems* (1955) 71.

The Reverend Julius H. Seelye was elected, 20 August 1858, to the chair in philosophy vacated by Professor Haven. Seelye preached in the First Church on February 6. Vinnie was in Boston with Mrs. Loring Norcross, who died in the following year.

205

To Samuel Bowles   *early April 1859*

Friend,

     Sir,

I did not see you. I am very sorry. Shall I keep the Wine till you come again, or send it in by "Dick?" It is now behind the door in the

Library, also an unclaimed flower. I did not know you were going so soon — Oh my tardy feet!

Will you not come again? Friends are gems – infrequent. Potosi is a care, Sir. I guard it reverently, for I could not afford to be poor now, after affluence. I hope the hearts in Springfield are not so heavy as they were — God bless the hearts in Springfield!

I am happy you have a "Horse." I hope you will get stalwart, and come and see us many years.

I have but two acquaintance, the "Quick and the Dead" — and would like more.

I write you frequently, and am much ashamed.

My voice is not quite loud enough to cross so many fields, which will, if you please, apologize for my pencil. Will you take my love to Mrs Bowles, whom I remember every day.

Emilie

Vinnie halloos from the world of nightcaps, "dont forget her love!"

MANUSCRIPT: AC. Ink and pencil. Undated. Reproduced in facsimile in *Letters* (1931) 188.

PUBLICATION: L (1894) 198–199; LL 221; L (1931) 188–189.

On 8 April 1859 Samuel Bowles wrote Charles Allen: "I had the present of a bottle of wine this week, from a woman, with an affectionate note. We had some good food Fast-day [April 7] and we drank the wine." (George S. Merriam, *Life and Times of Samuel Bowles* 296.)

207

To Dr. and Mrs. J. G. Holland   *September 1859*

Dear Hollands,

Belong to me! We have no fires yet, and the evenings grow cold. To-morrow, stoves are set. How many barefoot shiver I trust their Father knows who saw not fit to give them shoes.

Vinnie is sick to-night, which gives the world a russet tinge, usually so red. It is only a headache, but when the head aches next to you, it becomes important. When she is well, time leaps. When she is ill, he lags, or stops entirely.

Sisters are brittle things. God was penurious with me, which makes me shrewd with Him.

One is a dainty sum! One bird, one cage, one flight; one song in those far woods, as yet suspected by faith only!

This is September, and you were coming in September. Come! Our parting is too long. There has been frost enough. We must have summer now, and "whole legions" of daisies.

The gentian is a greedy flower, and overtakes us all. Indeed, this world is short, and I wish, until I tremble, to touch the ones I love before the hills are red—are gray—are white—are "born again"! If we knew how deep the crocus lay, we never should let her go. Still, crocuses stud many mounds whose gardeners till in anguish some tiny, vanished bulb.

We saw you that Saturday afternoon, but heedlessly forgot to ask where you were going, so did not know, and could not write. Vinnie saw Minnie flying by, one afternoon at Palmer. She supposed you were all there on your way from the sea, and untied her fancy! To say that her fancy wheedled her is superfluous.

We talk of you together, then diverge on life, then hide in you again, as a safe fold. Don't leave us long, dear friends! You know we're children still, and children fear the dark.

Are you well at home? Do you work now? Has it altered much since I was there? Are the children women, and the women thinking it will soon be afternoon? We will help each other bear our unique burdens.

Is Minnie with you now? Take her our love, if she is. Do her eyes grieve her now? Tell her she may have half ours.

Mother's favorite sister is sick, and mother will have to bid her good-night. It brings mists to us all;—the aunt whom Vinnie visits, with whom she spent, I fear, her last inland Christmas. Does God take care of those at sea? My aunt is such a timid woman!

Will you write to us? I bring you all their loves—*many*.

They tire me.

Emilie.

MANUSCRIPT: missing.
PUBLICATION: L (1894) 172–174; L (1931) 167–168; LH 57–58.

In New England the wild gentian does not bloom until August, and it here is alluded to as a harbinger of the season's end. On Saturday, 6 August 1859, the Hollands attended an excursion to Amherst of the

American Association for the Advancement of Science. Mrs. Dickinson's sister Lavinia Norcross, fatally ill, lived until the following April (see letter no. 217).

208

To Catherine Scott Turner (Anthon) 1859?

When Katie walks, this simple pair accompany her side,
When Katie runs unwearied they follow on the road,
When Katie kneels, their loving hands still clasp her pious knee —
Ah! Katie! Smile at Fortune, with *two* so *knit to thee!*

Emilie.

MANUSCRIPT: missing. The text is from a transcript (HCL) made by Mrs. Anthon.
PUBLICATION: L (1931) 146; *Poems* (1955) 159.
The transcript bears the notation: "Emily knitted a pair of *garters* for me & *sent them over* with these lines." Kate Turner visited Susan Dickinson some four or five times during the years 1859–1861. Any date for this note and for the letter following (no. 209) is conjectural, but the tone suggests that they were written near the beginning of the friendship.

209

To Catherine Scott Turner (Anthon) late 1859?

Katie —

Last year at this time I did not miss you, but positions shifted, until I hold your black in strong hallowed remembrance, and trust my colors are to you tints slightly beloved. You cease indeed to talk, which is a custom prevalent among things parted and torn, but shall I class this, dear, among elect exceptions, and bear you just as usual unto the kind Lord? — We dignify our Faith, when we can cross the ocean with it, though most prefer ships.

How do you do this year? I remember you as fires begin, and evenings open at Austin's, without the Maid in black, Katie, without the Maid in black. Those were unnatural evenings. – *Bliss* is unnatural –

How many years, I wonder, will sow the moss upon them, before we bind again, a little altered it may be, elder a little it *will* be, and yet the same as suns, which shine, between our lives and loss, and violets, not last years, but having the Mother's eyes. —

Do you find plenty of food at home? Famine is unpleasant. —

It is too late for "Frogs," or which pleases me better, dear – not quite early enough! The pools were full of you for a brief period, but that brief period blew away, leaving me with many stems, and but a few foliage! Gentlemen here have a way of plucking the tops of trees, and putting the fields in their cellars annually, which in point of taste is execrable, and would they please omit, I should have fine vegetation & foliage all the year round, and never a winter month. Insanity to the sane seems so unnecessary – but I am only one, and they are "four and forty," which little affair of numbers leaves me impotent. Aside from this dear Katie, inducements to visit Amherst are as they were. – I am pleasantly located in the deep sea, but love will row you out if her hands are strong, and don't wait till I land, for I'm going ashore on the other side —

Emilie.

MANUSCRIPT: missing.

PUBLICATION: *L* (1894) 149–150, in part; *LL* 221–222, in part; *L* (1931) 147–148, in part: dated "1861 ?."

The text is from the transcript (AC) made by Mrs. Anthon for Mrs. Todd. For the date, see the letter preceding. The phrase "I am pleasantly located in the deep sea" is similar to expressions used in letters written in 1864 and 1865, when ED's eyes were giving her trouble (nos. 294 and 306). But in context here the expression does not imply a physical handicap.

216

To Mrs. Samuel Bowles   *1860?*

Don't cry, dear Mary. Let us do that for you, because you are too tired now. We don't know how dark it is, but if you are at sea, perhaps when we say that we are there, you won't be as afraid.

The waves are very big, but every one that covers you, covers us, too.

[153]

Dear Mary, you can't see us, but we are close at your side. May we comfort you?

Lovingly,
Emily.

MANUSCRIPT: missing.
PUBLICATION: L (1894) 198; L (1931) 187.

Three Bowles children were stillborn. This note perhaps was written after the third occasion, prior to the birth of Charles, in December 1861.

217

To Lavinia N. Dickinson   *late April 1860*

Vinnie —

I can't believe it, when your letters come, saying what Aunt Lavinia said "just before she died." Blessed Aunt Lavinia now; all the world goes out, and I see nothing but her room, and angels bearing her into those great countries in the blue sky of which we don't know anything.

Then I sob and cry till I can hardly see my way 'round the house again; and then sit still and wonder if she sees us now, if she sees *me*, who said that she "loved Emily." Oh! Vinnie, it is dark and strange to think of summer afterward! How she loved the summer! The birds keep singing just the same. Oh! The thoughtless birds!

Poor little Loo! Poor Fanny! You must comfort them.

If you were with me, Vinnie, we could talk about her together.

And I thought she would live I wanted her to live so, I thought she could not die! To think how still she lay while I was making the little loaf, and fastening her flowers! Did you get my letter in time to tell her how happy I would be to do what she requested? Mr. Brady is coming to-morrow to bring arbutus for her. Dear little aunt! Will she look down? You must tell me all you can think about her. Did she carry my little bouquet? So many broken-hearted people have got to hear the birds sing, and see all the little flowers grow, just the same as if the sun hadn't stopped shining forever! . . . How I wish I could comfort you! How I wish you could comfort me, who weep at what I did not see and never can believe. I will try and share you a little longer, but it is so long, Vinnie.

[154]

We didn't think, that morning when I wept that you left me, and you, for other things, that we should weep more bitterly before we saw each other.

Well, she is safer now than "we know or even think." Tired little aunt, sleeping ne'er so peaceful! Tuneful little aunt, singing, as we trust, hymns than which the robins have no sweeter ones.

Good-night, broken hearts, Loo, and Fanny, and Uncle Loring. Vinnie, remember

Sister

MANUSCRIPT: missing.
PUBLICATION: *L* (1894) 233–234; *LL* 213–215; *L* (1931) 217–218.
Lavinia stayed on for a short time with her uncle Loring Norcross and the children after her aunt's death on April 17.

219

To Samuel Bowles *about 1860*

I cant explain it, Mr Bowles.

> Two swimmers wrestled on the spar
> Until the morning sun,
> When one turned, smiling, to the land –
> Oh God! the other One!
> The stray ships – passing, spied a face
> Upon the waters borne,
> With eyes, in death, still begging, raised,
> And hands – beseeching – thrown!

MANUSCRIPT: AC. Pencil.
PUBLICATION: *Home* 420.
The date is conjectured from the handwriting and from the fact that the same poem is included by ED in one of her packets (HCL) written about this time. The circumstances to which the poem appears to allude have not been identified. But it is clear that about this time she was undergoing a turbulent emotional disturbance (see letters no. 187 and 233). Early in 1862 she in fact made a confidant of Bowles (see letter no. 250).

To Catherine Scott Turner (Anthon)   *summer 1860?*

The prettiest of pleas, dear, but with a Lynx like me quite un-available, – Finding is slow, facilities for losing so frequent in a world like this, I hold with extreme caution, a prudence so astute may seem unnecessary, but plenty moves those most dear, who have been in want, and Saviour tells us, Kate, "the poor are always with us" – Were you ever poor? I *have* been a Beggar, and rich tonight, as by God's leave I believe I am, The "Lazzaroni's" faces haunt, pursue me still! You do not yet "dislimn," Kate, Distinctly sweet your face stands in its phantom niche – I touch your hand – my cheek your cheek – I stroke your vanished hair, Why did you enter, sister, since you must depart? Had not its heart been torn enough but *you* must send your shred? Oh! our Condor Kate! Come from your crags again! Oh: Dew upon the bloom fall yet again a summer's night. Of such have been the friends which have vanquished faces – sown plant by plant the church-yard plats and occasioned angels. – There is a subject dear – on which we never touch, Ignorance of its pageantries does not deter me – I, too went out to meet the "Dust" early in the morning, I, too in Daisy mounds possess hid treasure – therefore I guard you more – You did not tell me you had once been a "Millionaire." Did my sister think that opulence could be mistaken? – Some trinket will remain – some babbling plate or jewel! – I write you from the summer. The murmur-ing leaves fill up the chinks thro' which the winter red shone, when Kate was here, and Frank was here – and "Frogs" sincerer than our own splash in their Maker's pools – Its but a little past – dear – and yet how far from here it seems – fled with the snow! So through the snow go many loving feet parted by "Alps" how brief from Vineyards and the Sun! – Parents and Vinnie request love to be given Girl –

                                                  Emilie –

MANUSCRIPT: missing. The text is from a transcript (HCL) made by Mrs. Anthon for Susan Dickinson. Mrs. Anthon made another transcript (AC) for Mrs. Todd. There are slight variations in punctuation.

PUBLICATION: L (1894) 148–149; LL 212–213; L (1931) 145–146.

After Campbell Turner's death in 1857 his widow reverted to her maiden name, and ED seems to have been previously unaware that Kate

Scott had been married. Frank Gilbert had been visiting his sister Susan Dickinson on some occasion during the winter here recalled.

223

To Samuel Bowles   *early August 1860*

Dear Mr Bowles.

I am much ashamed. I misbehaved tonight. I would like to sit in the dust. I fear I am your little friend no more, but Mrs Jim Crow.

I am sorry I smiled at women.

Indeed, I revere holy ones, like Mrs Fry and Miss Nightingale. I will never be giddy again. Pray forgive me now: Respect little Bob o' Lincoln again!

My friends are a very few. I can count them on my fingers – and besides, have fingers to spare.

I am gay to see you – because you come so scarcely, else I had been graver.

Good night, God will forgive me – Will you please to *try?*

Emily.

MANUSCRIPT: Hooker. Ink. Dated: Sunday night. Addressed: Mr Bowles. Unpublished.

Bowles was in Amherst during the week of August 5 to report commencement festivities.

225

To Louise and Frances Norcross   *mid-September 1860*

Bravo, Loo, the cape is a beauty, and what shall I render unto Fanny, for all her benefits? I will take my books and go into a corner and give thanks! Do you think I am going "upon the boards" that I wish so smart attire? Such are my designs, though. I beg you not to disclose them! May I not secure Loo for drama, and Fanny for comedy? You are a brace of darlings, and it would give me joy to see you both, in any capacity. . . . Will treasure all till I see you. Never fear that I shall forget! In event of my decease, I will still exclaim "Dr. Thomp-

[157]

son," and he will reply, "Miss Montague." My little Loo pined for the hay in her last communication. Not to be saucy, dear, we sha'n't have any more before the first of March, Dick having hid it all in the barn in a most malicious manner; but he has not brought the sunset in, so there is still an inducement to my little girls. We have a sky or two, well worth consideration, and trees so fashionable they make us all *passés*.

I often remember you both, last week. I thought that flown mamma could not, as was her wont, shield from crowd, and strangers, and was glad Eliza was there. I knew she would guard my children, as she has often guarded me, from publicity, and help to fill the deep place never to be full. Dear cousins, I know you both better than I did, and love you both better, and always I have a chair for you in the smallest parlor in the world, to wit, my heart.

This world is just a little place, just the red in the sky, before the sun rises, so let us keep fast hold of hands, that when the birds begin, none of us be missing.

"Burnham" must think Fanny a scholastic female. I wouldn't be in her place! If she feels delicate about it, she can tell him the books are for a friend in the East Indies.

Won't Fanny give my respects to the "Bell and Everett party" if she passes that organization on her way to school? I hear they wish to make me Lieutenant-Governor's daughter. Were they cats I would pull their tails, but as they are only patriots, I must forego the bliss. . . .

Love to papa.

Emily.

MANUSCRIPT: destroyed.
PUBLICATION: L (1894) 234–236; LL 215–216; L (1931) 218–219.

The phrase "last week," in the beginning of the second paragraph is figurative, for more than a month had elapsed since commencement. The "Bell and Everett party" (John Bell and Edward Everett, respectively candidates for president and vice president on the short-lived Constitutional-Union party) was formed, September 12. Edward Dickinson declined the nomination for lieutenant governor of the state on their ticket, September 18. He was in Boston for the convention, staying with the Norcrosses, when this letter was written. John Dudley brought his fiancée, Eliza Coleman, to commencement in August, and Eliza had evidently chaperoned the Norcross girls, Louise and Frances, now respectively aged eighteen and thirteen. It is assumed that ED first met John Dudley on this occasion. Dr. Joseph P. Thompson had been a commencement speaker, and ED's comment on him suggests that he may have mistaken her for one of the Montague cousins. The Burnham Antique Book Shop was an established Boston store.

233

To recipient unknown   *about 1861*

Master.

If you saw a bullet hit a Bird – and he told you he was'nt shot – you might weep at his courtesy, but you would certainly doubt his word.

One drop more from the gash that stains your Daisy's bosom – then would you *believe?* Thomas' faith in Anatomy, was stronger than his faith in faith. God made me – [Sir] Master – I did'nt be – myself. I dont know how it was done. He built the heart in me – Bye and bye it outgrew me – and like the little mother – with the big child – I got tired holding him. I heard of a thing called "Redemption" – which rested men and women. You remember I asked you for it – you gave me something else. I forgot the Redemption [in the Redeemed – I did'nt tell you for a long time, but I knew you had altered me – I] and was tired – no more – [so dear did this stranger become that were it, or my breath – the Alternative – I had tossed the fellow away with a smile.] I am older – tonight, Master – but the love is the same – so are the moon and the crescent. If it had been God's will that I might breathe where you breathed – and find the place – myself – at night – if I (can) never forget that I am not with you – and that sorrow and frost are nearer than I – if I wish with a might I cannot repress – that mine were the Queen's place – the love of the Plantagenet is my only apology – To come nearer than presbyteries – and nearer than the new Coat – that the Tailor made – the prank of the Heart at play on the Heart – in holy Holiday – is forbidden me – You make me say it over – I fear you laugh – when I do not see – [but] "Chillon" is not funny. Have you the Heart in your breast – Sir – is it set like mine – a little to the left – has it the misgiving – if it wake in the night – perchance – itself to it – a timbrel is it – itself to it a tune?

[159]

These things are [reverent] holy, Sir, I touch them [reverently] hallowed, but persons who pray – dare remark [our] "Father"! You say I do not tell you all – Daisy confessed – and denied not.

Vesuvius dont talk – Etna – dont – [Thy] one of them – said a syllable – a thousand years ago, and Pompeii heard it, and hid forever – She could'nt look the world in the face, afterward – I suppose – Bashfull Pompeii! "Tell you of the want" – you know what a leech is, dont you – and [remember that] Daisy's arm is small – and you have felt the horizon hav'nt you – and did the sea – never come so close as to make you dance?

I dont know what you can do for it – thank you – Master – but if I had the Beard on my cheek – like you – and you – had Daisy's petals – and you cared so for me – what would become of you? Could you forget me in fight, or flight – or the foreign land? Could'nt Carlo, and you and I walk in the meadows an hour – and nobody care but the Bobolink – and *his* – a *silver* scruple? I used to think when I died – I could see you – so I died as fast as I could – but the "Corporation" are going Heaven too so [Eternity] wont be sequestered – now [at all] – Say I may wait for you – say I need go with no stranger to the to me – untried [country] fold – I waited a long time – Master – but I can wait more – wait till my hazel hair is dappled – and you carry the cane – then I can look at my watch – and if the Day is too far declined – we can take the chances [of] for Heaven – What would you do with me if I came "in white?" Have you the little chest to put the Alive – in?

I want to see you more – Sir – than all I wish for in this world – and the wish – altered a little – will be my only one – for the skies.

Could you come to New England – [this summer – could] would you come to Amherst – Would you like to come – Master?

[Would it do harm – yet we both fear God –] Would Daisy disappoint you – no – she would'nt – Sir – it were comfort forever – just to look in your face, while you looked in mine – then I could play in the woods till Dark – till you take me where Sundown cannot find us – and the true keep coming – till the town is full. [Will you tell me if you will?]

I did'nt think to tell you, you did'nt come to me "in white," nor ever told me why,

No Rose, yet felt myself a'bloom,
No Bird – yet rode in Ether.

[160]

MANUSCRIPT: AC. Ink. Words which ED crossed out are here enclosed in brackets; alternative readings are in parentheses.

PUBLICATION: L (1894) 422–423, six sentences only, and dated 1885; L (1931) 411, six sentences only, and dated "early 60's"; Home 422–430, entire, with facsimile in full.

For an earlier "Master" letter, see no. 187. The handwriting is the only clue to the date. This rough draft was left among ED's own papers, and no one knows whether a fair copy was made or sent to the person envisioned as the recipient.

238

To Susan Gilbert Dickinson   *summer 1861*

> Safe in their Alabaster Chambers,
> Untouched by morning
> And untouched by noon,
> Sleep the meek members of the Resurrection,
> Rafter of satin
> And Roof of stone.
>
> Light laughs the breeze
> In her Castle above them,
> Babbles the Bee in a stolid Ear,
> Pipe the Sweet Birds in ignorant cadence, –
> Ah, what sagacity perished here!

[The earlier version, above, ED sent to Sue during the summer of 1861. Sue appears to have objected to the second stanza, for ED sent her the following:]

> Safe in their Alabaster Chambers,
> Untouched by Morning –
> And untouched by Noon –
> Lie the meek members of the Resurrection –
> Rafter of Satin – and Roof of Stone –

Grand go the Years – in the Crescent – about them –
Worlds scoop their Arcs –
And Firmaments – row –
Diadems – drop – and Doges – surrender –
Soundless as dots – on a Disc of Snow –

Perhaps this verse would please you better – Sue –

Emily –

[The new version elicited an immediate response:]
   I am not suited dear Emily with the second verse – It is remarkable
as the chain lightening that blinds us hot nights in the Southern sky
but it does not go with the ghostly shimmer of the first verse as well
as the other one – It just occurs to me that the first verse is complete in
itself it needs no other, and can't be coupled – Strange things always
go alone – as there is only one Gabriel and one Sun – You never made
a peer for that verse, and I *guess* you[r] kingdom does'nt hold one –
I always go to the fire and get warm after thinking of it, but I never
can again – The flowers are sweet and bright and look as if they would
kiss one – ah, they expect a humming-bird – Thanks for them of course
– and not thanks only recognition either – Did it ever occur to you that
is all there is here after all – "Lord that I may receive my sight" –
   Susan is tired making *bibs* for her bird – her ring-dove – he will
paint my cheeks when I am old to pay me –

Sue –

Pony Express

[ED answered thus:]

Is *this frostier?*

Springs – shake the sills –
But – the Echoes – stiffen –
Hoar – is the Window –
And numb – the Door –
Tribes of Eclipse – in Tents of Marble –
Staples of Ages – have buckled – there –

Dear Sue –
   Your praise is good – to me – because I *know* it *knows* – and *suppose* – it *means* –

Could I make you and Austin – proud – sometime – a great way off – 'twould give me taller feet –

Here is a crumb – for the "Ring dove" – and a spray for *his* Nest, a little while ago – *just* – *"Sue."*

Emily.

MANUSCRIPTS: HCL (B 74a, 74b, 74c, and 203d). All are ink except 74a.

PUBLICATION: *FF* 164, in part; *Poems* (1955) 151–155, where the story of the development of the poem is told in full, but with portions of the letters – touching upon the infant Ned – omitted.

VII

1862–1865

"Perhaps you smile at me.
I could not stop for that –
My Business is Circumference."

The most crucial and — though she could not know it — historically eventful year in Emily Dickinson's life was 1862. She was undergoing an emotional disturbance of such magnitude that she feared for her reason. At the same time she had developed her poetic sensibilities to a degree that impelled her to write Thomas Wentworth Higginson in April to learn what a professional man of letters might have to say about her verses. In no other year did she ever write so much poetry.

There is no direct evidence that the Reverend Charles Wadsworth was the man with whom she fell in love, but the circumstantial evidence is impressive that such was true, and is at no point contradicted by other evidence.

By far the most important correspondence in these years are the letters to Higginson and to Samuel Bowles. She clearly made Bowles a confidant in the matter which touched her heart most closely, and when Higginson had made certain by midsummer 1862 that in his opinion her verses were not for publication, she continued to write him because his interest in her thoughts and her writing was genuine, and his concern somehow gave her the curative she sought. "You were not aware," she wrote him seven years later, "that you saved my Life."

The nature of the eye affliction which required a specialist's attention is not known, but her eyesight was not seriously impaired (she never wore glasses), and during the months she spent in Boston in 1864 and 1865 she continued to write both poems and letters.

The letters of this group are the most moving of all, for they reveal the pathos of unrequited yearning and the assurance of a mature artist who cannot expect fame in her lifetime.

To recipient unknown   *early 1862?*

Oh, did I offend it – [Did'nt it want me to tell it the truth] Daisy – Daisy – offend it – who bends her smaller life to his (it's) meeker (lower) every day – who only asks – a task – [who] something to do for love of it – some little way she cannot guess to make that master glad –

A love so big it scares her, rushing among her small heart – pushing aside the blood and leaving her faint (all) and white in the gust's arm –

Daisy – who never flinched thro' that awful parting, but held her life so tight he should not see the wound – who would have sheltered him in her childish bosom (Heart) – only it was'nt big eno' for a Guest so large – *this* Daisy – grieve her Lord – and yet it (she) often blundered – Perhaps she grieved (grazed) his taste – perhaps her odd – Backwoodsman [life] ways [troubled] teased his finer nature (sense). Daisy [fea] knows all that – but must she go unpardoned – teach her, preceptor grace – teach her majesty – Slow (Dull) at patrician things – Even the wren upon her nest learns (knows) more than Daisy dares –

Low at the knee that bore her once unto [royal] wordless rest [now] Daisy [stoops a] kneels a culprit – tell her her [offence] fault – Master – if it is [not so] small eno' to cancel with her life, [Daisy] she is satisfied – but punish [do not] dont banish her – shut her in prison, Sir – only pledge that you will forgive – sometime – before the grave, and Daisy will not mind – She will awake in [his] your likeness.

Wonder stings me more than the Bee – who did never sting me – but made gay music with his might wherever I [may] [should] did go – Wonder wastes my pound, you said I had no size to spare –

You send the water over the Dam in my brown eyes –

I've got a cough as big as a thimble – but I dont care for that – I've got a Tomahawk in my side but that dont hurt me much. [If you] Her master stabs her more –

Wont he come to her – or will he let her seek him, never minding [whatever] so long wandering [out] if to him at last.

Oh how the sailor strains, when his boat is filling – Oh how the dying tug, till the angel comes. Master – open your life wide, and take me in forever, I will never be tired – I will never be noisy when you want to be still. I will be [glad] [as the] your best little girl – nobody else will see me, but you – but that is enough – I shall not want any more – and all that Heaven only will disappoint me – will be because it's not so dear

MANUSCRIPT: AC. Penciled rough draft.
PUBLICATION: *Home* 430–431.

The alternative suggested changes are placed in parentheses; words crossed out, in brackets. Like the earlier "Master" letters (nos. 187 and 233) this draft was among ED's papers at the time of her death. Whether a fair copy was made and sent, or intended to be sent, is not known. Accurate dating is impossible. The letter may have been written earlier, but the characteristics of the handwriting make the present assignment reasonable.

248a

[*Charles Wadsworth to ED*]

My Dear Miss Dickenson

I am distressed beyond measure at your note, received this moment, – I can only imagine the affliction which has befallen, or is now befalling you.

Believe me, be what it may, you have all my sympathy, and my constant, earnest prayers.

I am very, very anxious to learn more definitely of your trial – and though I have no right to intrude upon your sorrow yet I beg you to write me, though it be but a word.

In great haste
Sincerely and most
Affectionately *Yours* ——

MANUSCRIPT: AC. It is unsigned and without date, but is in the handwriting of the Reverend Charles Wadsworth, with an embossed crest "C W."
PUBLICATION: *Home* 369–372, with facsimile reproduction.

This solicitous pastoral letter is placed here because it thus follows the last of the "Master" letters, and because the present assumption is that ED thought of Wadsworth as "Master." Actually the letter may have been written at a quite different time.

249

To Samuel Bowles   *early 1862*

Dear friend.

If I amaze[d] your kindness – My Love is my only apology. To the people of "Chillon" – this – is enoug[h] I have met – no othe[rs.] Would you – ask le[ss] for your *Queen* – M[r] Bowles?

Then – I mistake – [my] scale – To Da[?] 'tis *daily* – to be gran[ted] and not a "Sunday Su[m] [En]closed – is my [d]efence –

[F]orgive the Gills that ask for Air – if it is harm – to breathe!

To *"thank" you* – [s]hames my thought!

> [Sh]ould you but fail [at] – Sea –
> [In] sight of me –
> [Or] doomed lie –
> [Ne]xt Sun – to die –
> [O]r rap – at Paradise – unheard
> I'd *harass God*
> Until he let [you] in!

Emily.

MANUSCRIPT: Hooker. Ink. Outside edges torn away. Unpublished except for the poem, which is in *Poems* (1955) 162, and there dated 1861. There can be no exact date assigned. Here the letter is moved somewhat ahead, since the letter seems to be part of a sequence that ED wrote Bowles between January and early April, when he sailed for Europe.

250

To Samuel Bowles   *early 1862*

> Title divine – is mine!
> The Wife – without the Sign!
> Acute Degree – conferred on me –

[169]

Empress of Calvary!
Royal – all but the Crown!
Betrothed – without the swoon
God sends us Women –
When you – hold – Garnet to Garnet –
Gold – to Gold –
Born – Bridalled – Shrouded –
In a Day –
"My Husband" – women say –
Stroking the Melody –
Is *this* – the way?

Here's – what I had to "tell you" –
You will tell no other? Honor – is it's
own pawn –

MANUSCRIPT: AC. Ink.
PUBLICATION: *Poems* (1955) 758. A variant of the poem, sent to Susan
Dickinson about the same time, was first published in *LL* 49–50.
   The phrase "Honor is it's own pawn" ED used again, to conclude her
first letter to Higginson, written on 15 April 1862 (no. 260).

251

To Samuel Bowles   *early* 1862

Dear friend

   If you doubted my Snow – for a moment – you never will – again –
I know –
   Because I could not say it – I fixed it in the Verse – for you to
read – when your thought wavers, for such a foot as mine –

> Through the strait pass of suffering –
> The Martyrs – even – trod.
> Their feet – upon Temptation –
> Their faces – upon God –

A stately – shriven – Company –
Convulsion – playing round –
Harmless – as streaks of Meteor –
Upon a Planet's Bond –

Their faith – the everlasting troth –
Their Expectation – fair –
The Needle – to the North Degree –
Wades – so – thro' polar Air!

MANUSCRIPT: AC. Ink.

PUBLICATION: *Poems* (1955) 598. Another copy of the poem only furnished the text first published in 1891.

In *Poems* (1955) the letter is dated 1863. Since this group of notes and poems to Bowles can be dated by handwriting only, no date can be surely assigned. It cannot be said with assurance that this letter follows no. 250, but it certainly is an attempt to make her position clear, a position which the preceding letter makes ambiguous.

260

To T. W. Higginson   *15 April 1862*

Mr Higginson,

Are you too deeply occupied to say if my Verse is alive?

The Mind is so near itself – it cannot see, distinctly – and I have none to ask –

Should you think it breathed – and had you the leisure to tell me, I should feel quick gratitude –

If I make the mistake – that you dared to tell me – would give me sincerer honor – toward you –

I enclose my name – asking you, if you please – Sir – to tell me what is true?

That you will not betray me – it is needless to ask – since Honor is it's own pawn –

MANUSCRIPT: BPL (Higg 50). Ink. Envelope addressed: T. W. Higginson./Worcester./Mass. Postmarked: Amherst Ms Apr 15 1862.

PUBLICATION: *AM* LXVIII (October 1891) 444; *L* (1894) 301; *LL* 238; *L* (1931) 272.

In place of a signature, ED enclosed a card (in its own envelope) on which she wrote her name. This first letter to Higginson, which begins a correspondence that lasted until the month of her death, she wrote because she had just read his "Letter to a Young Contributor," the lead article in the *Atlantic Monthly* for April, offering practical advice to beginning writers. She also enclosed four poems: "Safe in their Alabaster Chambers," "The nearest Dream recedes unrealized," "We play at Paste," and "I'll tell you how the Sun rose." When Higginson first published the letter (in the first publication named above), he introduced it by saying: "On April 16, 1862, I took from the post office in Worcester, Mass., where I was then living, the following letter."

261

To T. W. Higginson   *25 April 1862*

Mr Higginson,

Your kindness claimed earlier gratitude – but I was ill – and write today, from my pillow.

Thank you for the surgery – it was not so painful as I supposed. I bring you others – as you ask – though they might not differ –

While my thought is undressed – I can make the distinction, but when I put them in the Gown – they look alike, and numb.

You asked how old I was? I made no verse – but one or two – until this winter – Sir –

I had a terror – since September – I could tell to none – and so I sing, as the Boy does by the Burying Ground – because I am afraid – You inquire my Books – For Poets – I have Keats – and Mr and Mrs Browning. For Prose – Mr Ruskin – Sir Thomas Browne – and the Revelations. I went to school – but in your manner of the phrase – had no education. When a little Girl, I had a friend, who taught me Immortality – but venturing too near, himself – he never returned – Soon after, my Tutor, died – and for several years, my Lexicon – was my only companion – Then I found one more – but he was not contented I be his scholar – so he left the Land.

You ask of my Companions Hills – Sir – and the Sundown – and a Dog – large as myself, that my Father bought me – They are better

[172]

than Beings – because they know – but do not tell – and the noise in the Pool, at Noon – excels my Piano. I have a Brother and Sister – My Mother does not care for thought – and Father, too busy with his Briefs – to notice what we do – He buys me many Books – but begs me not to read them – because he fears they joggle the Mind. They are religious – except me – and address an Eclipse, every morning – whom they call their "Father." But I fear my story fatigues you – I would like to learn – Could you tell me how to grow – or is it unconveyed – like Melody – or Witchcraft?

You speak of Mr Whitman – I never read his Book – but was told that he was disgraceful –

I read Miss Prescott's "Circumstance," but it followed me, in the Dark – so I avoided her –

Two Editors of Journals came to my Father's House, this winter – and asked me for my Mind – and when I asked them "Why," they said I was penurious – and they, would use it for the World –

I could not weigh myself – Myself –

My size felt small – to me – I read your Chapters in the Atlantic – and experienced honor for you – I was sure you would not reject a confiding question –

Is this – Sir – what you asked me to tell you?

Your friend,

E – Dickinson.

MANUSCRIPT: BPL (Higg 51). Ink. Envelope addressed: T. W. Higginson./Worcester./Mass. Postmarked: Amherst Ms Apr 26 1862.

PUBLICATION: AM LXVIII (Oct. 1891) 445–446; L (1894) 301–303; LL 238–240; L (1931) 372–374.

Higginson says in his Atlantic Monthly article introducing the letter (cited above) that the enclosed poems were two: "Your riches taught me poverty," and "A bird came down the walk." But the evidence after study of the folds in the letters and poems suggest that he was in error. The enclosures seem to have been: "There came a Day at Summer's full," "Of all the Sounds despatched abroad," and "South Winds jostle them." Harriet Prescott Spofford's "Circumstance" was published in the Atlantic Monthly for May 1860. Higginson's "Letter to a Young Contributor" quotes Ruskin and cites Sir Thomas Browne for vigor of style. The article's comment on "what a delicious prolonged perplexity it is to cut and contrive a decent clothing of words . . ." may explain ED's phrase "While my thought is undressed." The friend who taught her "Immortality" has generally been thought to be Benjamin Franklin Newton. The two editors who recently had asked her for her mind may have been Bowles and Holland.

Though ED frequently refers to the Brownings, she never again mentions Ruskin, and Keats but twice (see letters no. 1018 and 1034).

265

To T. W. Higginson   *7 June 1862*

Dear friend.

Your letter gave no Drunkenness, because I tasted Rum before – Domingo comes but once – yet I have had few pleasures so deep as your opinion, and if I tried to thank you, my tears would block my tongue –

My dying Tutor told me that he would like to live till I had been a poet, but Death was much of Mob as I could master – then – And when far afterward – a sudden light on Orchards, or a new fashion in the wind troubled my attention – I felt a palsy, here – the Verses just relieve –

Your second letter surprised me, and for a moment, swung – I had not supposed it. Your first – gave no dishonor, because the True – are not ashamed – I thanked you for your justice – but could not drop the Bells whose jingling cooled my Tramp – Perhaps the Balm, seemed better, because you bled me, first.

I smile when you suggest that I delay "to publish" – that being foreign to my thought, as Firmament to Fin –

If fame belonged to me, I could not escape her – if she did not, the longest day would pass me on the chase – and the approbation of my Dog, would forsake me – then – My Barefoot-Rank is better –

You think my gait "spasmodic" – I am in danger – Sir –

You think me "uncontrolled" – I have no Tribunal.

Would you have time to be the "friend" you should think I need? I have a little shape – it would not crowd your Desk – nor make much Racket as the Mouse, that dents your Galleries –

If I might bring you what I do – not so frequent to trouble you – and ask you if I told it clear – 'twould be control, to me –

The Sailor cannot see the North – but knows the Needle can –
The "hand you stretch me in the Dark," I put mine in, and turn
away – I have no Saxon, now –

> As if I asked a common Alms,
> And in my wondering hand
> A Stranger pressed a Kingdom,
> And I, bewildered, stand –
> As if I asked the Orient
> Had it for me a Morn –
> And it should lift it's purple Dikes,
> And shatter me with Dawn!

But, will you be my Preceptor, Mr Higginson?

Your friend

E Dickinson –

MANUSCRIPT: BPL (Higg 52). Ink. Envelope addressed: T. W. Higginson./Worcester./Mass. Postmarked: Amherst Ms Jun 7 1862.
PUBLICATION: *AM* LXVIII (Oct. 1891) 447; *L* (1894) 303–304; *LL* 240–241; *L* (1931) 274–275.
The phrase "I have no Saxon" means "Language fails me": see *Poems* (1955) 197, where in poem no. 276 she offers "English language" as her alternative for "Saxon." She enclosed no poems in this letter.

268

To T. W. Higginson   *July 1862*

Could you believe me – without? I had no portrait, now, but am small, like the Wren, and my Hair is bold, like the Chestnut Bur – and my eyes, like the Sherry in the Glass, that the Guest leaves – Would this do just as well?

It often alarms Father – He says Death might occur, and he has Molds of all the rest – but has no Mold of me, but I noticed the Quick wore off those things, in a few days, and forestall the dishonor – You will think no caprice of me –

You said "Dark." I know the Butterfly – and the Lizard – and the Orchis –

Are not those *your* Countrymen?

I am happy to be your scholar, and will deserve the kindness, I cannot repay.

If you truly consent, I recite, now –

Will you tell me my fault, frankly as to yourself, for I had rather wince, than die. Men do not call the surgeon, to commend – the Bone, but to set it, Sir, and fracture within, is more critical. And for this, Preceptor, I shall bring you – Obedience – the Blossom from my Garden, and every gratitude I know. Perhaps you smile at me. I could not stop for that – My Business is Circumference – An ignorance, not of Customs, but if caught with the Dawn – or the Sunset see me – Myself the only Kangaroo among the Beauty, Sir, if you please, it afflicts me, and I thought that instruction would take it away.

Because you have much business, beside the growth of me – you will appoint, yourself, how often I shall come – without your inconvenience. And if at any time – you regret you received me, or I prove a different fabric to that you supposed – you must banish me –

When I state myself, as the Representative of the Verse – it does not mean – me – but a supposed person. You are true, about the "perfection."

Today, makes Yesterday mean.

You spoke of Pippa Passes – I never heard anybody speak of Pippa Passes – before.

You see my posture is benighted.

To thank you, baffles me. Are you perfectly powerful? Had I a pleasure you had not, I could delight to bring it.

Your Scholar

MANUSCRIPT: BPL (Higg 54), dated by Higginson: July 1862. Ink. Envelope addressed: T. W. Higginson/Princeton/Massachusetts. Postmarked: Jul [?] 1862.

PUBLICATION: AM LXVIII (Oct. 1891) 447–448; L (1894), 305–306; LL 241–243; L (1931) 276–277.

"Pippa Passes," the first of the series in Browning's "Bells and Pomegranates," had been published in 1841. The letter enclosed four poems: "Of Tribulation these are they," "Your Riches taught me poverty," "Some keep the Sabbath going to Church," and "Success is counted sweetest."

To Dr. and Mrs. J. G. Holland   *summer 1862?*

Dear Friends,

I write to you. I receive no letter.

I say "they dignify my trust." I do not disbelieve. I go again. *Cardinals* wouldn't do it. Cockneys wouldn't do it, but I can't *stop* to strut, in a world where bells toll. I hear through visitor in town, that "Mrs. Holland is not strong." The little peacock in me, tells me not to inquire again. Then I remember my tiny friend – how brief she is – how dear she is, and the peacock quite dies away. Now, you need not speak, for perhaps you are weary, and "Herod" requires all your thought, but if you are *well* – let Annie draw me a little picture of an erect flower; if you are *ill*, she can hang the flower a little on one side!

Then, I shall understand, and you need not stop to write me a letter. Perhaps you laugh at me! Perhaps the whole United States are laughing at me too! *I* can't stop for that! *My* business is to love. I found a bird, this morning, down – down – on a little bush at the foot of the garden, and wherefore sing, I said, since nobody *hears*?

One sob in the throat, one flutter of bosom – "*My* business is to *sing*" – and away she rose! How do I know but cherubim, once, themselves, as patient, listened, and applauded her unnoticed hymn?

                                        Emily.

MANUSCRIPT: missing.

PUBLICATION: L (1894) 175–176; L (1931) 169; LH 55–56: dated (presumably by ED): Friday.

This letter is dated by conjecture only. Mrs. Ward, though placing it with a question mark in 1859 (in *LH*), now feels that 1862 is perhaps more likely. The evidence for the later date is in the phrase "in a world where bells toll" – suggesting the war period, and especially in the sentences: "Perhaps you laugh at me! . . . I can't stop for that! *My* business is to love . . . *My* business is to *sing*." The juxtaposition of the sentences closely follows that in the preceding letter to Higginson: "Perhaps you smile at me. I could not stop for that – My Business is Circumference." It was in 1862 that ED indeed felt that her business was to sing.

Bulwer-Lytton's widely popular drama *Richelieu* (1839) might account for ED's opinion of cardinals, and Emerson's *English Traits* (1856) could be the source of her opinion of "cockney conceit." In context, "Herod" seems to personify the persecution of illness. Annie was ten years old in the summer of 1862.

To T. W. Higginson   *August 1862*

Dear friend –

Are these more orderly? I thank you for the Truth –

I had no Monarch in my life, and cannot rule myself, and when I try to organize – my little Force explodes – and leaves me bare and charred –

I think you called me "Wayward." Will you help me improve?

I suppose the pride that stops the Breath, in the Core of Woods, is not of Ourself –

You say I confess the little mistake, and omit the large – Because I can see Orthography – but the Ignorance out of sight – is my Preceptor's charge –

Of "shunning Men and Women" – they talk of Hallowed things, aloud – and embarrass my Dog – He and I dont object to them, if they'll exist their side. I think Carl[o] would please you – He is dumb, and brave – I think you would like the Chestnut Tree, I met in my walk. It hit my notice suddenly – and I thought the Skies were in Blossom –

Then there's a noiseless noise in the Orchard – that I let persons hear – You told me in one letter, you could not come to see me, "now," and I made no answer, not because I had none, but did not think myself the price that you should come so far –

I do not ask so large a pleasure, lest you might deny me –

You say "Beyond your knowledge." You would not jest with me, because I believe you – but Preceptor – you cannot mean it? All men say "What" to me, but I thought it a fashion –

When much in the Woods as a little Girl, I was told that the Snake would bite me, that I might pick a poisonous flower, or Goblins kidnap me, but I went along and met no one but Angels, who were far shyer of me, than I could be of them, so I hav'nt that confidence in fraud which many exercise.

I shall observe your precept – though I dont understand it, always.

I marked a line in One Verse – because I met it after I made it – and never consciously touch a paint, mixed by another person –

I do not let go it, because it is mine.

Have you the portrait of Mrs Browning? Persons sent me three – If you had none, will you have mine?

Your Scholar –

MANUSCRIPT: BPL (Higg 55). Ink.

PUBLICATION: *AM* LXVIII (October 1891) 448–449; *L* (1894) 307–309; *LL* 243–244; *L* (1931) 277–278.

With this letter ED enclosed two poems: "Before I got my Eye put out," and "I cannot dance upon my Toes."

277

To Samuel Bowles   *late November 1862*

Dear friend.

I did not need the little Bat – to enforce your memory – for that can stand alone, like the best Brocade – but it was much – that far and ill, you recollected me – Forgive me if I prize the Grace – superior to the Sign. Because I did not see you, Vinnie and Austin, upbraided me – They did not know I gave my part that they might have the more – but then the Prophet had no fame in his immediate Town – My Heart led all the rest – I think that what we *know* – we can endure that others doubt, until their faith be riper. And so, dear friend, who knew me, I make no argument – to you –

Did I not want to see you? Do not the Phebes want to come? Oh They of little faith! I said I was glad that you were alive – Might it bear repeating? Some phrases are too fine to fade – and Light but just confirms them – Few absences could seem so wide as your's has done, to us – If 'twas a larger face – or we a smaller Canvas – we need not know – now you have come –

We hope often to see you – Our poverty – entitle us – and friends are nations in themselves – to supersede the Earth –

'Twould please us, were you well – and could your health be had by sacrifice of ours – 'twould be contention for the place – We used to tell each other, when you were from America – how failure in a Battle – were easier – and you here – I will not tell you further –

Perhaps you tire – now – A small weight – is obnoxious – upon a weary Rope – but had you Exile – or Eclipse – or so huge a Danger, as would dissolve all other friends – 'twould please me to remain –

Let others – show this Surry's Grace –
Myself – assist his Cross.

Emily –

MANUSCRIPT: Hooker. Ink. Unpublished.

Brocade that stands alone was probably suggested by a sentence in George Eliot's *The Mill on the Floss* (chapter 12), recently published (1860), which ED was perhaps now reading: "Mrs. Glegg . . . had inherited from her grandmother . . . a brocaded gown that would stand up empty, like a suit of armour. . ." (see also letter no. 368). Henry Howard, earl of Surrey (1517–1547), the first English writer of blank verse, was accused of high treason, tried before a packed jury, and beheaded.

278

To Louise and Frances Norcross   late January 1863

What shall I tell these darlings except that my father and mother are half their father and mother, and my home half theirs, whenever, and for as long as, they will. And sometimes a dearer thought than that creeps into my mind, but it is not for to-night. Wasn't dear papa so tired always after mamma went, and wasn't it almost sweet to think of the two together these new winter nights? The grief is our side, darlings, and the glad is theirs. Vinnie and I sit down to-night, while mother tells what makes us cry, though we know it is well and easy with uncle and papa, and only our part hurts. Mother tells how gently he looked on all who looked at him – how he held his bouquet sweet, as he were a guest in a friend's parlor and must still do honor. The meek, mild gentleman who thought no harm, but peace toward all.

Vinnie intended to go, but the day was cold, and she wanted to keep Uncle Loring as she talked with him, always, instead of this new way. She thought too, for the crowd, she could not see you, children, and she would be another one to give others care. Mother said Mr. V[aill], yes, dears, even Mr. V[aill], at whom we sometimes smile, talked about "Lorin' and Laviny" and his friendship towards them, to your father's guests. We won't smile at him any more now, will we? Perhaps he'll live to tell some gentleness of us, who made merry of him.

But never mind that now. When you have strength, tell us how it is, and what we may do for you, of comfort, or of service. Be sure you crowd all others out, precious little cousins. Good-night. Let Emily sing for you because she cannot pray:

> It is not dying hurts us so, –
> 'Tis living hurts us more;
> But dying is a different way,
> A kind, behind the door, –
> The southern custom of the bird
> That soon as frosts are due
> Adopts a better latitude.
> We are the birds that stay,
> The shiverers round farmers' doors,
> For whose reluctant crumb
> We stipulate, till pitying snows
> Persuade our feathers home.

Emily.

MANUSCRIPT: destroyed.
PUBLICATION: L (1894) 250–251; LL 252–253; L (1931) 228–229.
The girls were orphaned by the death of their father, Loring Norcross, on 17 January 1863. The service was conducted by the Reverend Joseph Vaill of Palmer.

280

To T. W. Higginson   *February 1863*
Dear friend

I did not deem that Planetary forces annulled – but suffered an Exchange of Territory, or World –

[181]

I should have liked to see you, before you became improbable. War feels to me an oblique place – Should there be other Summers, would you perhaps come?

I found you were gone, by accident, as I find Systems are, or Seasons of the year, and obtain no cause – but suppose it a treason of Progress – that dissolves as it goes. Carlo – still remained – and I told him –

> Best Gains – must have the Losses' Test –
> To constitute them – Gains –

My Shaggy Ally assented –

Perhaps Death – gave me awe for friends – striking sharp and early, for I held them since – in a brittle love – of more alarm, than peace. I trust you may pass the limit of War, and though not reared to prayer – when service is had in Church, for Our Arms, I include yourself – I, too, have an "Island" – whose "Rose and Magnolia" are in the Egg, and it's "Black Berry" but a spicy prospective, yet as you say, "fascination" is absolute of Clime. I was thinking, today – as I noticed, that the "Supernatural," was only the Natural, disclosed –

> Not "Revelation" – 'tis – that waits,
> But our unfurnished eyes –

But I fear I detain you –

Should you, before this reaches you, experience immortality, who will inform me of the Exchange? Could you, with honor, avoid Death, I entreat you – Sir – It would bereave

Your Gnome –

I trust the "Procession of Flowers" was not a premonition –

MANUSCRIPT: BPL (Higg 56). Ink. Dated: Amherst.

PUBLICATION: AM LXVIII (October 1891) 449; L (1894) 309–310, in part; LL 248–249, in part; L (1931) 278–279, entire.

In the letter ED enclosed "The Soul unto itself." Higginson had gone to South Carolina, in command of a Negro regiment, in November 1862. The *Springfield Republican* carried long items about Higginson and his troops in the issues of 1 January and 6 February 1863. Higginson's "Procession of Flowers" appeared in the December 1862, issue of the *Atlantic Monthly*. He could never explain the reason for the signature. One conjectures that perhaps he had earlier commented on the gnomic quality of her verses.

281

To Louise and Frances Norcross   *late May 1863*

I said I should come "in a day." Emily never fails except for a cause; that you know, dear Loo.

The nights turned hot, when Vinnie had gone, and I must keep no window raised for fear of prowling "booger," and I must shut my door for fear front door slide open on me at the "dead of night," and I must keep "gas" burning to light the danger up, so I could distinguish it – these gave me a snarl in the brain which don't unravel yet, and that old nail in my breast pricked me; these, dear, were my cause. Truth is so best of all I wanted you to know. Vinnie will tell of her visit. . . .

About Commencement, children, I can have no doubt, if you should fail me then, my little life would fail of itself. Could you only lie in your little bed and smile at me, that would be support. Tell the doctor I am inexorable, besides I shall heal you quicker than he. You need the balsam word. And who is to cut the cake, ask Fanny, and chirp to those trustees? Tell me, dears, by the coming mail, that you will not fail me. . . .

Jennie Hitchcock's mother was buried yesterday, so there is one orphan more, and her father is very sick besides. My father and mother went to the service, and mother said while the minister prayed, a hen with her chickens came up, and tried to fly into the window. I suppose the dead lady used to feed them, and they wanted to bid her good-by.

Life is death we're lengthy at, death the hinge to life.

Love from all,
Emily.

MANUSCRIPT: destroyed.
PUBLICATION: L (1894) 246–247; LL 249–250; L (1931) 231.
Professor Edward Hitchcock's wife died on 26 May 1863.

[183]

To Lavinia N. Dickinson   *Cambridge, about May 1864*

Dear Vinnie,

I miss you most, and I want to go Home and take good care of you and make you happy every day.

The Doctor is not willing yet, and He is not willing I should write. He wrote to Father, himself, because He thought it not best for me.

You wont think it strange any more, will you?

Loo and Fanny take sweet care of me, and let me want for nothing, but I am not at Home, and the calls at the Doctor's are painful, and dear Vinnie, I have not looked at the Spring.

Wont you help me be patient?

I cannot write but this, and send a little flower, and hope you wont forget me, because I want to come so much I cannot make it show.

                                                        Emily.

MANUSCRIPT: AC. Pencil.
PUBLICATION: *L* (1894) 153; *L* (1931) 150–151; *Home* 434.

The tone of the letter suggests that it was written shortly after ED arrived in Cambridge.

To T. W. Higginson   *Cambridge, early June 1864*

Dear friend,

Are you in danger—

I did not know that you were hurt. Will you tell me more? Mr Hawthorne died.

I was ill since September, and since April, in Boston, for a Physician's care—He does not let me go, yet I work in my Prison, and make Guests for myself—

Carlo did not come, because that he would die, in Jail, and the Mountains, I could not hold now, so I brought but the Gods—

I wish to see you more than before I failed—Will you tell me your health?

I am surprised and anxious, since receiving your note—

The only News I know
Is Bulletins all day
From Immortality.
Can you render my Pencil?
The Physician has taken away my Pen.
I enclose the address from a letter, lest my figures fail – Knowledge
of your recovery – would excel my own –

E – Dickinson

MANUSCRIPT: BPL (Higg 57). Pencil. Endorsed by TWH on last
(blank) page: Miss Dickinson/86 Austin St/Cambridgeport/Mass.
PUBLICATION: AM LXVIII (October 1891) 450; L (1894) 310–311;
LL 262; L (1931) 280.
Higginson had been wounded in July 1863, and left the army in May
1864. From 10 June until 2 September the Higginsons were at Pigeon
Cove; in November they settled at Newport, Rhode Island. Hawthorne
died on 19 May 1864.

291

To Edward (Ned) Dickinson   *Cambridge, 19 June 1864*

My little Uncle must remember me till I come Home a Hundred
miles to see his Braided Gown –
Emily knows a Man who drives a Coach like a Thimble, and turns
the Wheel all day with his Heel – His name is Bumblebee. Little Ned
will see Him before

His Niece.

MANUSCRIPT: HCL (B 16). Pencil.
PUBLICATION: LL 57–58, in part.
This was written for Ned on his third birthday. The Amherst dress-
maker's account (Jones Library) shows a dress made for him at this time.

294

To Susan Gilbert Dickinson   *Cambridge, September 1864*

At Centre of the Sea –
I am glad Mrs – Gertrude lived – I believed she would – Those

[185]

that are worthy of Life are of Miracle, for Life is Miracle, and Death, as harmless as a Bee, except to those who run –

It would be best to see you – it would be good to see the Grass, and hear the Wind blow the wide way in the Orchard – Are the Apples ripe – Have the Wild Geese crossed – Did you save the seed to the pond Lily?

Love for Mat, and John, and the Foreigner – And kiss little Ned in the seam in the neck, entirely for Me –

The Doctor is very kind –

I find no Enemy – Till the Four o'Clocks strike Five, Loo will last, she says. Do not cease, Sister. Should I turn in my long night I should murmur "Sue" –

Emily.

MANUSCRIPT: HCL (B 179). Pencil.
PUBLICATION: *FF* 231 and 266–267, excerpts only.
Susan's friend Gertrude Vanderbilt was accidentally wounded by a gun shot on 20 March 1864. A daughter, Susan Gilbert Smith, was born 8 September 1864 to Susan's sister, Martha Gilbert Smith. The phrase "At Centre of the Sea" forms the last line of the first stanza of the poem beginning "I many times thought Peace had come," written about 1863. This letter may or may not be complete.

305

To Susan Gilbert Dickinson   *March 1865*

Dear Sue –

> Unable are the Loved – to die –
> For Love is immortality –
> Nay – it is Deity –

Emily.

MANUSCRIPT: HCL (B 18). Pencil.
PUBLICATION: *FF* 263.
The date, conjectured from the handwriting, is confirmed by the circumstances. Susan's sister, Harriet Gilbert Cutler, died, 18 March 1865.

To Susan Gilbert Dickinson   *about March 1865*

You must let me go first, Sue, because I live in the Sea always and know the Road.

I would have drowned twice to save you sinking, dear, If I could only have covered your Eyes so you would'nt have seen the Water.

MANUSCRIPT: HCL (B 162). Pencil.
PUBLICATION: LL 100, in part; FF 270.

This is in the handwriting of the note preceding, and may have been written about the same time. The tropes involving water are especially predominant in messages written during the period that ED was under treatment for her eyes. See, for instance, letters no. 294 and 466.

To Mrs. J. G. Holland   *early November 1865*

Dear Sister,

Father called to say that our steelyard was fraudulent, exceeding by an ounce the rates of honest men. He had been selling oats. I cannot stop smiling, though it is hours since, that even our steelyard will not tell the truth.

Besides wiping the dishes for Margaret, I wash them now, while she becomes Mrs. Lawler, vicarious papa to four previous babes. Must she not be an adequate bride?

I winced at her loss, because I was in the habit of her, and even a new rolling-pin has an embarrassing element, but to all except anguish, the mind soon adjusts.

It is also November. The noons are more laconic and the sundowns sterner, and Gibraltar lights make the village foreign. November always seemed to me the Norway of the year. [Susan] is still with the sister who put her child in an ice nest last Monday forenoon. The redoubtable God! I notice where Death has been introduced, he frequently calls, making it desirable to forestall his advances.

It is hard to be told by the papers that a friend is failing, not even know where the water lies. Incidentally, only, that he comes to land. Is there no voice for these? Where is Love today?

Tell the dear Doctor we mention him with a foreign accent, party already to transactions spacious and untold. Nor have we omitted to breathe shorter for our little sister. Sharper than dying is the death for the dying's sake.

News of these would comfort, when convenient or possible.

Emily.

MANUSCRIPT: missing.
PUBLICATION: L (1894) 176–177; L (1931) 169–170; LH 69–70.

Letters written to Mrs. Holland in the three-year interval since the last (no. 269) do not survive, but the tone of this one certainly suggests that there had been no hiatus in their correspondence. Margaret O'Brien (sometimes O'Bryan) married Stephen Lawler on 18 October; it was her first marriage and his second. Martha Gilbert Smith's two-year-old daughter died on 3 November; an infant son had died in 1861.

The word *failing* in the fifth paragraph is probably a misprint for *sailing*. Samuel Bowles sailed from San Francisco on 28 October, and the *Republican* announced his return but did not name the port for which he was bound. (A photograph of Bowles made at this time is mentioned in letter no. 962.) The remark about Dr. Holland probably alludes to the fact that his *Life of Abraham Lincoln* (1865) was at the moment being translated into German, an item of news which one supposes Mrs. Holland had passed on to ED; the volume was issued in Springfield from the same press that published the version in English. Mrs. Holland must also have commented on the fact that a friend was dying, evidently a person unknown to ED.

VIII

1866–1869

*"A Letter always feels to me
like immortality because it is
the mind alone without corporeal friend."*

[1866–1869]

The total number of known letters for the four years that conclude the decade of the sixties is the smallest by far that Emily Dickinson is known to have written during her mature years. The reason probably is not that some letters of this period are irrecoverable. Psychologically she was dormant. The great poetic drive was suddenly at an end, and though she would continue to write poems, she would never again match the fecundity of the years just concluded.

Such a change must have been for her, in both her conscious and unconscious relations, a taxing experience which reflected itself in the pace of her living. The year 1867, for instance, remains almost totally blank. But one letter can assuredly be placed within it. A handful of poems are conjecturally so assigned simply because there is no reason to think that the year ceased to exist for her.

The eye affliction is never alluded to again, and seems not to have troubled her capacity to read and write with comfort. Her few correspondents at this time are the familiar ones, principally Colonel Higginson and Mrs. Holland. On the whole, this group suggests that she is trying to restore her strength and build up a new reserve.

To T. W. Higginson   *late January 1866*

Carlo died –

E. Dickinson

Would you instruct me now?

MANUSCRIPT: BPL (Higg 64). Ink. Dated: Amherst. Envelope addressed: Col. T. W. Higginson/Newport/Rhode Island. Postmarked: Hadley Ms Jan 27.

PUBLICATION: *AM* LXVIII (October 1891) 450; *L* (1931) 281.

This brief note, in which was enclosed the poem "Further in Summer than the Birds," attempts to reestablish a correspondence that had lapsed for eighteen months. ED's dog Carlo had been a favorite companion, and she never got another. (See letter no. 34.)

To Mrs. J. G. Holland   *early March 1866*

. . . the Sere.

Febuary passed like a Skate and I know March. Here is the "light" the Stranger said "was not on land or sea." Myself could arrest it but we'll not chagrin Him. Ned has been ill for a Week, maturing all our faces. He rides his Rocking-Horse today, though looking apparitional.

His Mama just called, leaving a Cashmere print.

Cousin Peter told me the Doctor would address Commencement. Trusting it insure you both for Papa's Fete, I endowed Peter.

We do not always know the source of the smile that flows to us. Ned tells that the Clock purrs and the Kitten ticks. He inherits his Uncle Emily's ardor for the lie.

My flowers are near and foreign, and I have but to cross the floor to stand in the Spice Isles.

The Wind blows gay today and the Jays bark like Blue Terriers.

I tell you what I see. The Landscape of the Spirit requires a lung, but no Tongue. I hold you few I love, till my heart is red as Febuary and purple as March.

Hand for the Doctor.

Emily.

MANUSCRIPT: HCL (H 20). Pencil. The opening of the letter is missing.

PUBLICATION: *L* (1894) 168–169, in part; *L* (1931) 170–171, in part; *LH* 73, in part.

ED's cousin Perez Cowan was a senior in Amherst College. "The light that never was, on sea or land" is from William Wordsworth's *Elegiac Stanzas*. ED has placed a "1" over *sea* and a "2" over *land*.

316

To T. W. Higginson   *early 1866*

Dear friend.

Whom my Dog understood could not elude others.

I should be glad to see you, but think it an apparitional pleasure – not to be fulfilled. I am uncertain of Boston.

I had promised to visit my Physician for a few days in May, but Father objects because he is in the habit of me.

Is it more far to Amherst?

You would find a minute Host but a spacious Welcome –

Lest you meet my Snake and suppose I deceive it was robbed of me – defeated too of the third line by the punctuation. The third and fourth were one – I had told you I did not print – I feared you might think me ostensible. If I still entreat you to teach me, are you much displeased?

I will be patient – constant, never reject your knife and should my my [sic] slowness goad you, you knew before myself that

> Except the smaller size
> No lives are round –
> These – hurry to a sphere
> And show and end –

The larger – slower grow
And later hang –
The Summers of Hesperides
Are long.

Dickinson

MANUSCRIPT: BPL (Higg 59). Ink. Dated: Amherst. Envelope addressed: Col. T. W. Higginson/Newport/Rhode Island.

PUBLICATION: *AM* LXVIII (October 1891) 451; in part; *L* (1894) 312, in part; *LL* 268–269, in part; *L* 281–282, entire, with facsimile reproduction of part, facing page 282. There is no stanza break in this version.

ED enclosed one poem in the letter: "A Death blow is a Life blow to some," together with a clipping of "The Snake" from the 17 February issue of the *Springfield Weekly Republican*. This replies to a letter from Higginson which expressed a desire to see her, and evidently called her "elusive." In the opening sentence it is to herself that she refers as "Whom." Her poem "A narrow Fellow in the Grass" appeared in both the *Daily* and the *Weekly Republican* during the week of the seventeenth (a Saturday). The full account of the publication is in *Poems* (1955) 713–714. But see also the correction noted by John L. Spicer in *Boston Public Library Quarterly* VIII (July 1956) 135–143.

319

To T. W. Higginson   *9 June 1866*

Dear friend

Please to thank the Lady. She is very gentle to care.

I must omit Boston. Father prefers so. He likes me to travel with him but objects that I visit.

Might I entrust you, as my Guest to the Amherst Inn? When I have seen you, to improve will be better pleasure because I shall know which are the mistakes.

Your opinion gives me a serious feeling. I would like to be what you deem me.

Thank you, I wish for Carlo.

Time is a test of trouble
But not a remedy –

[193]

If such it prove, it prove too
There was no malady.

Still I have the Hill, my Gibraltar remnant.
Nature, seems it to myself, plays without a friend.
You mention Immortality.
That is the Flood subject. I was told that the Bank was the safest place for a Finless Mind. I explore but little since my mute Confederate, yet the "infinite Beauty" – of which you speak comes too near to seek.
To escape enchantment, one must always flee.
Paradise is of the option.
Whosoever will Own in Eden notwithstanding Adam and Repeal.

Dickinson.

MANUSCRIPT: BPL (Higg 60). Ink. Dated: Amherst. Envelope addressed: Col. T. W. Higginson/Newport/Rhode Island. Postmarked: Hadley Ms Jun 9.

PUBLICATION: L (1931) 282–283.

Higginson has again urged her to come to Boston, and this is her second refusal. It is her first invitation that he visit Amherst. In the letter she enclosed four poems: "Blazing in Gold," "Ample make this Bed," "To undertake is to achieve," and "As imperceptibly as Grief."

320

To Susan Gilbert Dickinson   *about August 1866*

Sister

Ned is safe – Just "serenaded" Hannah, and is running off with a Corn Leaf "tail," looking back for cheers, Grandma "hoped" characteristically "he would be a very good Boy."

"Not very dood" he said, sweet defiant child! Obtuse ambition of Grandmamas! I kissed my hand to the early train but forgot to open the Blind, partly explaining your negligence.

Nothing is heard from Worcester though Father demanded a telegram, and the Dudleys delay for weather, so Susan shall see Hugh –

It rains in the Kitchen, and Vinnie trades Blackberries with a Tawny Girl – Guess I wont go out. My Jungle fronts on Wall St – Was the Sea cordial? Kiss him for Thoreau –

Do not fear for Home –
Be a bold Susan –
Clara sold the tobacco, and is good to Ned –
Dreamed of your meeting Tennyson in Ticknor and Fields –
Where the Treasure is, there the Brain is also –
Love for Boy –

Emily

MANUSCRIPT: HCL (B 59 and B 147). Pencil.
PUBLICATION: *AM* CXV (1915) 40, in part; *FF* 256, in part.

The date is conjectured from the handwriting. Evidently Susan and Austin were vacationing at the seashore, perhaps in Swampscott, where they sometimes went. Ned was now five. Edward Dickinson's brother William lived in Worcester. John and Eliza Dudley were expected for a visit. "Hugh" has not been identified.

Clara Newman, now twenty, was at this time living with Austin and Susan; the tobacco she has sold presumably was a crop which she herself had raised. The reference to Thoreau is one which Sue would be expected to understand. His *Cape Cod* had been published in 1865, and perhaps Sue and ED had been discussing it. Ticknor and Fields was a well known Boston publishing firm.

323

To T. W. Higginson   *mid-July 1867*

Bringing still my "plea for Culture,"
Would it teach me now?

MANUSCRIPT: BPL (Higg 63). Ink. Dated: Amherst. Envelope addressed: Col. T. W. Higginson/Newport/Rhode Island. Postmarked: Middletown Ct Jul 16.
PUBLICATION: *L* (1931) 284.

This brief note enclosed one poem: "The Luxury to apprehend." The postmark suggests that this letter was mailed by some member of the Dickinson family who was visiting the Dudleys in Middletown. No detail whatever, except what this letter reveals, is known about ED during the year 1867, but the probability is that she was not the visitor. Since the Dudleys left Middletown in June 1868, and since Higginson's essay "A Plea for Culture" had appeared in the January 1867, issue of the *Atlantic Monthly*, this letter almost certainly was written in 1867. It attempts to renew a correspondence with Higginson that apparently had lapsed after ED's second refusal, in the summer of 1866, to visit Boston (see letter no. 319). It is the only letter known which with reasonable certainty may be assigned to this year.

326

To Mrs. Luke Sweetser   *about 1868*

Dear Mrs Sweetser

My Breakfast surpassed Elijah's, though served by Robins instead of Ravens.   Affy
                                                          Emily.

MANUSCRIPT: Rosenbach 1170/18 (5). Pencil. Folded and addressed: Mrs Sweetser. Unpublished.

The letter is dated by handwriting, which is that of about 1868. The Sweetsers were near neighbors. Had the letter been sent to some other member of the Sweetser family, ED would have headed it "Mrs. Howard" ("Mrs. Nellie"), or "Aunt Katie." The allusion is to 1 Kings 17. 6: "And the ravens brought [Elijah] bread . . ."

330

To T. W. Higginson   *June 1869*

Dear friend

A Letter always feels to me like immortality because it is the mind alone without corporeal friend. Indebted in our talk to attitude and accent, there seems a spectral power in thought that walks alone – I would like to thank you for your great kindness but never try to lift the words which I cannot hold.

Should you come to Amherst, I might then succeed, though Gratitude is the timid wealth of those who have nothing. I am sure that you speak the truth, because the noble do, but your letters always surprise me. My life has been too simple and stern to embarrass any.

"Seen of Angels" scarcely my responsibility

It is difficult not to be fictitious in so fair a place, but test's severe repairs are permitted all.

[196]

When a little Girl I remember hearing that remarkable passage and preferring the "Power," not knowing at the time that "Kingdom" and "Glory" were included.

You noticed my dwelling alone – To an Emigrant, Country is idle except it be his own. You speak kindly of seeing me. Could it please your convenience to come so far as Amherst I should be very glad, but I do not cross my Father's ground to any House or town.

Of our greatest acts we are ignorant –

You were not aware that you saved my Life. To thank you in person has been since then one of my few requests. The child that asks my flower "Will you," he says – "Will you" – and so to ask for what I want I know no other way.

You will excuse each that I say, because no other taught me?

Dickinson

Manuscript: BPL (Higg 61). Ink. Dated by Higginson: June 1869.
Publication: *AM* LVXIII (October 1891) 451–452, in part; *L* (1894) 313–314, in part; *LL* 270, in part; *L* (1931) 283–284, entire.

ED echoes her opening sentence in a letter to James Clark which she wrote in 1882. This is her third refusal to go to Boston, and her second invitation to Higginson to come to Amherst, and it answers the letter which follows (HCL), written by Higginson and dated: May 11. 1869. ED's conviction that Higginson was the friend who saved her life must have been very deep, for she uses the same phrase in a letter written to him ten years later.

The woman Higginson mentions at the end of his first paragraph is Helen Hunt (Jackson). In 1890 Higginson wrote Mrs. Todd (*AB* 82): "H.H. did not know of her poems till I showed them to her (about 1866) and was very little in Amherst after that. But she remembered her at school."

330a

From T. W. Higginson

Sometimes I take out your letters & verses, dear friend, and when I feel their strange power, it is not strange that I find it hard to write & that long months pass. I have the greatest desire to see you, always feeling that perhaps if I could once take you by the hand I might be something to you; but till then you only enshroud yourself in this fiery mist & I cannot reach you, but only rejoice in the rare sparkles of light. Every year I think that I will contrive somehow to go to Amherst & see you: but that is hard, for I often am obliged to go away for lecturing, &c & rarely can go for pleasure. I would gladly go to Boston, at any practicable time, to meet you. I am always the same toward you, & never relax my interest in what you send to me. I should like to hear from you very often, but feel always timid lest what I *write* should be badly aimed & miss that fine edge of thought which you bear. It would be so easy, I fear, to miss you. Still, you see, I try. I think if I could once see you & know that you are real, I might fare better. It brought you nearer e[ven] to know that you had an actual [?] uncle, though I can hardly fancy [any?] two beings less alike than yo[u] [&?] him. But I have not seen him [for] several years, though I have seen [a lady] who once knew you, but could [not] tell me much.

It is hard [for me] to understand how you can live s[o alo]ne, with thoughts of such a [quali]ty coming up in you & even the companionship of your dog withdrawn. Yet it isolates one anywhere to think beyond a certain point or have such luminous flashes as come to you – so perhaps the place does not make much difference.

You must come down to Boston sometimes? All ladies do. I wonder if it would be possible to lure you [to] the meetings on the 3ᵈ Monday of every month at Mrs. [Sa]rgent's 13 Chestnut St. at 10 am – when somebody reads [a] paper & others talk or listen. Next Monday Mr. Emerson [rea]ds & then at 3½ P.M. there is a meeting of the Woman's [Cl]ub at 3 Tremont Place, where I read a paper on the [Gre]ek goddesses. That would be a good time for you to come [alth]ough I should still rather have you come on some [da]y when I shall not be so much taken up – for my object is to see you, more than to entertain you. I shall be in Boston also during anniversary week, June 25 * & 28, – or will the Musical Festival in June tempt you down. You see I am in earnest. Or don't you need sea air in summer. Write & tell me something in prose or verse, & I will be less fastidious in future & willing to write clumsy things, rather than none.

Ever your friend
[*signature cut out*]

* There is an extra meeting at Mrs. Sargent's that day & Mr. Weiss reads an essay. I have a right to invite you & you can merely ring & walk in.

332

To Perez Cowan   *October 1869*

These Indian-Summer Days with their peculiar Peace remind me of those stillest things that no one can disturb and knowing you are not at Home and have a sister less I liked to try to help you. You might not need assistance?

You speak with so much trust of that which only trust can prove, it makes me feel away, as if my English mates spoke sudden in Italian.

It grieves me that you speak of Death with so much expectation. I know there is no pang like that for those we love, nor any leisure like the one they leave so closed behind them, but Dying is a wild Night and a new Road.

I suppose we are all thinking of Immortality, at times so stimulatedly that we cannot sleep. Secrets are interesting, but they are also solemn – and speculate with all our might, we cannot ascertain.

I trust as Days go on your sister is more Peace than Pang – though to learn to spare is a sharp acquirement. The subject hurts me so that I will put it down, because it hurts you.

We bruise each other less in talking than in writing, for then a quiet accent helps words themselves too hard.

Do you remember Peter, what the Physician said to Macbeth? "That sort must heal itself."

I am glad you are working. Others are anodyne. You remembered Clara.

The Wedding was small, but lovely, and the sisters have gone. I give you a look of her flowers as Sue and Austin arranged them.

Tell us more of yourself, when you have time and please.

Emily.

MANUSCRIPT: NYPL (Berg Collection). Ink.

PUBLICATION: *Libbie Auction Catalogue* (of the Edward Abbott collection), 25, 26 February 1909, 6 pp.; *NEQ* 163:25 (1932), 441, in part.

Cowan was ordained 8 April 1869, and was still unmarried. Clara Newman married Sidney Turner, 14 October 1869.

To Louise Norcross   *late 1869*

Vinnie was "gone" indeed and is due to-day, and before the tumult that even the best bring we will take hold of hands. It was sweet and antique as birds to hear Loo's voice, worth the lying awake from five o'clock summer mornings to hear. I rejoice that my wren can rise and touch the sky again. We all have moments with the dust, but the dew is given. Do you wish you heard "A[ustin] talk"? Then I would you did, for then you would be here always, a sweet premium. Would you like to "step in the kitchen"? Then you shall by faith, which is the first sight. Mr. C[hurch] is not in the tree, because the rooks won't let him, but I ate a pear as pink as a plum that he made last spring, when he was ogling you. Mother has on the petticoat you so gallantly gathered while he sighed and grafted.

Tabby is eating a stone dinner from a stone plate, . . . Tim is washing Dick's feet, and talking to him now and then in an intimate way. Poor fellow, how he warmed when I gave him your message! The red reached clear to his beard, he was so gratified; and Maggie stood as still for hers as a puss for patting. The hearts of these poor people lie so unconcealed you bare them with a smile.

Thank you for recollecting my weakness. I am not so well as to forget I was ever ill, but better and working. I suppose we must all "ail till evening."

Read Mr. Lowell's *Winter*. One does not often meet anything so perfect.

In many little corners how much of Loo I have.

Maggie "dragged" the garden for this bud for you. You have heard of the "last rose of summer." This is that rose's son.

Into the little port you cannot sail unwelcome at any hour of day or night. Love for Fanny, and stay close to

Emily

Manuscript: destroyed.

PUBLICATION: *L* (1894) 258; *L* (1931) 237–238.

This letter, written with the casual intimacy which characterizes those addressed to the Norcross girls, draws to an unusual extent upon the literary and domestic associations which the girls will understand. At the household level ED speaks about the horse Dick, about Tim (Scannell?), Maggie Maher, and Horace Church. The phrase *"*ail till evening" recalls Browning's *Sordello*. Thomas Moore's "The Last Rose of Summer," set to music, was in any volume of familiar songs. The *Atlantic Almanac* (profusely illustrated and edited, with literary selections, by Oliver Wendell Holmes and Donald Grant Mitchell) in its issue for 1870 carried two prose essays that would have special appeal for ED: one by Higginson, titled "Swimming"; and one by James Russell Lowell, "A Good Word for Winter." It is this latter essay, almost certainly, which she here warmly recommends to Louise Norcross.

IX

1870–1874

"I find ecstasy in living —
the mere sense of living
is joy enough."

With the year 1870 the number of surviving letters markedly increases, and the fact is that events at this time helped to stimulate the flow of correspondence with the two friends to whom Emily Dickinson then was writing her most interesting letters. In May 1870 the Holland family returned from a two-year sojourn in Europe. In August Higginson paid his first and long hoped-for visit. After eight years of baffling correspondence, he found the meeting so stimulating that he recorded it fully in his diary and in letters to his wife and sister.

Important events in the lives of other friends called for attention, and the first letter in the group was written in response to the news of the death of a son of her favorite aunt.

But in 1870 she was in her fortieth year, and thus the important events in the lives of those in her own generation were usually leading to fulfillment. The death of her cousin Henry Sweetser did not touch her closely, for she scarcely knew him. The death of her father, in 1874, was the first major encroachment upon the routines of duty and love which she now made her total concern.

To Mrs. Joseph A. Sweetser   *late February 1870*

My sweet Aunt Katie.

When I am most grieved I had rather no one would speak to me, so I stayed from you, but I thought by today, perhaps you would like to see me, if I came quite soft and brought no noisy words. But when I am most sorry, I can say nothing so I will only kiss you and go far away. Who could ache for you like your little Niece – who knows how deep the Heart is and how much it holds?

I know we shall certainly see what we loved the most. It is sweet to think they are safe by Death and that that is all we have to pass to obtain their face.

There are no Dead, dear Katie, the Grave is but our moan for them.

> Were it to be the last
> How infinite would be
> What we did not suspect was marked
> Our final interview.

Henry had been a prisoner. How he had coveted Liberty probably his Redeemer knew – and as we keep surprise for those most precious to us, brought him his Ransom in his sleep.

Emily.

MANUSCRIPT: Rosenbach 1170/18 (27). Ink. Unpublished.

The Sweetser's eldest son, Henry Edwards, a young journalist of thirty-three, died on 17 February, after a long illness. He had collaborated with his cousin Charles Sweetser in founding the periodical *The Round Table*. The quatrain is in *Poems* (1955) 812.

To Louise and Frances Norcross   *early spring 1870*

Dear Children,

I think the bluebirds do their work exactly like me. They dart around just so, with little dodging feet, and look so agitated. I really feel for them, they seem to be so tried.

The mud is very deep – up to the wagons' stomachs – arbutus making pink clothes, and everything alive.

Even the hens are touched with the things of Bourbon, and make republicans like me feel strangely out of scene.

Mother went rambling, and came in with a burdock on her shawl, so we know that the snow has perished from the earth. Noah would have liked mother.

I am glad you are with Eliza. It is next to shade to know that those we love are cool on a parched day.

Bring my love to —— and Mr. ——. You will not need a hod. C[lara] writes often, full of joy and liberty. I guess it is a case of peace. . . .

Pussy has a daughter in the shavings barrel.

Father steps like Cromwell when he gets the kindlings.

Mrs. S[weetser] gets bigger, and rolls down the lane to church like a reverend marble. Did you know little Mrs. Holland was in Berlin for her eyes? . . .

Did you know about Mrs. J——? She fledged her antique wings. 'Tis said that "nothing in her life became her like the leaving it."

> Great Streets of Silence led away
> To Neighborhoods of Pause –
> Here was no Notice – no Dissent,
> No Universe – no Laws –
>
> By Clocks – 'twas Morning, and for Night
> The Bells at Distance called –
> But Epoch had no basis here,
> For Period exhaled.

Emily.

MANUSCRIPT: destroyed. The text of *Letters* (1931), where the letter but not the poem is published, is followed here. The poem follows the AC autograph, as published in *Poems* (1955) 810.

PUBLICATION: L (1894) 259–260; LL 271–272, in part; L (1931) 238–239. In all three the poem is omitted, but in both editions of L it is indicated as being part of the letter.

In the early spring of 1870 the Norcross sisters went to Milwaukee to be with their cousin Eliza Dudley, now an invalid. The Hollands returned from their trip to Europe in May. The person identified as C[lara] is probably Clara Newman Turner, who married Sidney Turner of Norwich, Connecticut, 14 October 1869. Mrs. Luke Sweetser was a rotund lady whose interest in fashions was locally recognized. (See letter no. 389.) The paraphrase in the last sentence is from *Macbeth*, I, iv, 7–8: "Nothing in his life/Became him like the leaving it. . ."

342

To T. W. Higginson   *16 August 1870*

Dear friend

I will be at Home and glad.

I think you said the 15th. The incredible never surprises us because it is the incredible.

                         E. Dickinson

MANUSCRIPT: BPL (Higg 62). Ink. Envelope addressed: Mr Higginson.

PUBLICATION: L (1894) 314; LL 275; L (1931) 284.
This note was delivered evidently by hand at the Amherst House, in response to one Higginson sent ED on his arrival, asking if he might call. She had expected him on the previous day, Monday. The following letter (BPL) Higginson wrote his wife that evening, dating it: Amherst/Tuesday 10 P.M.:

342a

I shan't sit up tonight to write you all about E.D. dearest but if you had read Mrs. Stoddard's novels you could understand a house where each member runs his or her own selves. Yet I only saw her.

A large county lawyer's house, brown brick, with great trees & a garden — I sent up my card. A parlor dark & cool & stiffish, a few books & engravings & an open piano — Malbone & O D [Out Door] Papers among other books.

A step like a pattering child's in entry & in glided a little plain woman with two smooth bands of reddish hair & a face a little like Belle Dove's; not plainer — with no good feature — in a very plain & exquisitely clean white pique & a blue net worsted shawl. She came to me with two day lilies which she put in a sort of childlike way into my hand & said "These are my introduction" in a soft frightened breathless childlike voice — & added under her breath Forgive me if I am frightened; I never see strangers & hardly know what I say — but she talked soon & thenceforward continuously — & deferentially — sometimes stopping to ask me to talk instead of her — but readily recommencing. Manner between Angie Tilton & Mr. Alcott — but thoroughly ingenuous & simple which they are not & saying many things which you would have thought foolish & I wise — & some things you wd. hv. liked. I add a few over the page.

This is a lovely place, at least the view Hills everywhere, hardly mountains. I saw Dr. Stearns the Pres't of College — but the janitor cd. not be found to show me into the building I may try again tomorrow. I called on Mrs. Banfield & saw her five children — She looks much like H. H. *when ill* & was very cordial & friendly. Goodnight darling I am very sleepy & do good to write you this much. Thine am I

I got here at 2 & leave at 9. E.D. dreamed all night of *you* (not me) & next day got my letter proposing to come here!! She only knew of you through a mention in my notice of Charlotte Hawes.

"Women talk: men are silent: that is why I dread women.

"My father only reads on Sunday — he reads *lonely* & *rigorous* books."

"If I read a book [and] it makes my whole body so cold no fire ever can warm me I know *that* is poetry. If I feel physically as if the top of my head were taken off, I know *that* is poetry. These are the only way I know it. Is there any other way."

"How do most people live without any thoughts. There are many people in the world (you must have noticed them in the street) How do they live. How do they get strength to put on their clothes in the morning"

"When I lost the use of my Eyes it was a comfort to think there were so few real *books* that I could easily find some one to read me all of them"

"Truth is such a *rare* thing it is delightful to tell it."

"I find ecstasy in living—the mere sense of living is joy enough"

I asked if she never felt want of employment, never going off the place & never seeing any visitor "I never thought of conceiving that I could ever have the slightest approach to such a want in all future time" (& added) "I feel that I have not expressed myself strongly enough."

She makes all the bread for her father only likes hers & says "& people must have puddings" this *very* dreamily, as if they were comets —so she makes them.

[That evening Higginson made this entry in his diary (HCL):]

To Amherst, arrived there at 2 Saw Prest Stearns, Mrs. Banfield & Miss Dickinson (twice) a remarkable experience, quite equalling my expectation. A pleasant country town, unspeakably quiet in the summer aftn.

[Next day he wrote his wife again, enclosing further notes (BPL), on ED. He dated the letter: Wednesday noon]:

342b

I am stopping for dinner at White River Junction, dearest, & in a few hours shall be at Littleton thence to go to Bethlehem. This morning at 9 I left Amherst & sent you a letter last night. I shall mail this at L. putting with it another sheet about E.D. that is in my valise.

She said to me at parting "Gratitude is the only secret that cannot reveal itself."

I talked with Prest Stearns of Amherst about her—& found him a very pleasant companion in the cars. Before leaving today, I got in to the Museums & enjoyed them much; saw a meteoric stone almost as long as my arm & weighing 436 lbs! a big slice of some other planet. It fell in Colorado. The collection of bird tracks of extinct birds in stone is very wonderful & unique & other good things. I saw Mr. Dickinson this morning a little—thin dry & speechless—I saw what her life has been. Dr. S. says her sister is proud of her.

I wd. have stolen a *totty* meteor, dear but they were under glass.

Mrs. Bullard I have just met in this train with spouse & son—I shall ride up with her.

Some pretty glimpses of mts. but all is dry and burnt I never saw the river at Brattleboro so low.

Did I say I staid at Sargent's in Boston & she still hopes for Newport.

This picture of Mrs Browning's tomb is from E.D. "Timothy Titcomb" [Dr. Holland] gave it to her.

I think I will mail this here as I hv. found time to write so much. I miss you little woman & wish you were here but you'd hate travelling.

Ever

E D again

"Could you tell me what home is"

"I never had a mother. I suppose a mother is one to whom you hurry when you are troubled."

"I never knew how to tell time by the clock till I was 15. My father thought he had taught me but I did not understand & I was afraid to say I did not & afraid to ask any one else lest he should know."

Her father was not severe I should think but remote. He did not wish them to read anything but the Bible. One day her brother brought home Kavanagh hid it under the piano cover & made signs to her & they read it: her father at last found it & was displeased. Perhaps it was before this that a student of his was amazed that they had never heard of Mrs. [Lydia Maria] Child & used to bring them books & hide in a bush by the door. They were then little things in short dresses with their feet on the rungs of the chair. After the first book she thought in ecstasy "This then is a book! And there are more of them!"

"Is it oblivion or absorption when things pass from our minds?"

Major Hunt interested her more than any man she ever saw. She remembered two things he said – that her great dog "understood gravitation" & when he said he should come again "in a year. If I say a shorter time it will be longer."

When I said I would come again *some time* she said "Say in a long time, that will be nearer. Some time is nothing."

After long disuse of her eyes she read Shakespeare & thought why is any other book needed.

I never was with any one who drained my nerve power so much. Without touching her, she drew from me. I am glad not to live near her. She often thought me *tired* & seemed very thoughtful of others.

[210]

[The postscript of a letter Higginson wrote his sisters (HCL) on Sunday, 21 August, adds:]

Of course I hv. enjoyed my trip very very much. In Amherst I had a nice aftn & evng with my singular poetic correspondent & the remarkable cabinets of the College.

[Recalling the interview twenty years later, Higginson wrote in the *Atlantic Monthly* LXVIII (October 1891) 453:]

The impression undoubtedly made on me was that of an excess of tension, and of an abnormal life. Perhaps in time I could have got beyond that somewhat overstrained relation which not my will, but her needs, had forced upon us. Certainly I should have been most glad to bring it down to the level of simple truth and every-day comradeship; but it was not altogether easy. She was much too enigmatical a being for me to solve in an hour's interview, and an instinct told me that the slightest attempt at direct cross-examination would make her withdraw into her shell; I could only sit still and watch, as one does in the woods; I must name my bird without a gun, as recommended by Emerson.

354

To Mrs. J. G. Holland   *early October 1870*

I guess I wont send that note now, for the mind is such a new place, last night feels obsolete.

Perhaps you thought dear Sister, I wanted to elope with you and feared a vicious Father.

It was not quite that.

The Papers thought the Doctor was mostly in New York. Who then would read for you? Mr Chapman, doubtless, or Mr Buckingham! The Doctor's sweet reply makes me infamous.

Life is the finest secret.

So long as that remains, we must all whisper.

With that sublime exception I had no clandestineness.

It was lovely to see you and I hope it may happen again. These beloved accidents must become more frequent.

We are by September and yet my flowers are bold as June. Amherst has gone to Eden.

To shut our eyes is Travel.

The Seasons understand this.

How lonesome to be an Article! I mean – to have no soul.

An Apple fell in the night and a Wagon stopped.

I suppose the Wagon ate the Apple and resumed it's way.

How fine it is to talk.

What Miracles the News is!

Not Bismark but ourselves.

> The Life we have is very great.
> The Life that we shall see
> Surpasses it, we know, because
> It is Infinity.
> But when all Space has been beheld
> And all Dominion shown
> The smallest Human Heart's extent
> Reduces it to none.

Love for the Doctor, and the Girls.

Ted might not acknowledge me.

Emily.

MANUSCRIPT: HCL (H 24). Ink.
PUBLICATION: LH 84–86.

The Hollands had returned to Springfield in the spring of 1870, and visited in Amherst during the summer. A new enterprise kept Dr. Holland much in New York during October, when the first issue of the magazine he edited, *Scribner's Monthly*, was being prepared for the press. In the person of Bismark, ED alludes to the principal news of the day, the Franco-Prussian war.

356

To Susan Gilbert Dickinson   *19 December 1870*

Lest any doubt that we are glad that they were born Today
Whose having lived is held by us in noble Holiday
Without the date, like Consciousness or Immortality –

Emily –

MANUSCRIPT: HCL (B 33). Pencil.

PUBLICATION: FF 225, with note: "To Sue with flowers on her birthday"; *Poems* (1955) 809.

The handwriting suggests 1870, the year in which Sue celebrated her fortieth birthday.

359

To Mrs. J. G. Holland   *early January 1871*

I have a fear I did not thank you for the thoughtful Candy.
Could you conscientiously dispel it by saying that I did?
Generous little Sister!
I will protect the Thimble till it reaches Home —
Even the Thimble has it's Nest!
The Parting I tried to smuggle resulted in quite a Mob at last!
The Fence is the only Sanctuary. That no one invades because no one suspects it.
Why the Thief ingredient accompanies all Sweetness Darwin does not tell us.
Each expiring Secret leaves an Heir, distracting still.
Our unfinished interview like the Cloth of Dreams, cheapens other fabrics.
That Possession fairest lies that is least possest.
Transport's mighty price is no more than he is worth –
Would we sell him for it? That is all his Test.
Dont affront the Eyes –
Little Despots govern worst.
Vinnie leaves me Monday – Spare me your remembrance while I buffet Life and Time without –

Emily.

MANUSCRIPT: HCL (H 26). Ink.
PUBLICATION: LH 87.
Early in January Vinnie went to New York to visit the Hills. Mrs. Holland had evidently, on a recent call, forgotten her thimble, which she has asked ED to forward. The expression "Mob at last" implies that ED and Mrs. Holland had tried to converse privately when they parted after Mrs. Holland's call, but had been interrupted. The place probably was the little back hall connected with the kitchen, which had come to be known as the "Northwest Passage" (see FF 25).

[213]

To Louise and Frances Norcross   *early October 1871*

We have the little note and are in part relieved, but have been too alarmed and grieved to hush immediately. The heart keeps sobbing in its sleep. It is the speck that makes the cloud that wrecks the vessel, children, yet no one fears a speck. I hope what is not lost is saved. Were any angel present, I feel it could not be allowed. So grateful that our little girls are not on fire too. Amherst would have quenched them. Thank you for comforting innocent blamed creatures. We are trying, too. The mayor of Milwaukee cuts and you and Loo sew, don't you? The *New York Times* said so. Sorrow is the "funds" never quite spent, always a little left to be loaned kindly. We have a new cow. I wish I could give Wisconsin a little pail of milk. Dick's Maggie is wilting. Awkward little flower, but transplanting makes it fair. How are the long days that made the fresh afraid?

                                                    Brother Emily.

MANUSCRIPT: destroyed.
PUBLICATION: L (1894) 264–265; L (1931) 242.
The great Chicago fire was on 8–9 October 1871, but there were forest fires in Wisconsin that month at exactly the same time, less publicized but involving much greater loss of life.

368

To T. W. Higginson   *November 1871*

I did not read Mr Miller because I could not care about him –
Transport is not urged –
Mrs Hunt's Poems are stronger than any written by Women since Mrs – Browning, with the exception of Mrs Lewes – but truth like Ancestor's Brocades can stand alone – You speak of "Men and Women." That is a broad Book – "Bells and Pomegranates" I never saw but have Mrs Browning's endorsement. While Shakespeare remains Literature is firm –
An Insect cannot run away with Achilles' Head. Thank you for having written the "Atlantic Essays." They are a fine Joy – though to

possess the ingredient for Congratulation renders congratulation superfluous.

Dear friend, I trust you as you ask – If I exceed permission, excuse
the bleak simplicity that knew no tutor but the North. Would you
but guide

Dickinson

MANUSCRIPT: BPL (Higg 74). Ink. Envelope addressed: Mr Higginson.

PUBLICATION: L (1894) 320, garbled; LL 293–294, garbled; L (1931)
295.

Four poems are enclosed: "When I hoped I feared," "The Days that
we can spare," "Step lightly on this narrow spot," and "Remembrance has
a Rear and Front." Joaquin Miller's *Songs of the Sierras* appeared in 1871.
Helen Hunt's *Verses* had appeared the year before. Browning is referred
to by *Men and Women* (1855) and *Bells and Pomegranates* (1846). Higginson's *Atlantic Essays* was issued in September 1871.

369

To Mrs. J. G. Holland   *late November 1871*

Dear Sister.

Bereavement to yourself your faith makes secondary. We who
cannot hear your voice are chastened indeed —

"Whom he loveth, he punisheth," is a doubtful solace finding tart
response in the lower Mind.

I shall cherish the Stripes though I regret that your latest Act
must have been a Judicial one. It comforts the Criminal little to know
that the Law expires with him.

Beg the Oculist to commute your Sentence that you may also
commute mine. Doubtless he has no friend and to curtail Communion is all that remains to him.

This transitive malice will doubtless retire – offering you anew
to us and ourselves to you.

I am pleased the Gingerbread triumphed.

Let me know your circumstance through some minor Creature,
abler in Machinery if unknown to Love.

[215]

Steam has his Commissioner, tho' his substitute is not yet disclosed of God.

Emily.

MANUSCRIPT: HCL (H 27). Ink.
PUBLICATION: *LH* 88–89.
A friend of both Bowles and Holland, Albert D. Briggs of Springfield, was appointed one of the Massachusetts railroad commissioners on 22 November. The quotation is from Hebrews 12.6: ". . . whom the Lord loveth he chasteneth. . ." This letter implies that ED had sent Mrs. Holland her recipe for gingerbread, doubtless the same as that which she supplied Susan Dickinson, who added it to her manuscript cookbook.

373

To Edward (Ned) Dickinson　　　　　　　　　　*mid-May 1872?*

Neddie never would believe that Emily was at his Circus, unless she left a fee—

MANUSCRIPT: HCL (L 52). Pencil. Envelope addressed: Neddie. Unpublished. The impression of a coin still shows in the note. Ned may have had his circus soon after the visiting circus had been in Amherst, 14 May.

389

To Louise and Frances Norcross　　　　　　　　　*late April 1873*

. . . There is that which is called an "awakening" in the church, and I know of no choicer ecstasy than to see Mrs. [Sweetser] roll out in crape every morning, I suppose to intimidate antichrist; at least it would have that effect on me. It reminds me of Don Quixote demanding the surrender of the wind-mill, and of Sir Stephen Toplift, and of Sir Alexander Cockburn.

Spring is a happiness so beautiful, so unique, so unexpected, that I don't know what to do with my heart. I dare not take it, I dare not leave it—what do you advise?

Life is a spell so exquisite that everything conspires to break it.

"What do I think of *Middlemarch*?" What do I think of glory – except that in a few instances this "mortal has already put on immortality."

George Eliot is one. The mysteries of human nature surpass the "mysteries of redemption," for the infinite we only suppose, while we see the finite. . . . I launch Vinnie on Wednesday; it will require the combined efforts of Maggie, Providence and myself, for whatever advances Vinnie makes in nature and art, she has not reduced departure to a science. . . .

Your loving
Emily.

MANUSCRIPT: destroyed.

PUBLICATION: L (1894) 279; L (1931) 254.

There were evangelical meetings in Amherst during the week of 22 April 1873. A card (HCL) written and signed by Edward Dickinson is dated 1 May, and says: "I hereby give myself to God." Vinnie made her visit, here spoken about, to the Hollands, now living in New York; she probably left Amherst in May. For an earlier description of Mrs. Luke Sweetser, written in similar vein, see letter no. 339. Sir Alexander Cockburn (1802–1880), the lord chief justice of England from 1859 until his death, is here alluded to as the epitome of awesome sedateness. Sir Stephen Toplift has not been identified. Since no person of that name is known, he presumably is a somewhat modish character from fiction, familiar to ED and the Norcrosses. The quotation used to characterize *Middlemarch* is adapted from 1 Corinthians 15.53: ". . . and this mortal must put on immortality." The final quotation may be ED's attempt to recall Matthew 13.11: "Because it is given unto you to know the mysteries of the kingdom of heaven, but to them it is not given."

391

To Mrs. J. G. Holland   *early summer 1873*

I was thinking of thanking you for the kindness to Vinnie.

She has no Father and Mother but me and I have no Parents but her.

She has been very happy and returns with her Sentiments at rest. Enclosed please find my gratitude.

You remember the imperceptible has no external Face.

Vinnie says you are most illustrious and dwell in Paradise. I have never believed the latter to be a superhuman site.

Eden, always eligible, is peculiarly so this noon. It would please you to see how intimate the Meadows are with the Sun. Besides—

> The most triumphant Bird I ever knew or met
> Embarked upon a twig today
> And till Dominion set
> I famish to behold so eminent a sight
> And sang for nothing scrutable
> But intimate Delight.
> Retired, and resumed his transitive Estate—
> To what delicious Accident
> Does finest Glory fit!

While the Clergyman tells Father and Vinnie that "this Corruptible shall put on Incorruption"—it has already done so and they go defrauded.

Emily—

MANUSCRIPT: Holland. Ink.
PUBLICATION: *LH* 92–93.
Written after Vinnie's return from her visit. The poem had been sent to the Norcrosses earlier. The scripture quotation is from 1 Corinthians 15.42.

392

To Susan Gilbert Dickinson   *August 1873*

Sister

Our parting was somewhat interspersed and I cannot conclude which went. I shall be cautious not to so as to miss no one.

Vinnie drank your Coffee and has looked a little like you since, which is nearly a comfort.

Austin has had two calls and is very tired—One from Professor Tyler, and the other from Father. I am afraid they will call here.

Bun has run away—

Disaffection – doubtless – as to the Supplies. Ned is a better Quarter Master than his vagrant Papa.

The little Turkey is lonely and the Chickens bring him to call. His foreign Neck in familiar Grass is quaint as a Dromedary. I suppose the Wind has chastened the Bows on Mattie's impudent Hat and the Sea presumed as far as he dare on her stratified Stockings.

If her Basket wont hold the Boulders she picks, I will send a Bin.

Ned is much lamented and his Circus Airs in the Rowen will be doubly sweet.

Bela Dickinson's son is the only Basso remaining. It rains every pleasant Day now and Dickens' Maggie's Lawn will be green as a Courtier's.

Love for your Brother and Sister – please – and the dear Lords.

Nature gives her love –

Twilight touches Amherst with his yellow Glove.

Miss me sometimes, dear – Not on most occasions, but the Seldoms of the Mind.

Emily.

MANUSCRIPT: HCL (B 150). Ink.
PUBLICATION: LL 63, ending only; FF 234–235, in part.

The date is conjectured from the handwriting. Susan took the children to Swampscott in the summer of 1873, where they visited as guests of one of her brothers.

408

To Mrs. Joseph A. Sweetser   *late January 1874*

Saying nothing, My Aunt Katie, sometimes says the Most.

> Death's Waylaying not the sharpest
> Of the thefts of Time –
> There Marauds a sorer Robber,
> Silence – is his name –
> No Assault, nor any Menace
> Doth betoken him.
> But from Life's consummate Cluster –
> He supplants the Balm.

Emily.

MANUSCRIPT: missing. The text is from a transcript of the autograph made when it was on exhibit at the Jones Library in 1935.

PUBLICATION: Kate Dickinson Sweetser, *Great American Girls* (1931) 135; *Poems* (1955) 899.

Joseph Sweetser walked out of his New York apartment on the evening of 21 January 1874, and was never subsequently traced. Many papers carried the account. The *Springfield Republican* noted it on 29 January.

412

To Mrs. J. G. Holland   *May 1874*

Little Sister.

I hope you are safe and distinguished. Is the latter the former? Experience makes me no reply.

Nature begins to work and I am assisting her a little, when I can be spared.

It is pleasant to work for so noble a Person.

Vinnie and "Pat" are abetting the Farm in Papa's absence. A Triumph of Schemes, if not of Executions. Pat is as abnegating as a Dromedary and I fear will find his Lot as unique.

When you were here – there were Flowers and there are Flowers now, but those were the Nosegays of Twilight and these – are the Nosegays of Dawn –

It is plain that some one has been asleep!

Suffer Rip – Van Winkle!

Vinnie says Maggie is "Cleaning House." I should not have suspected it, but the Bible directs that the "Left Hand" circumvent the Right!

We are to have another "Circus," and again the Procession from Algiers will pass the Chamber-Window.

The Minor Toys of the Year are alike, but the Major – are different.

But the dimensions of each subject admonish me to leave it.

Love, though, for your own. When a Child and fleeing from Sacrament I could hear the Clergyman saying "All who loved the Lord Jesus Christ – were asked to remain –"

My flight kept time to the Words.

Emily.

MANUSCRIPT: HCL (H 33). Ink.
PUBLICATION: *LH* 97.
In 1874 Maginley's Circus came to town on 23 May.

413

To T. W. Higginson   *late May 1874*

I thought that being a Poem one's self precluded the writing Poems, but perceive the Mistake. It seemed like going Home, to see your beautiful thought once more, now so long forbade it – Is it Intellect that the Patriot means when he speaks of his "Native Land"? I should have feared to "quote" to you what you "most valued."

You have experienced sanctity.

It is to me untried.

> Of Life to own –
> From Life to draw –
> But never touch the Reservoir –

You kindly ask for my Blossoms and Books – I have read but a little recently – Existence has overpowered Books. Today, I slew a Mushroom –

> I felt as if the Grass was pleased
> To have it intermit.
> This Surreptitious Scion
> Of Summer's circumspect.

The broadest words are so narrow we can easily cross them – but there is water deeper than those which has no Bridge. My Brother and Sisters would love to see you. Twice, you have gone – Master –

Would you but once come –

MANUSCRIPT: BPL (Higg 88). Ink.
PUBLICATION: *L* (1931) 304–305.
Higginson's poem "Decoration," appropriate to Memorial Day, appeared in the June issue of *Scribner's Monthly.*

To Louise and Frances Norcross   *summer 1874*

You might not remember me, dears. I cannot recall myself. I thought I was strongly built, but this stronger has undermined me.

We were eating our supper the fifteenth of June, and Austin came in. He had a despatch in his hand, and I saw by his face we were all lost, though I didn't know how. He said that father was very sick, and he and Vinnie must go. The train had already gone. While horses were dressing, news came he was dead.

Father does not live with us now – he lives in a new house. Though it was built in an hour it is better than this. He hasn't any garden because he moved after gardens were made, so we take him the best flowers, and if we only knew he knew, perhaps we could stop crying. . . . The grass begins after Pat has stopped it.

I cannot write any more, dears. Though it is many nights, my mind never comes home. Thank you each for the love, though I could not notice it. Almost the last tune that he heard was, "Rest from thy loved employ."

                                                        Emily.

MANUSCRIPT: destroyed.
PUBLICATION: L (1894) 280; LL 290–291; L (1931) 255.
Edward Dickinson died on 16 (not 15) June. ED concludes her letter by recalling the James Montgomery hymn (which she had evidently played for her father):

Servant of God, well done!
Rest from thy loved employ.
The battle fought, the victory won,
Enter thy Master's joy!

To Samuel Bowles   *late June 1874*

I should think you would have few Letters for your own are so noble that they make men afraid – and sweet as your Approbation is – it is had in fear – lest your depth convict us.

You compel us each to remember that when Water ceases to rise – it has commenced falling. That is the law of Flood. The last Day that I saw you was the newest and oldest of my life.

Resurrection can come but once – first – to the same House. Thank you for leading us by it.

Come always, dear friend, but refrain from going. You spoke of not liking to be forgotten. Could you, tho' you would? Treason never knew you.

Emily.

MANUSCRIPT: AC. Ink.
PUBLICATION: *L* (1894) 220; *LL* 271; *L* (1931) 206.
The Bowleses had been with the Dickinson family at the time of the funeral of Edward Dickinson. Bowles sailed for Europe in mid-July.

418

To T. W. Higginson   *July 1874*

The last Afternoon that my Father lived, though with no premonition – I preferred to be with him, and invented an absence for Mother, Vinnie being asleep. He seemed peculiarly pleased as I oftenest stayed with myself, and remarked as the Afternoon withdrew, he "would like it to not end."

His pleasure almost embarrassed me and my Brother coming – I suggested they walk. Next morning I woke him for the train – and saw him no more.

His Heart was pure and terrible and I think no other like it exists.

I am glad there is Immortality – but would have tested it myself – before entrusting him.

Mr Bowles was with us – With that exception I saw none. I have wished for you, since my Father died, and had you an Hour unengrossed, it would be almost priceless. Thank you for each kindness.

My Brother and Sister thank you for remembering them.

Your beautiful Hymn, was it not prophetic? It has assisted that Pause of Space which I call "Father" –

MANUSCRIPT: BPL (Higg 68). Ink. Endorsed by TWH: July 1874 Her father's death.

PUBLICATION: *AM* LXVIII (October 1891) 455, in part; *L* (1894) 317–318; *LL* 291–292; *L* (1931) 291–292.
In her final paragraph ED again alludes to Higginson's poem "Decoration" (see letter no. 413).

425

To Clara Newman Turner   *December 1874*
I am sure you must have remembered that Father had "Become as Little Children," or you would never have dared send him a Christmas gift, for you know how he frowned upon Santa Claus – and all such prowling gentlemen –

MANUSCRIPT: missing.
PUBLICATION: *L* (1894) 372; *LL* 294; *L* (1931) 362.
The text is from a transcript (AC) given to Mrs. Todd by Mrs. Turner, who states in her reminiscences (HCL) that the letter was sent to her in thanks for a Christmas wreath for Edward Dickinson's grave. The quotation is from Matthew 18.3.

X

1875–1879

"Nature is a Haunted House – but Art –
a House that tries to be haunted."

During the final decade of her life Emily Dickinson's withdrawal from outside association became nearly absolute. She chose now communication through the medium of letters, and more than half of all that survive were written in the brief span of years that remain. She wrote few poems after 1874, but among them are some of her finest genre sketches of movement and color observed from the world of nature, for this world had become an awesome reality into which she projected her imagination with an artist's mature skill.

The birth of her nephew Gilbert in 1875 was an event which increased in importance, for it brought members of the two houses closer together as the boy grew. He was not destined to survive his ninth year. The death of Samuel Bowles from sheer exhaustion, in 1878, closed a chapter in her life, for he had been the friend whom she had always treated with affectionate deference, as a much-loved elder brother.

Two events now occurred of far reaching consequence. She came to know Helen Hunt Jackson, and her love for Judge Otis Lord became important. Helen Jackson by this time was acclaimed the leading woman poet in America and had become a most successful writer of stories. She had learned about Emily Dickinson's poetry through Colonel Higginson, and she was the only qualified contemporary who believed Dickinson to be an authentic poet. That opinion was of no small moment to the woman who now and then is signing her letters "Dickinson."

Judge Lord had been a lifelong friend of Edward Dickinson. He and his wife had been frequent overnight guests in the Dickinson house and thus Emily had always known him. His wife died in 1877. The attachment between the Judge and Emily became intimate soon thereafter. Marriage may have been contemplated; the nature and degree of her affection is patent in the letters that she wrote him.

Though the outer manifestations of what is commonly called an active life are now absent, the inner never abate, as the letters, particularly those to Mrs. Holland and to Colonel Higginson, make amply clear.

To Mrs. J. G. Holland   *late January 1875*

Sister.

This austere Afternoon is more becoming to a Patriot than to one whose Friend is it's sole Land.

No event of Wind or Bird breaks the Spell of Steel.

Nature squanders Rigor – now – where she squandered Love.

Chastening – it may be – the Lass that she receiveth.

My House is a House of Snow – true – sadly – of few.

Mother is asleep in the Library – Vinnie – in the Dining Room – Father – in the Masked Bed – in the Marl House.

> How soft his Prison is —
> How sweet those sullen Bars —
> No Despot – but the King of Down
> Invented that Repose!

When I think of his firm Light – quenched so causelessly, it fritters the worth of much that shines. "Dust unto the Dust" indeed – but the final clause of that marvelous sentence – who has rendered it?

"I say unto you," Father would read at Prayers, with a militant Accent that would startle one.

Forgive me if I linger on the first Mystery of the House.

It's specific Mystery – each Heart had before – but within this World. Father's was the first Act distinctly of the Spirit.

Austin's Family went to Geneva, and Austin lived with us four weeks. It seemed peculiar – pathetic – and Antediluvian. We missed him while he was with us and missed him when he was gone.

All is so very curious.

Thank you for that "New Year" – the first with a fracture. I trust it is whole and hale – to you.

"Kingsley" rejoins "Argemone" —

Thank you for the Affection. It helps me up the Stairs at Night, where as I passed my Father's Door – I used to think was safety. The Hand that plucked the Clover – I seek, and am

                                                        Emily.

MANUSCRIPT: HCL (H 34). Ink.
PUBLICATION: *LH* 102–103.
Mrs. Holland had plucked a spray of clover from Edward Dickinson's grave, which ED never visited, and gave it to her. Argemone is the heroine of Kingsley's first novel, *Yeast*. Kingsley died, 23 January 1875.

438

To Samuel Bowles   *about 1875*

Dear friend.

It was so delicious to see you — a Peach before the time, it makes all seasons possible and Zones – a caprice.

We who arraign the "Arabian Nights" for their under statement, escape the stale sagacity of supposing them sham.

We miss your vivid Face and the besetting Accents, you bring from your Numidian Haunts.

Your coming welds anew that strange Trinket of Life, which each of us wear and none of us own, and the phosphorescence of your's startles us for it's permanence. Please rest the Life so many own, for Gems abscond –

In your own beautiful words, for the Voice is the Palace of all of us, "Near, but remote,"

Emily.

If we die, will you come for us, as you do for Father?
"Not born" yourself, "to die," you must reverse us all.

———

MANUSCRIPT: AC. Ink.
PUBLICATION: *L* (1894) 221–222; *LL* 284–285; *L* (1931) 207: – the body of the letter and the signature. The postscript is printed as a separate message: *L* (1894) 222–223; *LL* 285; *L* (1931) 208.
The date, conjectured from the handwriting, is almost certainly 1875. It was Bowles's custom to be present at commencement exercises in August. The first sentence together with the postscript suggest that perhaps this year he came during the spring, his first visit since he was present with the family at the time of Edward Dickinson's funeral in June 1874.

Letters (1894) and subsequent editions print the following as a separate letter.

If we die, will you come for us, as you do for father? "Not born," yourself "to die," you must reverse us all.

Last to adhere
When summers swerve away –
Elegy of
Integrity.

To remember our own Mr. Bowles is all we can do.
With grief it is done, so warmly and long, it can never be new.

Emily.

It is not dated, but is placed as one sent to Bowles, presumably in his last illness. The "letter" is in fact a montage of three separate items. The first two sentences conclude this letter. The stanza (AC) is on a separate sheet. The last two sentences constitute the letter sent to Mrs. Bowles after the death of her husband (no. 532). The provenance of the verse is almost certainly Bingham 99–7, described in *Poems* (1955), 964, as written on a sheet of note paper and folded as if enclosed in an envelope. The lines may in fact have been enclosed with letter no. 532, or sent to Mrs. Bowles about the same time, for they are in the handwriting of about 1878. At the time *Poems* was published, the "letter" was thought to be lost; thus the concluding version of the lines as printed in *Poems*, deriving from the montage, is a duplication of the version (Bingham 99–7) already described.

440

To T. W. Higginson   *mid-June 1875*

Dear friend –

Mother was paralyzed Tuesday, a year from the evening Father died. I thought perhaps you would care –

Your Scholar.

MANUSCRIPT: BPL (Higg 71). Pencil.
PUBLICATION: *AM* LXVIII (October 1891) 455; *L* (1894) 319; *LL* 293; *L* (1931) 293.
This note was evidently written during the week of the fifteenth.

441

To T. W. Higginson   *July 1875*

Dear friend.

Mother was very ill, but is now easier, and the Doctor thinks that in more Days she may partly improve. She was ignorant at the time and her Hand and Foot left her, and when she asks me the name of her sickness – I deceive for the first time. She asks for my Father, constantly, and thinks it rude he does not come – begging me not to retire at night, lest no one receive him. I am pleased that what grieves ourself so much – can no more grieve him. To have been immortal transcends to become so. Thank you for being sorry.

I thought it value to hear your voice, though at so great distance – Home is so far from Home, since my Father died.

The courtesy to my Brother and Sisters I gave and replace, and think those safe who see your Face.

Your Scholar.

MANUSCRIPT: BPL (Higg 72). Ink.
PUBLICATION: L (1931) 293–294.
This letter responds to a note of sympathy from Higginson, written after he had received the preceding note.

442

To Louise and Frances Norcross   *summer 1875*

Dear Children,

I decided to give you one more package of lemon drops, as they only come once a year. It is fair that the bonbons should change hands, you have so often fed me. This is the very weather that I lived with you those amazing years that I had a father. W[illie] D[ickinson']s wife came in last week for a day and a night, saying her heart drove her. I am glad that you loved Miss Whitney on knowing her nearer. Charlotte Brontë said "Life is so constructed that the event does not, cannot, match the expectation."

The birds that father rescued are trifling in his trees. How flippant are the saved! They were even frolicking at his grave, when Vinnie went there yesterday. Nature must be too young to feel, or many years too old.

Now children, when you are cutting the loaf, a crumb, peradventure a crust, of love for the sparrows' table. . . .

MANUSCRIPT: destroyed.

PUBLICATION: *L* (1894) 281; *LL* 298; *L* (1931) 256.
The date Mrs. Todd assigned is retained; the tone of the letter suggests that it was written in the year following her father's death. For a note relating to the Brontë quotation, see letter no. 459.

443

To Susan Gilbert Dickinson   *early August 1875*

Emily and all that she has are at Sue's service, if of any comfort to Baby—
Will send Maggie, if you will accept her—

Sister—

MANUSCRIPT: HCL (B 42). Pencil.
PUBLICATION: *FF* 244.
Susan's third child, Thomas Gilbert Dickinson, was born 1 August 1875.

444

To Helen Hunt Jackson   *late October 1875*

Have I a word but Joy?
                E. Dickinson.
            Who fleeing from the Spring
            The Spring avenging fling
            To Dooms of Balm—

MANUSCRIPT: HCL (L 51). Ink.
PUBLICATION: *Poems* (1955) 924.
On the last blank page a note in Helen Jackson's hand reads: "This is *mine*, remember, You must send it back to me, or else you will be a robber." (Helen Jackson returned the letter to ED, who kept it, for an explanation of the three lines of verse). The letter was written when ED learned of the marriage of Helen Hunt to William S. Jackson, 22 October 1875. The earliest evidence of a correspondence between them is an envelope (AC), never sent, addressed in the handwriting of about 1868 to Mrs. Helen Hunt. That summer she was in Amherst. Another envelope never sent (AC) is addressed, about 1872, to Bethlehem, New Hampshire, where Mrs. Hunt then summered.

After Mrs. Jackson returned the letter above, ED must have written her again, as the following letter (HCL) from Helen Jackson, dated Colorado Springs, 20 March 1876, indicates:

444a

But you did not send it back, though you wrote that you would.
Was this an accident, or a late withdrawal of your consent?
Remember that it is mine — not yours — and be honest.

Thank you for not being angry with my impudent request for interpretations.

I do wish I knew just what "dooms" you meant, though!

A very clever man — one of the cleverest I ever met — a Mr. Dudley of Milwaukee, spent a day with us last week, and we talked about you. So threads cross, even on the outermost edges of the web.

I hope some day, somewhere I shall find you in a spot where we can know each other. I wish very much that you would write to me now and then, when it did not bore you. I have a little manuscript volume with a few of your verses in it — and I read them very often — You are a great poet — and it is a wrong to the day you live in, that you will not sing aloud. When you are what men call dead, you will be sorry you were so stingy.

Yours truly
Helen Jackson.

450

To T. W. Higginson   *February 1876*

There is so much that is tenderly profane in even the sacredest Human Life — that perhaps it is instinct and not design, that dissuades us from it.

> The Treason of an accent
> Might Ecstasy transfer —
> Of her effacing Fathom
> Is no Recoverer —

It makes me happy to send you the Book. Thank you for accepting it, and please not to own "Daniel Deronda" till I bring it, when it is done. You ask me if I see any one – Judge Lord was with me a week in October and I talked with Father's Clergyman once, and once with Mr Bowles. Little – wayfaring acts – comprise my "pursuits" – and a few moments at night, for Books – after the rest sleep. Candor – my Preceptor – is the only wile. Did you not teach me that yourself, in the "Prelude" to "Malbone"? You once told me of "printing but a few Poems." I hoped it implied you possessed more ——

Would you show me – one? You asked me if I liked the cold – but it is warm now. A mellow Rain is falling.

It wont be ripe till April – How luscious is the dripping of February eaves! It makes our thinking Pink –

It antedates the Robin – Bereaving in prospective that Febuary leaves ——

Thank you for speaking kindly.

I often go Home in thought to you.

Your Scholar –

MANUSCRIPT: BPL (Higg 81). Ink.
PUBLICATION: L (1931) 297–298.
Daniel Deronda began running serially in the March issue of *Harper's Monthly*, and this letter may well have been written after ED had seen an announcement of its impending publication (in book form later in the year), but before she had read the first installment of it (see letter no. 457). "Father's Clergyman" was the pastor of the First Church, the Reverend Jonathan L. Jenkins (see letter no. 464). The expression "Candor is the only wile" is ED's succinct rephrasing of the following thought, in Higginson's "Prelude" to his novel *Malbone: An Oldport Romance* (1869): "One learns, in growing older, that no fiction can be so strange nor appear so improbable as would the simple truth. . ."

457

To T. W. Higginson   *spring 1876*

But two had mentioned the "Spring" to me – yourself and the Revelations. "I – Jesus – have sent mine Angel."

[233]

I inferred your touch in the Papers on Lowell and Emerson – It is delicate that each Mind is itself, like a distinct Bird –

I was lonely there was an "Or" in that beautiful "I would go to Amherst," though grieved for it's cause. I wish your friend had my strength for I dont care for roving – She perhaps might, though to remain with you is Journey – To abstain from "Daniel Deronda" is hard – you are very kind to be willing. I would have liked to wait, but "Sue" smuggled it under my Pillow, and to wake so near it overpowered me – I am glad "Immortality" pleased you. I believed it would. I suppose even God himself could not withhold that now – When I think of my Father's lonely Life and his lonelier Death, there is this redress –

> Take all away –
> The only thing worth larceny
> Is left – the Immortality –

My earliest friend wrote me the week before he died "If I live, I will go to Amherst – if I die, I certainly will."

Is your House deeper off?

Your Scholar

MANUSCRIPT: BPL (Higg 78). Ink.

PUBLICATION: AM LXVIII (October 1891) 455, in part; L (1894) 323, in part; LL 302, in part; L (1931) 301, in part.

This and the following letter to Higginson and his wife (no. 459) were written about the same time in the spring of 1876.

ED correctly guessed that Higginson wrote the unsigned review of Lowell's *Among My Books: Second Series* for the March 1876 issue of *Scribner's Monthly*. (It is so identified in Mary Thacher Higginson, *Thomas Wentworth Higginson* . . . , Boston, 1914, 413). The review of Emerson's *Letters and Social Aims* in the April issue, likewise unsigned, may be Higginson's but has not been so identified. The "friend" referred to in the third paragraph is Mrs. Higginson, whose illness was increasing. Higginson's reply to the letter ED wrote to him in February (no. 450) told her that he would be glad to refrain from reading *Daniel Deronda* until he had received the copy she wished to send him. It was published late in the year, after being completed serially in the October issue of *Scribner's Monthly*. The second volume of the presentation set, containing Higginson's signature, is now among the books from his library at HCL. The comment on "Immortality" might apply to the poem " 'Faithful to the end' Amended." "My earliest friend" in all probability was B. F. Newton. The quotation in the first paragraph is from Revelation 22.16.

To T. W. Higginson   *spring 1876*

I am glad to have been of joy to your friend, even incidentally, and greedy for the supplement of so sweet a privilege. I hope that you had a happy trip, and became refreshed. Labor might fatigue, though it is Action's rest.

> The things we thought that we should do
> We other things have done
> But those peculiar industries
> Have never been begun –
>
> The Lands we thought that we should seek
> When large enough to run
> By Speculation ceded
> To Speculation's Son –
>
> The Heaven, in which we hoped to pause
> When Discipline was done
> Untenable to Logic
> But possibly the one –

I am glad you remember the "Meadow Grass."
That forestalls fiction.
I was always told that conjecture surpassed Discovery, but it must have been spoken in caricature, for it is not true –

> The long sigh of the Frog
> Upon a Summer's Day
> Enacts intoxication
> Upon the Passer by.
>
> But his receding Swell
> Substantiates a Peace
> That makes the Ear inordinate
> For corporal release –

> Would you but guide
>   Your scholar

MANUSCRIPT: BPL (Higg 85). Ink.
PUBLICATION: L (1931) 296, in part.

Higginson's trips in 1876, according to his diary (HCL), were short ones to fill speaking engagements.

In this letter ED says that conjecture (anticipation, expectation) does not match or surpass discovery (the event). But see letter no. 442, where she seems to imply the opposite.

459A

To T. W. Higginson   *1876*

Nature is a Haunted House – but Art – a House that tries to be haunted.

MANUSCRIPT: BPL (Higg 42). Ink.
PUBLICATION: L (1931) 295.
This may have been sent as a separate message or it may have accompanied the preceding letter, for it has the same folds.

464

To Jonathan L. Jenkins   *about 1876*

It will make Today more homelike, that he who first made Heaven homelike to Father, is with his Children.

Emily.

MANUSCRIPT: Howe. Ink. Addressed on the fold: Mr Jenkins.
PUBLICATION: FN 109.
The date is conjectured from the handwriting. Perhaps the note was written on the anniversary of her father's death, 16 June. Jenkins had officiated at Edward Dickinson's funeral. The note was perhaps sent to him at a family gathering at Austin's, which ED did not attend.

465

To Samuel Bowles   *about 1876*

Of your exquisite Act there can be no Acknowledgment but the Ignominy that Grace gives.

Emily.

MANUSCRIPT: AC. Pencil.
PUBLICATION: L (1894) 221; LL 284; L (1931) 207.
The date is conjectured from the handwriting. Perhaps this note thanks Bowles for flowers sent on the second anniversary of her father's death, 16 June 1874.

466

To Samuel Bowles   *about 1876*

We part with the River at the Flood through a timid custom, though with the same Waters we have often played.

Emily.

MANUSCRIPT: AC. Pencil.
PUBLICATION: L (1894) 210; LL 267; L (1931) 205.
The handwriting of this message, like that of the message preceding, is almost certainly about 1876, but the occasion which prompted it has not been identified. Perhaps both were written with her father in mind.

489

To Samuel Bowles   *about 1877*

Dear friend,

You have the most triumphant Face out of Paradise – probably because you are there constantly, instead of ultimately –

Ourselves – we do inter – with sweet derision
The Channel of the Dust – who once achieves –
Invalidates the Balm of that Religion
That doubts – as fervently as it believes.

Emily.

MANUSCRIPT: AC. Pencil.
PUBLICATION: L (1894) 220; LL 271; L (1931) 206-207.
The date is conjectured from the handwriting. A photograph of Bowles taken about this time — he was just past fifty — is reproduced in this volume. This letter may acknowledge receipt of a copy of it.

To Sally Jenkins   *about 1877?*

Will the sweet child who sent me the butterflies, herself a member of the same ethereal nation, accept a rustic kiss, flavored, we trust, with clover?

MANUSCRIPT: missing.
PUBLICATION: *L* (1894) 371; *FN* 64–65; *L* (1931) 361.
An empty envelope (HCL – L 48) survives, addressed in pencil: Katie "Did,"/from/Katie did'nt –. If the above letter was sent in this envelope – and it was about this time that ED was writing notes to the Jenkins children – the letter belongs here. Sally's nickname was "Did."

To Mrs. Jonathan L. Jenkins   *late May 1877*
Dear friend,

It was pathetic to see your Voice instead of hearing it, for it has grown sweetly familiar in the House, as a Bird's. Father left us in June – you leave us in May. I am glad there will be no April till another year. Austin brought the note and waited like a hungry Boy for his crumb of words. Be sure to speak his name next time, he looks so solitary.

He told me that he could not sleep Friday night or Saturday night, and so rose and read lethargic Books to stupefy himself.

Sorrow is unsafe when it is real sorrow. I am glad so many are counterfeits – guileless because they believe themselves.

Kiss Diddie and Mac for us, precious Refugees, with love for our Brother whom with you we follow in the peculiar distance, "even unto the end."

Perhaps it is "the end" now. I think the Bell thought so because it bade us all goodbye when you stood in the Door.

You concealed that you heard it. Thank you.

                                                                         Emily.

MANUSCRIPT: missing.

PUBLICATION: *L* (1894) 374, in part; *FN* 134–135, in part; *L* (1931) 364–365, in part.

The *Amherst Record* for Wednesday 18 April 1877, announced that Jenkins preached his first sermon in the First Church at Pittsfield on the previous Sunday. This letter, with its clear reference to the growing breach between Austin and Susan, evidently acknowledges a call that Mrs. Jenkins made shortly before the family left Amherst in May. The scripture quotation is from Matthew 28.20.

511

To Edward (Ned) Dickinson   *July 1877*

Dear Ned –

You know I never liked you in those Yellow Jackets.

Emily.

MANUSCRIPT: HCL (B 83). Pencil.
PUBLICATION: *AM* CXV (1915) 37; LL 60.

An item in the *Springfield Republican*, 19 July 1877, reported that Ned had been stung by a hornet on the day preceding.

515

To Samuel Bowles   *about 1877*

Dear friend.

Vinnie accidentally mentioned that you hesitated between the "Theophilus" and the "Junius."

Would you confer so sweet a favor as to accept that too, when you come again?

I went to the Room as soon as you left, to confirm your presence – recalling the Psalmist's sonnet to God, beginning

> I have no Life but this –
> To lead it here –
> Nor any Death – but lest
> Dispelled from there –

Nor tie to Earths to come —
Nor Action new
Except through this extent
The love of you.

It is strange that the most intangible thing is the most adhesive.

Your "Rascal."

I washed the Adjective.

MANUSCRIPT: AC. Ink.
PUBLICATION: L (1894) 219–220; LL 267; L (1931) 205–206.

Gertrude M. Graves wrote "A Cousin's Memories of Emily Dickinson," *Boston Sunday Globe*, 12 January 1930, telling how Bowles once called upstairs to ED: "Emily, you wretch! No more of this nonsense! I've traveled all the way from Springfield to see you. Come down at once." She is said to have complied and never have been more witty. The conclusion to this letter suggests that Bowles had said "You damned rascal."

525

To Mrs. J. G. Holland   *December 1877*

I always feel that the Minutest Effort of the dear Eyes, demands a peculiarly immediate reply—and internally it receives it, but time to say we are sorry, is sometimes withheld—

Wrenched from my usual Route by Vinnie's singular illness—and Mother's additional despair—I have felt like a troubled Top, that spun without reprieve. Vinnie's relief is slow—She has borne more than she could, as you and I know more of, than her Physician does—

Torture for worthless sakes is equally Torture—

I shall try superhumanly to save her, and believe I shall, but she has been too lacerated to revive immediately.

Mrs Lord—so often with us—has fled—as you know—Dear Mr Bowles is hesitating—God help him decide on the Mortal Side!

This is Night—now—but we are not dreaming. Hold fast to your Home, for the Darling's stealthy momentum makes each moment—Fear—

I enclose a Note, which if you would lift as far as Philadelphia, if it did not tire your Arms—would please me so much.

Would the Doctor be willing to address it? Ask him, with my love.

Maggie remembers you with fondness – and Mother gives her love – Vinnie longs for you.

Is not the distinction of Affection, almost Realm enough?

Emily.

MANUSCRIPT: HCL (H 44). Ink.
PUBLICATION: LH 118–119.

Mrs. Holland's eyesight was seriously impaired after her operation in 1872, and many letters from ED allude to it in this manner. Mrs. Otis P. Lord died on 10 December. The letter enclosed for Dr. Holland to address and forward to Philadelphia was presumably intended for Charles Wadsworth.

532

To Mrs. Samuel Bowles   *about 16 January 1878*

To remember our own Mr Bowles is all we can do.

With grief it is done, so warmly and long, it can never be new.

Emily.

MANUSCRIPT: AC. Pencil.
PUBLICATION: L (1894) 223; LL 286; L (1931) 208.

These "broken words" (see letter no. 536) were probably written on the day that Samuel Bowles died, 16 January 1878. Mrs. Bowles answered the note soon after, eliciting ED's reply in the letter referred to above. On this letter, see the note to letter no. 438.

536

To Mrs. Samuel Bowles   *early 1878*

I hasten to you, Mary, because no moment must be lost when a heart is breaking, for though it broke so long, each time is newer than the last, if it broke truly. To be willing that I should speak to you was so generous, dear.

Sorrow almost resents love, it is so inflamed.

I am glad if the broken words helped you. I had not hoped so much, I felt so faint in uttering them, thinking of your great pain. Love makes us "heavenly" without our trying in the least. 'Tis easier than a Saviour – it does not stay on high and call us to its distance; its low "Come unto me" begins in every place. It makes but one mistake, it tells us it is "rest" – perhaps its toil is rest, but what we have not known we shall know again, that divine "again" for which we are all breathless.

I am glad you "work." Work is a bleak redeemer, but it does redeem; it tires the flesh so that can't tease the spirit.

Dear "Mr. Sam" is very near, these midwinter days. When purples come on Pelham, in the afternoon we say "Mr. Bowles's colors." I spoke to him once of his Gem chapter, and the beautiful eyes rose till they were out of reach of mine, in some hallowed fathom.

> Not that he goes – we love him more
> Who led us while he stayed.
> Beyond earth's trafficking frontier,
> For what he moved, he made.

Mother is timid and feeble, but we keep her with us. She thanks you for remembering her, and never forgets you. . . . Your sweet "and left me all alone," consecrates your lips.

Emily.

MANUSCRIPT: missing.
PUBLICATION: L (1894) 223–224; LL 314–315; L (1931) 209–210.
See the note to letter no. 532. Mr. Bowles's "Gem chapter" may have been Revelation 21, of which ED herself was particularly fond.

537

To Maria Whitney   *early 1878*

Dear friend,

I have thought of you often since the darkness, – though we cannot assist another's night. I have hoped you were saved. That he has received Immortality who so often conferred it, invests it with a more sudden charm. . . .

I hope you have the power of hope, and that every bliss we know or guess hourly befalls you.

E. Dickinson.

MANUSCRIPT: missing.
PUBLICATION: L (1894) 336; L (1931) 325.
ED knew that Bowles's death was poignantly felt by Maria Whitney. This and the three following extracts, dated by Mrs. Todd "1878," evidently were written about the same time.

547

To Mrs. J. G. Holland   *about March 1878*

Dear Sister.

I take Mrs Browning's little Basket to bring the note to you – and when you find it is not her, you will be disappointed, but there is many a discipline before we obtain Heaven – Your little Note protected, as it always does, and the "Whips of Time" felt a long way off.

Your little Trip still lingers, for is not all petite you do – you are such a Linnet?

Vinnie was much elated by your rogueries. She thinks you are stealthy as Talleyrand –

We learn of you in the Papers and of your new House, of which it is said there will be a Portrait – "so I shall see it in just three Days," though I would rather see it's vital inhabitants.

I gave your words to Ned – who bowed and seemed much raised –

Baby does all the errands now – and I enclose a Circular, setting forth his wants.

To see the little Missionary starting with his Basket, would warm the chillest Heart.

I know you will do what I ask you, and so I only thank you, and make no outer remarks.

Lovingly,

Emily.

MANUSCRIPT: HCL (H 47). Ink.
PUBLICATION: LH 124–125.
The "Portrait" was an article in the *Springfield Republican* of some

[243]

length, in the 24 July issue, describing the Hollands' new house in the Thousand Islands. The last sentence evidently asks Mrs. Holland to forward an enclosure, probably a letter intended for Dr. Wadsworth. "Whips of Time" paraphrases Hamlet's "whips and scorns of time" (III, i, 70). The second quotation paraphrases the opening line of Browning's "In Three Days": "So, I shall see her in three days." Mrs. Ward conjectures that "Mrs Browning's little Basket" means that ED folded the letter in a circular notice or the wrapping from a copy of Elizabeth Barrett Browning's *Earlier Poems*, first published in the United States in March 1878.

559

To Otis P. Lord   *about 1878*

[*fair copy — first two pages only extant*]

My lovely Salem smiles at me. I seek his Face so often – but I have done with guises.

I confess that I love him – I rejoice that I love him – I thank the maker of Heaven and Earth – that gave him me to love – the exultation floods me. I cannot find my channel – the Creek turns Sea – at thought of thee –

Will you punish me? "Involuntary Bankruptcy," how could that be Crime?

Incarcerate me in yourself – rosy penalty – threading with you this lovely maze, which is not Life or Death – though it has the intangibleness of one, and the flush of the other – waking for your sake on Day made magical with you before I went

[*rough draft of fair copy above*]

My lovely Salem smiles at me I seek his Face so often – but I am past disguises (have dropped –) (have done with guises –)

I confess that I love him – I rejoice that I love him – I thank the maker of Heaven and Earth that gave him me to love – the exultation floods me – I can not find my channel – The Creek turned Sea at thoughts of thee – will you punish it – [turn I] involuntary Bankruptcy as the Debtors say. Could that be a Crime – How could that be crime – Incarcerate me in yourself – that will punish me – Threading with you this lovely maze which is not Life or Death tho it has

[244]

the intangibleness of one and the flush of the other waking for your sake on Day made magical with [before] you before I went to sleep – What pretty phrase – we went to sleep as if it were a country – let us make it one – we could (will) make it one, my native Land – my Darling come oh *be* a patriot now – Love is a patriot now Gave her life for its (its) country Has it meaning now – Oh nation of the soul thou hast thy freedom now

MANUSCRIPTS: AC. Both are in pencil.

PUBLICATION: *Revelation* 78–81, with facsimile.

The rough draft is on a discarded envelope addressed in Lord's hand: Miss Vinnie Dickinson,/Amherst/By Mr Cooper's Kindness. (James I. Cooper was Austin Dickinson's law partner.)

The letters, and drafts and fragments of letters, to Lord were found among ED's papers after her death, and given to Mrs. Todd by Austin Dickinson (*Revelation* 1–2). It would appear that ED and Lord in time came to make a practice of writing each other weekly — or intending to do so. The intimacy of the relationship continued until his death in 1884. This letter and the four that follow are in the handwriting of about 1878. They are here grouped, since no specific time of the year is indicated in the letters.

560

To Otis P. Lord   *about 1878*

Ned and I were talking about God and Ned said "Aunt Emily – does Judge Lord belong to the Church"?

"I think not, Ned, technically."

"Why, I thought he was one of those Boston Fellers who thought it the respectable thing to do." "I think he does nothing ostensible – Ned." "Well – my Father says if there were another Judge in the Commonwealth like him, the practice of Law would amount to something." I told him I thought it probable – though recalling that I had never tried any case in your presence but my own, and that, with your sweet assistance – I was murmurless.

I wanted to fondle the Boy for the fervent words – but made the distinction. Dont you know you have taken my will away and I "know

[245]

not where" you "have laid" it? Should I have curbed you sooner? "Spare the 'Nay' and spoil the child"?

Oh, my too beloved, save me from the idolatry which would crush us both —

"And very Sea — Mark of my utmost Sail" —

MANUSCRIPT: AC. Pencil. It is a fair copy.
PUBLICATION: *Revelation* 77–82.

561

To Otis P. Lord   *about 1878*

To beg for the Letter when it is written, is bankrupt enough, but to beg for it when it is'nt, and the dear Donor is sauntering, mindless of it's worth, *that* is bankrupter.

Sweet One — to make the bright week noxious, that was once so gay, have you quite the warrant? Also, my Naughty one, too seraphic Naughty, who can sentence you? Certainly not my enamored Heart. Now my blissful Sophist, you that can make "Dont" "Do" — though forget that I told you so, [*part of two pages cut out*]

Perhaps, please, you are sinful? Though of power to make Perdition divine, who can punish you?

MANUSCRIPT: AC. Pencil. Fair copy.
PUBLICATION: *Revelation* 82.

562

To Otis P. Lord   *about 1878*

Dont you know you are happiest while I withhold and not confer — dont you know that "No" is the wildest word we consign to Language?

You do, for you know all things — [*top of sheet cut off*] . . . to lie so near your longing — to touch it as I passed, for I am but a restive sleeper and often should journey from your Arms through the happy night, but you will lift me back, wont you, for only there I ask to be —

I say, if I felt the longing nearer – than in our dear past, perhaps I could not resist to bless it, but must, because it would be right

The "Stile" is God's – My Sweet One – for your great sake – not mine – I will not let you cross – but it is all your's, and when it is right I will lift the Bars, and lay you in the Moss – You showed me the word.

I hope it has no different guise when my fingers make it. It is Anguish I long conceal from you to let you leave me, hungry, but you ask the divine Crust and that would doom the Bread.

That unfrequented Flower
Embellish thee – (deserving be) [*sheet cut off*]

I was reading a little Book – because it broke my Heart I want it to break your's – Will you think that fair? I often have read it, but not before since loving you – I find that makes a difference – it makes a difference with all. Even the whistle of a Boy passing late at Night, or the Low [?] of a Bird – [*sheet cut away*] Satan" – but then what I have not heard is the sweet majority – the Bible says very roguishly, that the "wayfaring Man, though a Fool – need not err therein"; need the "wayfaring" Woman? Ask your throbbing Scripture.

It may surprise you I speak of God – I know him but a little, but Cupid taught Jehovah to many an untutored Mind – Witchcraft is wiser than we –

Manuscript: AC. Pencil.

Publication: *Revelation* 83, with the first page reproduced in facsimile.

563

To Otis P. Lord   *about 1878*

Tuesday is a deeply depressing Day – it is not far enough from your dear note for the embryo of another to form, and yet what flights of Distance – and so I perish softly and spurn the Birds (spring) and spurn the Sun – with pathetic (dejected) malice – but when the Sun begins to turn the corner Thursday night – everything refreshes – the soft uplifting grows till by the time it is Sunday night, all my Life (Cheek) is Fever with nearness to your blissful words – (rippling words)

MANUSCRIPT: AC. Pencil. Jotted on a discarded scrap of letter.
PUBLICATION:*Revelation* 94, with facsimile reproduction.
It is written on a scrap of letter from Maggie Maher.

573

To Maria Whitney   *late 1878*

Dear friend,

   I had within a few days a lovely hour with Mr and Mrs Jackson
of Colorado, who told me that love of Mr Bowles and longing for
some trace of him, led them to his house, and to seek his wife. They
found her, they said, a stricken woman, though not so ruthless as they
feared. That of ties remaining, she spoke with peculiar love of a Miss
Whitney of Northampton, whom she would soon visit, and almost
thought of accompanying them as far as yourself.

   To know that long fidelity in ungracious soil was not wholly squandered, might be sweet to you.

   I hope that you are well, and in full receipt of the Great Spirit
whose leaving life was leaving you.

Faithfully

MANUSCRIPT: missing.
PUBLICATION: *L* (1931) 327. The present text derives from a transcript
(AC) made by Mrs. Todd when she saw the letter.
   The Jacksons had been in Amherst for a few days, leaving there on
24 October. It is significant that ED received not only Mrs. Jackson but
her husband, a total stranger. Such an act for ED this late in her life was
unprecedented (see letter no. 573c). The second paragraph makes it
clear that ED was aware that Maria Whitney's devotion to Samuel
Bowles had not always been appreciated.
   ED's letters to Helen Jackson written during 1878 are missing, but the
contents of them can be inferred from those Mrs. Jackson wrote ED
(HCL). The first, dated Colorado Springs, 29 April 1878, asks for a poem
to be included in a volume of the No Name series. The full story of Mrs.
Jackson's effort to get it is told in *Poems* (1955) xxx–xxxiii, and begins
with the following letter (unpublished), which returns a photograph of
Gilbert.

[248]

My dear friend,

My face was not "averted" in the least. It was only that I did not speak: and of my not speaking, I ought to be very much ashamed, and should be, if I had not got past being ashamed of my delinquencies in the matter of letter writing. But I assure you I have never forgotten that you kindly wrote one day, asking if all were well with me: and I have all along meant to write and say "yes," if no more.

All last summer and autumn I was very busy, in altering over and fitting up our cottage. I think to alter one house is equal to building ten! and to do any such work in Colorado is ten times harder than to do it any where else in the world. But now it is all done, and we are "settled" — (odd word that and does a good deal of double duty in the language) — I can hardly recollect the fatigues and discomforts which went before. It is a very picturesque and cozy little house, and I enjoy it unspeakably. I should like to see all my Eastern friends in it.

Would it be of any use to ask you once more for one or two of your poems, to come out in the volume of "no name" poetry which is to be published before long by Roberts Bros.? If you will give me permission I will copy them — sending them in my own handwriting — and promise never to tell any one, not even the publishers, whose the poems are. Could you not bear this much of publicity? only you and I would recognize the poems. I wish very much you would do this — and I think you would have much amusement in seeing to whom the critics, those shrewd guessers would ascribe your verses.

I am hoping to come East with Mr. Jackson, before next winter: but we have no fixed plan — and may not get off. It is a long way to come.

I wish you would give my love to Doctor Cate — I was about to say "when you see him," but you never see anybody! Perhaps however you have improved. I send back the little baby face to tell you that I had not "averted" my face — only the habit of speaking. It is an earnest and good little face: your brother's child I presume. — Will you ask Mrs. Dickinson some day, if she still hears from Jane Goodenow — I would like very much to know where and how she is. Goodbye —

Always cordially yours –

Helen Jackson

On her October visit Mrs. Jackson pursued her effort to secure a poem. From Hartford, Connecticut, where she and Mr. Jackson were sojourning at the home of Charles Dudley Warner, she wrote on 25 October, the day following her Amherst visit, the following note, pressing her request.

573b

My dear Friend —

Here comes the line I promised to send — we had a fine noon on Mt. Holyoke yesterday — and took the 5 o clk train to Springfield –; but there, Mr. Jackson found a telegram from New York which compelled him to go on without stopping here — and so I came alone to Mr. Warners, which was a disappointment.

Now — will you send me the poem? No — will you let me send the "Success" — which I know by heart — to Roberts Bros for the Masque of Poets? If you will, it will give me a great pleasure. I ask it as a personal favor to myself – Can you refuse the only thing I perhaps shall ever ask at your hands?

Yours ever

Helen Jackson

ED must have granted permission, for Mrs. Jackson wrote the following letter, dated Colorado Springs, 8 December 1878:

573c

My dear friend,

I suppose by this time you have seen the Masque of Poets. I hope you have not regretted giving me that choice bit of verse for it. I was pleased to see that it had in a manner, a special place, being chosen to end the first part of the volume, — on the whole, the volume is a disappointment to me. Still I think it has much interest for all literary people. I confess myself quite unable to conjecture the authorship of most of the poems.

Colorado is as lovely as ever: — our mountains are white with snow now, but there is no snow in the town: at noon one can have windows open, if the fires blaze well on the hearths. What would you think of that in N. England.

I am very glad that I saw you this autumn: also that you saw my husband and liked him, as I perceived that you did –

Thank you once more for the verses.

Yours always
Helen Jackson

The story of the publishing of "Success" comes to an end with the following letter (HCL), written to ED by Thomas Niles, the publisher of Roberts Brothers. It is dated 15 January 1879, and was a reply to one from ED, written to thank him for a copy of *A Masque of Poets*.

573d

Dear Miss Dickinson

You were entitled to a copy of "A Masque of Poets" without thanks, for your valuable contribution which for want of a known sponsor Mr Emerson has generally had to father.

I wanted to send you a proof of your poem, wh. as you have doubt-less perceived was slightly changed in phraseology

Yrs very truly
T. Niles

Typical of the reviews of *A Masque of Poets* which attributed "Success" to Emerson is that which appeared in the influential *Literary World,* 10 December 1878 (IX, 118): "If anything in the volume was contributed by Emerson, we should consider these lines upon 'Success' most probably his." And the comment is followed with a quotation of the whole poem.

592

To Mrs. Jonathan L. Jenkins   *late January 1879*

Would you feel more at Home with a Flower from Home, in your Hand, dear?

Manuscript: HCL (L 39). Pencil.

PUBLICATION: *L* (1894) 364; *L* (1931) 364; *FN* 123.
Probably this note was sent on the occasion of the birth of Austin Dickinson Jenkins, 19 January 1879.

593

To T. W. Higginson   *February 1879*

Dear friend,

To congratulate the Redeemed is perhaps superfluous for Redemption leaves nothing for Earth to add – It is very sweet and serious to suppose you at Home, and reverence I cannot express is all that remains – I have read of Home in the Revelations —— "Neither thirst any more" –

You speak very sweetly of the Stranger –

I trust the Phantom Love that enrolls the "Sparrow" – enfolds her softer than a Child –

The name of the "little Book she wrote," I do not quite decipher – "– and Prairie"? Should you perhaps tell me, I think I could see her Face in that – I am sorry not to have seen your "Hawthorne," but have known little of Literature since my Father died – that and the passing of Mr Bowles, and Mother's hopeless illness, overwhelmed my Moments, though your Pages and Shakespeare's, like Ophir – remain –

To see you seems improbable, but the Clergyman says I shall see my Father –

The subterranean stays –

MANUSCRIPT: HCL – the first two pages; and BPL (Higg 117) – the last two pages. Pencil.
PUBLICATION: *AM* CXXXIX (June 1927) 800; *L* (1931) 312–313.
Higginson's marriage to Mary Potter Thacher took place during the first week in February, 1879. The book she had written and to which he had alluded was a small collection of discursive essays, *Seashore and Prairie*, published in 1877. Higginson's *Short Studies of American Authors*, which contains a brief estimate of Hawthorne, Higginson sent to ED as soon as it was published; however, this had not yet been written. He had published two earlier essays on Hawthorne: "An Evening with Mrs. Hawthorne," *Atlantic Monthly*, XXVIII (October 1871), 432–433; and "Hawthorne's Last Bequest," *Scribner's Monthly*, V (November 1872),

100–105. He had evidently alluded to one of these, probably to the second, since it deals more directly with Hawthorne. The quotation in the first paragraph is from Revelation 7.16: "They shall hunger no more, neither thirst any more. . ."

595

To Mrs. Henry Hills   *1879?*

"Come unto me." Beloved Commandment. The Darling obeyed.

MANUSCRIPT: missing.
PUBLICATION: *L* (1894) 398; *L* (1931) 387.
An infant, Samuel, died, 23 February, 1879.

601

To Helen Hunt Jackson   *about mid-April 1879*

Spurn the temerity –
Rashness of Calvary –
Gay were Gethsemene
Knew we of Thee –

MANUSCRIPT: HCL (Higginson). Pencil.
PUBLICATION: *AM* CXXXIX (June 1927) 801; *L* (1931) 318; *Poems* (1955) 992.
This may have been an Easter greeting and a reminder to Mrs. Jackson that ED has not recently heard from her. At the bottom of the sheet Mrs. Jackson wrote: "Wonderful twelve words! – H. J.," and evidently sent the message to Higginson, for it now rests among his papers. Mrs. Jackson wrote the following letter (HCL) to ED, dated Colorado Springs, 12 May 1879:

601a

My dear friend,

I know your "Blue bird" by heart — and that is more than I do of any of my own verses. —

I also want your permission to send it to Col. Higginson to read. These two things are my testimonial to its merit.

We have blue birds here — I might have had the sense to write something about one myself, but I never did: and now I never can. For which I am inclined to envy, and perhaps hate you.

"The man I live with" (I suppose you recollect designating my husband by that curiously direct phrase) is in New York, — and I am living alone, — which I should find very insupportable except that I am building on a bath room, & otherwise setting my house to rights. To be busy is the best help I know of, for all sorts of discomforts. —

What should you think of trying your hand on the oriole? He will be along presently

Yours ever —

Helen Jackson

P.S. Write & tell me if I may pass the Blue Bird along to the Col? —

604

To Edward (Ned) Dickinson   *about 1879*

> Ned —
>
> Time's wily Chargers will not wait
> At any Gate but Woe's —
> But there — so gloat to hesitate
> They will not stir for blows —
>
> Dick —
> Jim —

MANUSCRIPT: HCL (B 45). Pencil.
PUBLICATION: *FF* 251; *Poems* (1955) 1008.

Mrs. Bianchi's note in *FF* says the lines were sent after Ned's horses Dick and Jim had run away with him. The verses, however, would seem more appropriate to an occasion when Ned inadvertently found himself in a funeral procession from which he could not extricate himself by whipping up the horses.

To Mrs. J. G. Holland *October 1879*

Little Sister,

I was glad you wrote – I was just about addressing the Coroner of Alexandria – You spared me the melancholy research –

Are you pretty well – have you been happy –

Are your Eyes safe?

A thousand questions rise to my lips, and as suddenly ebb – for how little I know of you recently — An awkward loneliness smites me – I fear I must ask with Mr Wentworth, "Where are our moral foundations?"

Should you ask what had happened here, I should say nothing perceptible. Sweet latent events – too shy to confide –

It will vivify us to your remembrance to tell you that Austin and Sue have just returned from Belchertown Cattle Show –

Austin brought me a Balloon and Vinnie a Watermelon and each of his family a Whip – Wasn't it primitive?

When they drove away in the dust this morning, I told them they looked like Mr and Mrs "Pendexter," turning their backs upon Long-fellow's Parish –

Brave Vinnie is well – Mother does not yet stand alone and fears she never shall walk, but I tell her we all shall fly so soon, not to let it grieve her, and what indeed is Earth but a Nest, from whose rim we are all falling?

One day last Summer I laughed once like "Little Mrs Holland," Vinnie said I did – how much it pleased us all –

I ask you to ask your Doctor will he be so kind as to write the name of my Philadelphia friend on the Note within, and your little Hand will take it to him –

You were so long so faithful, Earth would not seem homelike without your little sunny Acts –

Love for you each —

Emily.

MANUSCRIPT: HCL (H 51). Pencil.

PUBLICATION: *LH* 129–130.

The Belchertown Cattle Show took place on 9 October 1879. Mr. Wentworth is a character in Henry James's *The Europeans,* serialized at this time in *Scribner's Monthly.* Mr. Pendexter is a character in Longfellow's *Kavanagh.*

XI

1880–1883

*"I hesitate which word to take,
as I can take but few and each
must be the chiefest . . ."*

The letters which comprise this group show an increased nervous tension brought on in part by the frictions between the two houses — particularly between Vinnie and Sue, and in part by the death of friends. Dr. Holland's death in 1881 was not the personal loss that Bowles's death had been; it chiefly touched her through her deep affection for Mrs. Holland, who in these years seems to have been her staunchest comforter and most steady correspondent. The extent of her correspondence with Lord can never be known, since presumably the bulk of it has been long destroyed, but its nature is clear from the surviving fragments.

Charles Wadsworth's death in April 1882 concluded one of the meaningful associations of her life, and served to open a new correspondence. James Clark had been a lifelong friend of Wadsworth's, and the spate of letters she now wrote James Clark (and later his brother Charles) are almost solely testimonials to the departed friend. Her mother survived into November of that year, and the letters of this period are clear evidence that the demands made on Emily by a helpless invalid strengthened the bond between mother and daughter.

The most shattering experience proved to be, not the death of an adult friend, but that of her eight-year-old nephew Gilbert, in the autumn of 1883. With his departure went a certain inner light. She still groped for words with which to form poems, now chiefly elegies, but hardly more than fragments were produced. There are, however, noble utterances in the letters.

To Mrs. Lucius Boltwood   *March 1880?*

The Spring of which dear Mrs Boltwood speaks, is not so brave as herself, and should bring her of right, it's first flower.

Though a Pie is far from a flower, Mr Howells implies in his "Undiscovered Country," that "our relation to Pie" will unfold in proportion to finer relations.

With sweet thoughts from us all, and thanks for the charming Butter, and the gallant notes,

Very faithfully,
Emily

MANUSCRIPT: missing. The text is from a transcript in the Jones Library, made when the autograph was on loan exhibit in 1929.

PUBLICATION: *Amherst Graduates' Magazine* XXVI (1937) 297-307; Adèle Allen: *Around a Village Green*, pp. 54-55.

A note from Vinnie to Mrs. Boltwood, dated 8 March 1880, expresses sympathy for an accident to her son, who had been thrown from a carriage. This note may have been written then. Howells's *Undiscovered Country* was published serially in *Scribner's Monthly*, beginning in January. This note, accompanying a pie, acknowledges the gift of butter.

To T. W. Higginson   *spring 1880*

Dear friend –

Most of our Moments are Moments of Preface – "Seven Weeks" is a long Life – if it is all lived –

The little Memoir was very touching. I am sorry she was not willing to stay –

The flight of such a fraction takes all our Numbers Home –

"Room for one more" was a plea for Heaven –

I misunderstood – Heaven must be a lone exchange for such a parentage –

These sudden intimacies with Immortality, are expanse – not Peace – as Lightning at our feet, instills a foreign Landscape. Thank you for the Portrait – it is beautiful, but intimidating – I shall pick "May flowers" more furtively, and feel new awe of "Moonlight."

The route of your little Fugitive must be a tender wonder – and yet

> A Dimple in the Tomb
> Makes that ferocious Room
> A Home –

Your Scholar –

MANUSCRIPT: Hallowell. Pencil.
PUBLICATION: *AM* CXXXIX (1927) 800; *L* (1931) 315.
Higginson sent ED a "memoir" of the baby that died in March. In 1879 Mary Thacher Higginson published *Room for One More*, a story for children.

642

To Edward (Ned) Dickinson   *mid-May 1880*

Phoebus – "I'll take the Reins."

Phaeton.

MANUSCRIPT: HCL (B 86). Pencil. Unpublished. Addressed: Ned.
Amherst Record, 12 May: "W. A. Dickinson has just purchased a fine young stepper to take the place of his old family carriage horse, and shows plenty of style as well as life."

646

To Mrs. Jonathan L. Jenkins   *about 1880*

Hope they are with each other – Never saw a little Boy going Home to Thanksgiving, so happy as Austin, when he passed the Door –

Emily.

MANUSCRIPT: Sister Mary James. Pencil.
PUBLICATION: *FN* 112.
Austin had gone to visit Mr. Jenkins, who was his close friend.

To Mrs. J. G. Holland   *July 1880*

Dear friend,

While Little Boys are commemorating the advent of their Country, I have a Letter from "Aunt Glegg" saying "Summer is nearly gone," so I thought I would pick a few Seeds this Afternoon and bid you Good bye as you would be off for Winter. I think Persons dont talk about "Summer stopping" this time o' year, unless they are inclement themselves.

I wish you would speak to the Thermometer about it – I dont like to take the responsibility.

Perhaps you never received a Note I sent you or you would have answered the little question was in it?

It was not about the "promised Messiah –"

The Weather is like Africa and the Flowers like Asia and the Numidian Heart of your "Little Friend" neither slow nor chill –

> The Road to Paradise is plain,
> And holds scarce one.
> Not that it is not firm
> But we presume
> A Dimpled Road
> Is more preferred.
> The Belles of Paradise are few –
> Not me – nor you –
> But unsuspected things –
> Mines have no Wings.

July 15th

You see I have been delayed – but we will begin where we left off –

Austin and I were talking the other Night about the Extension of Consciousness, after Death and Mother told Vinnie, afterward, she thought it was "very improper."

She forgets that we are past "Correction in Righteousness –"

I dont know what she would think if she knew that Austin told me confidentially "there was no such person as Elijah."

I suppose Doctor is catching Trout and Convalescence and wish I could meet them both at Breakfast – and bid my very little Sister a most sweet Good Night –

MANUSCRIPT: HCL (H 52). Pencil.
PUBLICATION: LH 131–132.

ED dated the letter "July 4th" but put it aside and finished it on "July 15th." Aunt Glegg, a character in George Eliot's *The Mill on the Floss*, cast a shadow over members of the family, whether she was present or absent; ED undoubtedly has in mind her Aunt Elizabeth Currier. The scripture allusion is to 2 Timothy 3.16: "All scripture is given . . . for correction, for instruction in righteousness."

651

To Samuel Bowles the younger   *early August 1880*

Dear friend,

Our friend your Father was so beautifully and intimately recalled Today that it seemed impossible he had experienced the secret of Death – A servant who had been with us a long time and had often opened the Door for him, asked me how to spell "Genius," yesterday – I told her and she said no more – Today, she asked me what "Genius" meant? I told her none had known –

She said she read in a Catholic Paper that Mr Bowles was "the Genius of Hampshire," and thought it might be that past Gentleman – His look could not be extinguished to any who had seen him, for "Because I live, ye shall live also," was his physiognomy –

I congratulate you upon his immortality, which is a constant stimulus to my Household – and upon your noble perpetuation of his cherished "Republican."

Please remember me tenderly to your Mother –

With honor,
Emily Dickinson –

MANUSCRIPT: Bowles. Pencil.
PUBLICATION: *L* (1894) 349; *LL* 342–343; *L* (1931) 337.

ED got Maggie Maher to address the envelope, probably because Maggie had called attention to the tribute to Bowles: Saml Bowles Esq/ Republican/Springfield/Mass. Postmarked: Amherst Mass Aug 2.

653

To T. W. Higginson   *August 1880*

Dear friend,

I was touchingly reminded of your little Louisa this Morning by an Indian Woman with gay Baskets and a dazzling Baby, at the Kitchen Door – Her little Boy "once died," she said, Death to her dispelling him – I asked her what the Baby liked, and she said "to step." The Prairie before the Door was gay with Flowers of Hay, and I led her in – She argued with the Birds – she leaned on Clover Walls and they fell, and dropped her – With jargon sweeter than a Bell, she grappled Buttercups – and they sank together, the Buttercups the heaviest – What sweetest use of Days!

'Twas noting some such Scene made Vaughn humbly say "My Days that are at best but dim and hoary" –

I think it was Vaughn –

It reminded me too of "Little Annie," of whom you feared to make the mistake in saying "Shoulder Arms" to the "Colored Regiment" – but which was the Child of Fiction, the Child of Fiction or of Fact, and is "Come unto me" for Father or Child, when the Child precedes?

MANUSCRIPT: HCL (Higginson). Pencil.
PUBLICATION: *AM* LXVIII (October 1891) 455–456, in part; *L* (1894) 330–331, in part; *LL* 325, in part; *AM* CXXXIX (June 1927) 801, entire; *L* (1931) 316–317, entire.

The *Amherst Record* for 18 August 1880 notes: "The poor Indian has arrived and a party of some such nationality is in camp at East Street." "Little Annie" was "The Baby of the Regiment" in Higginson's *Army Life in a Black Regiment* (1870). The quotation from Henry Vaughan is from the third stanza of "They are all gone into the world of light," and reads: "My days, which are at best but dull and hoary."

To Martha Gilbert Smith   *August 1880*

It was like my Mattie to send the Peaches, pink as the Heart they indorse –

I wish I had something as sumptuous to enclose to her –

I have, but it is anonymous –

I love to hear you are growing better – I hope you may be a hale Mattie before you go away – vast as Vinnie and I, who tower like Acorns – Thank you from each, delightedly – If the transitive be but the minor, we shall need a large accession of strength, for the major sweetness –

Lovingly,
Emily –

MANUSCRIPT: HCL (L 30). Pencil.
PUBLICATION: FF 252–253.

Mattie was visiting her sister Sue in Amherst. Her husband had died in December 1878.

To Susan Gilbert Dickinson   *about 1880*

Memoirs of Little Boys that live –

"Were'nt you chasing Pussy," said Vinnie to Gilbert?

"No – she was chasing herself" –

"But was'nt she running pretty fast"? "Well, some slow and some fast" said the beguiling Villain – Pussy's Nemesis quailed –

Talk of "hoary Reprobates"!

Your Urchin is more antique in wiles than the Egyptian Sphinx –

Have you noticed Granville's Letter to Lowell?

"Her Majesty" has contemplated you, and reserves her decision!

Emily –

MANUSCRIPT: HCL (B 72). Pencil.
PUBLICATION: AM CXV (1915) 37–38; LL 58.

Lowell went as minister to England in 1880, the year that Granville took over the Foreign Office.

666

To Louise and Frances Norcross   *about September 1880*

I have only a moment, exiles, but you shall have the largest half. Mother's dear little wants so engross the time, – to read to her, to fan her, to tell her health will come tomorrow, to explain to her *why* the grasshopper is a burden, because he is not so new a grasshopper as he was, – this is so ensuing, I hardly have said "Good-morning, mother," when I hear myself saying "Mother, good-night."

MANUSCRIPT: destroyed.
PUBLICATION: L (1894) 294; L (1931) 266.
This letter was written on the day preceding that on which ED wrote the following letter to Mrs. Holland. The scripture allusion to the grasshopper is from Ecclesiastes 12.5.

667

To Mrs. J. G. Holland   *about September 1880*

Dear Sister –

The responsibility of Pathos is almost more than the responsibility of Care. Mother will never walk. She still makes her little Voyages from her Bed to her Chair in a Strong Man's Arms – probably that will be all.

Her poor Patience loses it's way and we lead it back – I was telling her Nieces yesterday, who wrote to ask for her, that to read to her – to fan her – to tell her "Health would come Tomorrow," and make the Counterfeit look real – to explain *why* "the Grasshopper is a Burden" – because it is not as new a Grasshopper as it was – this is so ensuing, that I hardly have said, "Good Morning, Mother," when I hear myself saying "Mother, – Good Night –"

Time is short and full, like an outgrown Frock –

[265]

You are very kind to give me leave to ask "the question" again, but on renewed self examination I find I have not the temerity –

I thought of your Garden in the Rocks those unfeeling Nights – perhaps it had "Watchers" as Vinnie's did –

I hope the Doctor is improving – in his health – I mean – his other perfections precluding the suggestion, and that my little Sister is in sweet robustness –

Vinnie is far more hurried than Presidential Candidates – I trust in more distinguished ways, for *they* have only the care of the Union, but Vinnie the Universe –

With her love and mine,

Emily –

Manuscript: HCL (H 53). Pencil.
Publication: *LH* 133.

This letter was written in response to one from Mrs. Holland which evidently invited ED to repeat the question now lost (see letter no. 650). It had also described her flowerbeds at Bonniecastle in the Thousand Islands after the first September frosts. The political campaigns of a presidential election year, ED's letter notes, are gathering momentum.

668

To Mrs. Joseph A. Sweetser   *autumn 1880*

Aunt Katie and the Sultans have left the Garden now, and parting with my own, recalls their sweet companionship –

Mine were not I think as exuberant as in other Years – Perhaps the Pelham Water shocked their stately tastes – but cherished avariciously, because less numerous. I trust your Garden was willing to die – I do not think that mine was – it perished with beautiful reluctance, like an evening star –

I hope you were well since we knew of you, and as happy as Sorrow would allow –

There are Sweets of Pathos, when Sweets of Mirth have passed away –

Mother has had a weary Cold, and suffers much from Neuralgia, since the changing Airs, though I trust is no feebler than when you were here –

She has her little pleasures as the patient have – the voices of Friends – and devotion of Home.

The "Ravens" must "cry," to be ministered to – she – need only sigh.

Vinnie knows no shadow – brave – faithful – punctual – and courageous Maggie not yet caught in the snares of Patrick – Perhaps it is quite the Home it was when you last beheld it –

I hope your Few are safe, and your Flowers encouraging –

News of your Sultans and yourself, would be equally lovely, when you feel inclined. Blossoms have their Leisures –

Lovingly,
Emily –

MANUSCRIPT: Jones Library. Pencil.
PUBLICATION: L (1894) 407–408; L (1931) 398–399.
Water was first brought by pipes from Pelham in June 1880. The allusion to ravens is from Psalms 147.9: "He giveth to the beast his food, and to the young ravens which cry."

674

To T. W. Higginson   *November 1880*

Dear friend,

You were once so kind as to say you would advise me – Could I ask it now –

I have promised three Hymns to a charity, but without your approval could not give them –

They are short and I could write them quite plainly, and if you felt it convenient to tell me if they were faithful, I should be very grateful, though if public cares too far fatigue you, please deny

Your Scholar –

MANUSCRIPT: BPL (Higg 110). Pencil.
PUBLICATION: L (1894) 330; LL 324; L (1931) 315–316.
The Annual Sale of the Mission Circle, for the support of children in India and other Far Eastern countries, was held in the First Church, 30 November. The "public cares" refers to the election of Higginson, 4 November, to the Massachusetts legislature.

To T. W. Higginson   *November 1880*

Dear friend,

I am tenderly happy that you are happy – Thank you for the Whisper –

If I dared to give the Madonna my love –

The thoughtfulness I may not accept is among my Balms – Grateful for the kindness, I enclose those you allow, adding a fourth, lest one of them you might think profane –

They are Christ's Birthday – Cupid's Sermon – A Humming-Bird – and My Country's Wardrobe –

Reprove them as your own –

To punish them would please me, because the fine conviction I had so true a friend –

Your Scholar –

MANUSCRIPT: Porter. Pencil.
PUBLICATION: *AM* CXXXIX (June 1927) 800; *L* (1931) 314.
The poems enclosed, in the order ED names them, were: "The Savior must have been," "Dare you see a Soul at the White Heat," "A Route of Evanescence," and "My country need not change her gown."

To T. W. Higginson   *November 1880*

Dear friend,

Thank you for the advice – I shall implicitly follow it –

The one who asked me for the Lines, I had never seen –

He spoke of "a Charity" – I refused but did not inquire – He again earnestly urged, on the ground that in that way I might "aid unfortunate Children" – The name of "Child" was a snare to me and I hesitated – Choosing my most rudimentary, and without criterion, I inquired of you – You can scarcely estimate the opinion to one utterly guideless –

Again thank you –

Your Scholar –

MANUSCRIPT: BPL (Higg 111). Pencil.
PUBLICATION: *AM* LXVIII (October 1891) 451; *L* (1894) 330; *LL* 324–325; *L* (1931) 316.

This letter concludes the correspondence with Higginson relative to the selection of poems to be donated to the Mission Circle. One infers that Higginson advised her to offer one or more. Of the persons in Amherst who might have urged ED to contribute poems, the one who most nearly fits the description is Joseph K. Chickering, professor of English in Amherst College. ED in fact never saw him, then or later, though he was especially thoughtful at the time of Mrs. Dickinson's death in 1882. He unsuccessfully tried, more than once, to call on ED.

682

To Sally Jenkins   *late December 1880*

Dear "Did" –

Atmospherically it was the most beautiful Christmas on record – The Hens came to the Door with Santa Claus, and the Pussies washed themselves in the open Air without chilling their Tongues – and Santa Claus himself – sweet old Gentleman, was even gallanter than usual – Visitors from the Chimney were a new dismay, but all of them brought their Hands so full, and behaved so sweetly – only a Churl could have turned them away – And then the ones at the Barn, were so happy – Maggie gave her Hens a Check for Potatoes, and each of the Cats a Gilt Edged Bone – and the Horses had both new Blankets from Boston – Do you remember Dark Eyed Mr – Dickinson, who used to shake your Hand when it was so little it had hardly a Stem – He too had a beautiful Gift of Roses – from a friend away –

It was a lovely Christmas –

Please give my love to your Father and Mother – and the "Lantern" Brother, and the Lad unknown – But what made you remember me? Tell me, with a kiss, or is it a secret?

Emily –

[269]

MANUSCRIPT: HCL (L 36). Pencil.

PUBLICATION: *L* (1894) 371, in part; *LL* 295, in part; *FN* 63, in part; *L* (1931) 362, in part.

The "Lad unknown" is Austin Dickinson Jenkins, born in January 1879. Sally ("Did") was about fourteen; her brother Mac (MacGregor), eleven.

685

To Mrs. J. G. Holland   *early January 1881*

Sister Golconda must look very burnished in her Christmas Gifts, and the bashful Gem that the Scripture enjoins, "a meek and lowly Spirit," must be quite obscured – but one must clad demurely to please the Scripture's taste, a very plain Old Gentleman, with few Expenses out –

Your sweet light-hearted manner informed me more than statements, that the Doctor was better – the inferential Knowledge – the distinctest one, and I congratulate you – and not omit ourselves –

How sweet the "Life that now is," and how rugged to leave it – and ruggeder to stay behind when our Dear go –

A Little Boy ran away from Amherst a few Days ago, and when asked where he was going, replied, "Vermont or Asia." Many of us go farther. My pathetic Crusoe –

Vinnie had four Pussies for Christmas Gifts – and two from her Maker, previous, making six, in toto, and finding Assassins for them, is my stealthy Aim – Mother, we think unchanged – Vinnie's ideal "Irons" in the ideal "Fire" and me, prancing between – a Gymnastic Destiny –

Vails of Kamtchatka dim the Rose – in my Puritan Garden, and as a farther stimulus, I had an Eclipse of the Sun a few Mornings ago, but every Crape is charmed –

I knew a Bird that would sing as firm in the centre of Dissolution, as in it's Father's nest –
Phenix, or the Robin?
While I leave you to guess, I will take Mother her Tea –

Emily.

MANUSCRIPT: HCL (H 56). Pencil.

PUBLICATION: *LH* 137–138.
Dr. Holland had given his wife a pair of diamond earrings for Christmas. The *Amherst Record* for 29 December reports the disappearance of Jerry Scanlan (Scannell), aged fourteen. A few days later he turned up in Springfield. The new year opened with a few days of intense cold. There had been a partial eclipse of the sun on 31 December.

The "lowly Spirit" alludes to Matthew 11.29.

692

To Mrs. J. G. Holland   *spring 1881*

Dear Sister.

We are making a few simple repairs, what Dickens would call qualifications and aspects – and looking in Vinnie's Basket for the Lightning Rod, which she had mislaid, "What *would* Mrs Holland think" said Vinnie?

"I would inquire," I said.

I can always rely on your little Laugh, which is what the Essayist calls "the immortal Peewee."

Did you know that Father's "Horace" had died – the "Cap'n Cuttle" of Amherst? He had lived with us always, though was not congenial – so his loss is a pang to Tradition, rather than Affection – I am sure you remember him – He is the one who spoke patronizingly of the Years, of Trees he sowed in "26," or Frosts he met in "20," and was so legendary that it seems like the death of the College Tower, our first Antiquity – I remember he was at one time disinclined to gather the Winter Vegetables till they had frozen, and when Father demurred, he replied "Squire, ef the Frost is the Lord's Will, I dont popose to stan in the way of it." I hope a nearer inspection of that "Will" has left him with as ardent a bias in it's favor.

Vinnie is under terrific headway, but finds time to remember you with vivid affection – and Mother is unchanged, though my new gratitude every morning, that she is still with us, convinces me of her frailty.

Vinnie is eager to see the Face of George Eliot which the Doctor promised, and I wince in prospective, lest it be no more sweet. God chooses repellant settings, dont he, for his best Gems?

[271]

All you will say of yourselves is dear to Emily and Vinnie, and is'nt to say it soon – prudent – in so short a Life?

MANUSCRIPT: HCL (H 60). Pencil.
PUBLICATION: *LH* 143–144.

Horace Church, gardener and sexton of the First Church, died, 7 April 1881. Higginson's essay "The Life of Birds," published in the *Atlantic Monthly*, September, 1862, has the sentence: "And penetrating to some yet lonelier place, we find it consecrated to that life-long sorrow . . . which is made immortal in the plaintive cadence of the Peewee-Flycatcher." Cap'n Cuttle is a character in *Dombey and Son*. The picture of George Eliot which Dr. Holland had promised may have been the one used as a frontispiece in the first issue of the *Century Magazine*, November 1881, which Holland was preparing for the press.

714

To Susan Gilbert Dickinson   *about 1881*

Doctor –

How did you snare Howells?

                              Emily –

"Emily –

Case of Bribery – Money did it –
                              Holland –["]

MANUSCRIPT: HCL (B 17). Pencil.
PUBLICATION: LL 83, altered.

The date is conjectured from the handwriting. During the summer of 1881 William D. Howells's novel *A Fearful Responsibility* was appearing in installment in Holland's *Scribner's Monthly*. ED's note to Dr. Holland probably elicited the reply here quoted to Sue. The letter following, to Dr. Holland, seems to answer it.

715

To Dr. J. G. Holland   *about 1881*

Dear Doctor,

Your small Note was as merry as Honey, and enthralled us all – I sent it over to Sue, who took Ned's Arm and came across – and we talked of Mr Samuel and you, and vital times when you two bore the Republican, and came as near sighing – all of us – as would be often wise – I should say next door – Sue said she was homesick for those "better Days," hallowed be their name.

Amazing Human Heart – a syllable can make to quake like jostled Tree – what Infinite – for thee!

I wish you were rugged, and rejoice you are gay, and am re-convinced by your arch note that Unless we become as Rogues, we cannot enter the Kingdom of Heaven –

Emily.

MANUSCRIPT: HCL (H 58). Pencil.
PUBLICATION: *LH* 140–141.
This was evidently written shortly after ED received the "small Note," a copy of which she sent over to Sue. There is a hint toward the end of the first paragraph, which ED knew would be clear to the Hollands, that the stresses at the house next door have not abated.

719

To Jonathan L. Jenkins and family   *about 1881*

Dear friends,

You have our sympathy. When an old friend like the Decalogue, turns his back on us, who then can we trust?

Emily.

MANUSCRIPT: HCL (L 47). Pencil.
PUBLICATION: *FN* 98–99.
ED pasted this unidentified clipping onto the letter:
> John Jenkins, hailing from Philadelphia, was arrested
> at Baltimore yesterday on charge of passing counterfeit
> half and quarter-dollar pieces, and 200 pieces of counter-
> feit coin were found on his person. It is suspected that
> he is employed by a gang of counterfeiters.

721

To Mrs. J. G. Holland   *August 1881*

Dear Sister.

I think everything will get ripe today so it can be Autumn tomorrow if it would like, for such heat was never present and I think of your Forest and Sea as a far off Sherbet.

We have an artificial Sea, and to see the Birds follow the Hose for a Crumb of Water is a touching Sight. They wont take it if I hand it to them – they run and shriek as if they were being assassinated, but oh, to steal it, that is bliss – I cant say that their views are not current.

When I look in the Morning Paper to see how the President is, I know you are looking too, and for once in the Day I am sure where you are, which is very friendly.

The Pilgrim's Empire seems to stoop – I hope it will not fall –

We have a new Black Man and are looking for a Philanthropist to direct him, because every time he presents himself, I run, and when the Head of the Nation shies, it confuses the Foot –

When you read in the "Massachusetts items" that he has eaten us up, a memorial merriment will invest these preliminaries.

Who wrote Mr Howells' story? Certainly he did not. Shakespeare was never accused of writing Bacon's works, though to have been suspected of writing his, was the most beautiful stigma of Bacon's Life – Higher, is the doom of the High.

Doctor's betrothal to "Blanco" I trust you bear unmurmuringly. Mother and Vinnie wept – I read it to both at their request –

Thank you for surviving the duplicity – Thank you for not stopping being anxious about us. Not to outgrow Suspense, is beloved indeed.

Emily.

MANUSCRIPT: HCL (H 61). Pencil.
PUBLICATION: *LH* 145–146.
President Garfield, shot on 2 July, lingered through the summer and died, 19 September. On Howells's *A Fearful Responsibility*, which ED was finding not to her taste, see letter no. 714. The August issue of *Scribner's Monthly*, in which the Howells novel was concluded, also contained a poem by Holland: "To My Dog Blanco."

724

To Mrs. Samuel Bowles   *6 September 1881*

Dear Mary,

I give you only a word this mysterious morning in which we must light the lamps to see each other's faces, thanking you for the trust too confiding for speech.

You spoke of enclosing the face of your child. As it was not there, forgive me if I tell you, lest even the copy of sweetness abscond; and may I trust you received the flower the mail promised to take you, my foot being incompetent?

The timid mistake about being "forgotten," shall I caress or reprove? Mr. Samuel's "sparrow" does not "fall" without the fervent "notice."

"Would you see us, would Vinnie?" Oh, my doubting Mary! Were you and your brave son in my father's house, it would require more prowess than mine to resist seeing you.

Shall I still hope for the picture? And please address to my full name, as the little note was detained and opened, the name being so frequent in town, though not an Emily but myself.

Vinnie says "give her my love, and tell her I would delight to see her;" and mother combines.

There should be no tear on your cheek, dear, had my hand the access to brush it away.

Emily.

MANUSCRIPT: missing.
PUBLICATION: *L* (1894) 227; *LL* 331; *L* (1931) 212, where it is dated "Tuesday."

The phenomenon which ED records, known as "yellow day," occurred on Tuesday, 6 September 1881. The allusion to the sparrow recalls one of Hamlet's final remarks (*Hamlet*, V, ii, 229–233): ". . . there's a special providence in the fall of a sparrow. . . The readiness is all. . . ."

727

To Louise and Frances Norcross   *24 September 1881*

Dear Ones,

If I linger, this will not reach you before Sunday; if I do not, I must write you much less than I would love. "Do unto others as ye would that they should do unto you." I would rather they would do unto me *so*.

After infinite wanderings the little note has reached us. It was mailed the twelfth – we received it the twenty-third. The address "Misses Dickinson" misled the rustic eyes – the postmaster knows Vinnie, also by faith who Emily is, because his little girl was hurt, and Emily sent her juleps – but he failed of the intellectual grasp to combine the names. So after sending it to all the *Mrs.* Dickinsons he could discover, he consigned it to us, with the request that we would speedily return it if not ours, that he might renew his research. Almost any one under the circumstances would have doubted if it were theirs, or indeed if they were themself – but to us it was clear. Next time, dears, direct Vinnie, or Emily, and perhaps Mr. [Jameson]'s astuteness may be adequate. I enclose the battered remains for your Sabbath perusal, and tell you we think of you tenderly, which I trust you often believe.

Maggie is making a flying visit to cattle-show, on her very robust wings – for Maggie is getting corpulent. Vinnie is picking a few seeds – for if a pod "die, shall he not live again"; and with the shutting mail I go to read to mother about the President. When we think of the lone effort to live, and its bleak reward, the mind turns to the myth "for His mercy endureth forever," with confiding revulsion. Still, when Professor Fisk died on Mount Zion, Dr. Humphrey prayed "to whom shall we turn but thee"? "I have finished," said Paul, "the faith." We rejoice that he did not say discarded it.

The little postman has come – Thomas's "second oldest," and I close with reluctant and hurrying love.

Emily.

MANUSCRIPT: destroyed.

PUBLICATION: *L* (1894) 290–291; *L* (1931) 263–264, where it is dated: "Saturday," presumably the date given by ED.

The Cattle Show in 1881 took place on Saturday, 24 September. Garfield died, 19 September. The postmaster was John Jameson. Thomas Kelley was Maggie Maher's brother-in-law. For a note on Professor Fiske, which will explain the allusion here, see letter no. 1042. Most of the scriptural quotations are too well known to need identification. The last one, from 2 Timothy 4.7, may have been purposely altered: "I have fought a good fight, I have finished my course, I have kept the faith."

729

To Mrs. J. G. Holland   *October 1881*

We read the words but know them not. We are too frightened with sorrow. If that dear, tired one must sleep, could we not see him first?

Heaven is but a little way to one who gave it, here. "Inasmuch," to him, how tenderly fulfilled!

Our hearts have flown to you before — our breaking voices follow. How can we wait to take you all in our sheltering arms?

Could there be new tenderness, it would be for you, but the heart is full — another throb would split it — nor would we dare to speak to those whom such a grief removes, but we have somewhere heard "A little child shall lead them."

Emily.

MANUSCRIPT: missing.
PUBLICATION: L (1894) 183; L (1931) 176; LH 149.

Dr. Holland died of a heart attack, 12 October 1881. This letter was written immediately upon receipt of the telegram which notified the Dickinsons of his death. This and letter no. 730 were written to Mrs. Holland before the end of the month.

730

To Mrs. J. G. Holland　　　　　　　　　　　　　　　*October 1881*

Panting to help the dear ones and yet not knowing how, lest any voice bereave them but that loved voice that will not come, if I can rest them, here is down — or rescue, here is power.

One who only said "I am sorry" helped me the most when father ceased — it was too soon for language.

Fearing to tell mother, some one disclosed it unknown to us. Weeping bitterly, we tried to console her. She only replied "I loved him so."

Had he a tenderer eulogy?

Emily.

MANUSCRIPT: missing.
PUBLICATION: L (1894) 184; L (1931) 177; LH 149.

750

To Otis P. Lord　　　　　　　　　　　　　　　*30 April 1882*

His little "Playthings" were very sick all the Week that closed, and except the sweet Papa assured them, they could not believe – it had one grace however, it kept the faint Mama from sleep, so she could dream of Papa awake – an innocence of fondness.

To write you, not knowing where you are, is an unfinished pleasure – Sweeter of course than not writing, because it has a wandering Aim, of which you are the goal – but far from joyful like yourself, and moments we have known – I have a strong surmise that moments we have *not* known are tenderest to you. Of their afflicting Sweetness, you only are the judge, but the moments we had, were very good – they were quite contenting.

Very sweet to know from Morn to Morn what you thought and said – the Republican told us – though that Felons could see you and we could not, seemed a wondering fraud. I feared for your sweet Lungs in the crowded Air, the Paper spoke of "Throngs" – We were much amused at the Juror's "cough" you thought not pulmonary, and when you were waiting at your Hotel for the Kidder Verdict, and the Jury decided to go to sleep, I thought them the loveliest Jury I had ever met. I trust you are "at Home," though my Heart spurns the suggestion, hoping all – absence – but itself.

I am told it is only a pair of Sundays since you went from me. I feel it many years. Today is April's last – it has been an April of meaning to me. I have been in your Bosom. My Philadelphia [Charles Wadsworth] has passed from Earth, and the Ralph Waldo Emerson – whose name my Father's Law Student taught me, has touched the secret Spring. Which Earth are we in?

Heaven, a Sunday or two ago – but that also has ceased –

Momentousness is ripening. I hope that all is firm. Could we yield each other to the impregnable chances till we had met once more?

Monday –

Your's of a Yesterday is with me. I am cruelly grieved about the "Cold." I feared it, but entreated it to wrong some other one. Must it of all the Lives have come to trouble your's? Be gentle with it – Coax it – Dont drive it or 'twill stay – I'm glad you are "at Home." Please think it with a codicil. My own were homeless if you were. Was my sweet "Phil" "proud"? What Hour? Could you tell me? A momentary gleam of him between Morning . . .

. . . Door either, after you have entered, nor any Window, except in the Chimney, and if Folks knock at the Grass, the Grass can let them in. I almost wish it would, sometimes – with reverence I say it. That was a big – sweet Story – the number of times that "Little Phil" read his Letter, and the not so many, that Papa read his, but I am prepared for falsehood.

On subjects of which we know nothing, or should I say *Beings* – is "Phil" a "Being" or a "Theme," we both believe, and disbelieve a hundred times an Hour, which keeps Believing nimble.

But how can "Phil" have one opinion and Papa another – I thought the Rascals were inseparable – "but there again," as Mr New Bedford Eliot used to say, "I may be mistaken."

Papa has still many Closets that Love has never ransacked. I do – do want you tenderly. The Air is soft as Italy, but when it touches me, I spurn it with a Sigh, because it is not you. The Wanderers came last Night – Austin says they are brown as Berries and as noisy as Chipmunks, and feels his solitude much invaded, as far as I can learn. These dislocations of privacy among the *Privateers* amuse me very much, but "the Heart knoweth its own" Whim – and in Heaven they neither woo nor are given in wooing – what an imperfect place!

Mrs Dr Stearns called to know if we didnt think it very shocking for [Benjamin F.] Butler to "liken himself to his Redeemer," but we thought Darwin had thrown "the Redeemer" away. Please excuse the wandering writing. Sleeplessness makes my Pencil stumble. Affection clogs it – too. Our Life together was long forgiveness on your part toward me. The trespass of my rustic Love upon your Realms of Ermine, only a Sovreign could forgive – I never knelt to other – The Spirit never twice alike, but every time another – that other more divine. Oh, had I found it sooner! Yet Tenderness has not a Date – it comes – and overwhelms.

The time before it was – was naught, so why establish it? And all the time to come it is, which abrogates the time.

MANUSCRIPT: AC. Pencil. One page or more in the middle is missing; it is impossible to know whether pages are missing at the beginning and end. The letter is not a rough draft but a fair copy. It is dated: Sunday (and half way through): Monday. It was written on 30 April and 1 May.

PUBLICATION: *Revelation* 85–87.

Judge Lord presided at a murder trial which opened at Springfield, 25 April; on April 29 Dwight Kidder was convicted of manslaughter in the death of his half-brother Charles, and sentenced to prison for twenty years. The *Republican* reported the case in detail. In his own letter of 30 April, written from Salem, Lord evidently had mentioned a slight indisposition. On 1 May, the day ED concluded her letter, Lord was seriously stricken and lapsed into unconsciousness. On 3 May the *Republican* said that little hope was held for his recovery, but by 8 May he was reported past the crisis.

This letter was written two weeks after Lord had sojourned in Amherst for a few days in mid-April, before going to Springfield. Charles Wadsworth died 1 April; Emerson on 27 April.

751

To Abbie C. Farley   8 *May 1882*

Monday –

Dear Abby –

This was all the Letter we had this Morning – Was it not enough? Oh no – a tiding every Hour would not be enough – I hoped to hear nothing yesterday unless it were through you –

The last we knew was Hope, and that would last till Monday, but Austin brought a Morning Paper as soon as I was down – "I hope there'll be something of Mr Lord – I'll look it over here," he said – "Couldn't I find it quicker," I inquired timidly – Searching and finding nothing he handed the Paper to me – I found nothing, also – and felt relieved and disturbed too – Then I knew I should hear Monday, but Morning brought me nothing but just this little general Note to a listening World – Were our sweet Salem safe, it would be "May" indeed – I shall never forget "May Day."

All our flowers were draped –

Is he able to speak or to hear voices or to say "Come in," when his Amherst knocks?

Fill his Hand with Love as sweet as Orchard Blossoms, which he will share with each of you – I know his boundless ways –
As it was too much sorrow, so it is almost too much joy –

Lovingly,
Emily.

MANUSCRIPT: HCL. Pencil.
PUBLICATION: *Revelation* 62.

[280]

ED pasted at the top of the first page of the letter a clipping from the *Springfield Republican* for Monday, 8 May, reading: "Judge Lord has passed the crisis at Salem, and there is hope that he will soon be about again."

Among the rough drafts in the Bingham collection (AC) is the poem beginning "The Pile of Years is not so high." It is written on the verso of a discarded sheet of stationery, in the handwriting of about this time, that starts and ends thus:

> Dear Abby,
>   I am [gri]eved for Mary

Abbie Farley's cousin, another niece of the Judge, also lived with him.

752

To Otis P. Lord   *14 May 1882*

To remind you of my own rapture at your return, and of the loved steps, retraced almost from the "Undiscovered Country," I enclose the Note I was fast writing, when the fear that your Life had ceased, came, fresh, yet dim, like the horrid Monsters fled from in a Dream.

Happy with my Letter, without a film of fear, Vinnie came in from a word with Austin, passing to the Train. "Emily, did you see anything in the Paper that concerned us"? "Why no, Vinnie, what"? "Mr Lord is very sick." I grasped at a passing Chair. My sight slipped and I thought I was freezing. While my last smile was ending, I heard the Doorbell ring and a strange voice said "I thought first of you." Meanwhile, Tom [Kelley] had come, and I ran to his Blue Jacket and let my Heart break there – that was the warmest place. "He will be better. Dont cry Miss Emily. I could not see you cry."

Then Vinnie came out and said "Prof. Chickering thought we would like to telegraph." He "would do it for us."

"Would I write a Telegram"? I asked the Wires how you did, and attached my name.

The Professor took it, and Abby's brave – refreshing reply I shall remember

MANUSCRIPT: AC. Pencil. Dated: Sunday. The letter, which seems to be incomplete, is a fair copy.

PUBLICATION: *Revelation* 87.

ED received an immediate reply from Abbie Farley, and wrote this letter on the Sunday following.

The nature of the next letter, from Washington Gladden, dated Springfield, 27 May 1882 (HCL – unpublished), suggests that when ED made the inquiry which his reply answers, she did so having in mind the death of Wadsworth and the serious illness of Lord.

752a

My friend:

"Is immortality true?" I believe that it is true – the only reality – almost; a thousand times truer than mortality, which is but a semblance after all. I believe that virtue is deathless; that God who is the source of virtue, gave to her "the glory of going on, and not to die"; that the human soul, with which virtue is incorporate, cannot perish. I believe in the life everlasting, because Jesus Christ taught it. Say what you will about him, no one can deny that he knew the human soul, its nature, its laws, its destinies, better than any other being who ever trod this earth; and he testifies, and his testimony is more clear, more definite, more positive on this than on any other subject, that there is life beyond the grave.

"In my Father's house are many mansions: if it were not so I would have told you."

Absolute demonstration there can be none of this truth; but a thousand lines of evidence converge toward it; and I believe it. It is all I can say. God forbid that I should flatter one who is dying with any illusive hope; but this hope is not illusive. May God's spirit gently lead this hope into the heart of your friend, and make it at home there, so that in the last days it shall be an anchor to the soul, sure and steadfast –

Your friend
Washington Gladden

757

To Susan Gilbert Dickinson   *about* 1882

Dear Sue –

With the exception of Shakespeare, you have told me of more

knowledge than any one living – To say that sincerely is strange praise.

MANUSCRIPT: missing. The text derives from a photostat reproduction (HCL B 2).
PUBLICATION: LL 64; FF 176 (facsimile reproduction).
The strain between the two houses about this time had perhaps a temporary fission. Mrs. Bingham quotes a conversation between her mother and Susan Dickinson in the fall of 1881, when the Todds first arrived in Amherst. Lavinia had asked Mrs. Todd to call. "Sue said at that, 'You will not allow your husband to go there, I hope! . . . I went in there one day, and in the drawing room I found Emily reclining in the arms of a man.'" (*Revelation* 59). It is probable that Sue's resentment concerning the attachment of Emily to Judge Lord was made clear to Emily, and may account for this note of "strange praise."

769

To Mabel Loomis Todd   *late September 1882*

Dear Friend,

That without suspecting it you should send me the preferred flower of life, seems almost supernatural, and the sweet glee that I felt at meeting it, I could confide to none. I still cherish the clutch with which I bore it from the ground when a wondering Child, an unearthly booty, and maturity only enhances mystery, never decreases it. To duplicate the Vision is almost more amazing, for God's unique capacity is too surprising to surprise.

I know not how to thank you. We do not thank the Rainbow, although it's Trophy is a snare.

To give delight is hallowed – perhaps the toil of Angels, whose avocations are concealed –

I trust that you are well, and the quaint little Girl with the deep Eyes, every day more fathomless.

With joy,

E. Dickinson.

MANUSCRIPT: AC. Pencil. Envelope addressed (by George Montague): Mrs. Todd/#1413 College Hill Terrace/Washington/D. C. Postmarked: Brat. & Palmer Jct. Sep 30.
PUBLICATION: L (1894) 430–431; L (1931) 419–420.

Mrs. Todd was in Washington at the time, and sent a panel of Indian pipes, which she had painted. On 2 October she recorded receipt of this letter.

772

To Mrs. William F. Stearns   *October 1882*

Dear friend,

Affection wants you to know it is here. Demand it to the utmost.

Tenderly,
E. Dickinson.

MANUSCRIPT: missing.
PUBLICATION: *L* (1894) 407; *LL* 335; *L* (1931) 396.
Mrs. Stearns's daughter Ethel died, 15 October.

773

To James D. Clark   *1882*

Dear friend,

Perhaps Affection has always one question more which it forgot to ask.

I thought it possible you might tell me if our lost one had Brother or Sister.

I knew he once had a Mother, for when he first came to see me, there was Black with his Hat. "Some one has died" I said. "Yes" — he said, "his Mother."

"Did you love her," I asked. He replied with his deep "Yes." I felt too that perhaps you, or the one you confidingly call "Our Charlie," might know if his Children were near him at last, or if they grieved to lose that most sacred Life. Do you know do they resemble him? I hoped that "Willie" might, to whom he clung so tenderly. How irreparable should there be no perpetuation of a nature so treasured! [Wh] Please forgive the requests which I hope have not wearied you, except as bereavement always wearies.

The sharing a sorrow never lessens, but when a Balm departs, the Plants that nearest grew have a grieved significance and you cherished my friend. My Sister gives her love to you. We hope you are more strong.

E. Dickinson.

MANUSCRIPT: AC. Pencil. (ED wrote, then crossed out, the letters in brackets.)
PUBLICATION: L (1931) 345.
Wadsworth's mother died, 1 October 1859.

777

To Maria Whitney   *14 November 1882*

Tuesday

Sweet friend,

Our Mother ceased –

While we bear her dear form through the Wilderness, I am sure you are with us.

Emily.

MANUSCRIPT: Princeton University Library. Pencil.
PUBLICATION: L (1894) 340; LL 344; L (1931) 329.
This was written on the day Mrs. Dickinson died.

779

To Mrs. J. G. Holland   *November 1882*

The dear Mother that could not walk, has *flown*. It never occurred to us that though she had not Limbs, she had *Wings* – and she soared from us unexpectedly as a summoned Bird – She had a few weeks since a violent cold, though so had we all, but our's recovered apparently, her's seemed more reluctant – but her trusted Physician was with her, who returned her to us so many times when she thought to go, and he felt no alarm – After her cough ceased she suffered much from neuralgic pain, which as nearly as we can know, committed the last wrong – She seemed entirely better the last Day of her Life and took Lemonade – Beef Tea and Custard with a pretty ravenousness that delighted us. After a restless Night, complaining of great weariness, she was lifted earlier than usual from her Bed to her Chair, when a few quick breaths and a "Dont leave me, Vinnie" and her sweet being closed – That the one we have cherished so softly so long, should be in that great Eternity without our simple Counsels, seems frightened and foreign, but we hope that Our Sparrow has ceased to fall, though at first we believe nothing –

Thank you for the Love — I was sure whenever I lost my own I should find your Hand –

The Clover you brought me from Father's Grave, Spring will sow on Mother's – and she carried Violets in her Hand to encourage her.

Remember me to your Annie and Kate. Tell them I envy them their Mother. "Mother"! What a Name!

Emily.

MANUSCRIPT: HCL (H 72). Pencil.
PUBLICATION: LH 165.
The second paragraph suggests that this is a reply to a letter of condolence from Mrs. Holland.

813

To Thomas Niles   *mid-March 1883*

Dear friend.

I bring you a chill Gift – My Cricket and the Snow. A base return indeed, for the delightful Book, which I infer from you, but an earnest one.

With thanks,
E. Dickinson.

MANUSCRIPT: AC. Pencil.
PUBLICATION: L (1894) 416; LL 341; L (1931) 406.
This letter was written in response to the letter following, from Thomas Niles, dated 13 March 1883. His letter was soon followed by a copy of Mathilde Blind's *Life of George Eliot*, published by Roberts Brothers on 17 March. The poems ED enclosed were "Further in Summer than the Birds" (incorporated in the letter preceding the signature), and "It sifts from Leaden Sieves" (separately enclosed). This letter exchange was prob-

ably initiated by ED in a letter (now missing) to Niles inquiring — as she had done a year before — whether Cross's *Life* of George Eliot was in progress.

813a

Dear Miss Dickinson

I do not hear anything about the Life of George Eliot by Mr Cross — at least only rumors that he is at work upon it.

We shall publish on Saturday a life of her by Mathilde Blind wh. will be worth your reading.

I shall be glad at any time to answer your inquiries

Very truly
T. Niles

As a further mark of her appreciation, ED sent Niles her own copy of the Brontë sisters' poems, which on 31 March the publisher acknowledged thus (all Niles's letters to ED are at HCL in the Dickinson collection, and are unpublished).

813b

My dear Miss Dickinson

I received the copy of "Currer, Ellis & Acton Bells Poems." I already have a copy of a later Ed. which contains all of these and additional poems by Ellis & Acton.

Surely you did not mean to present me with your copy — if you did, I thank you heartily, but in doing so I must add that I would not for the world rob you of this very rare book, of which this is such a nice copy.

If I may presume to say so, I will take instead a M.S. collection of your poems, that is, if you want to give them to the world through the medium of a publisher

Very truly yours
T. Niles

I return the precious little volume by mail.

ED made no response to this request for a manuscript collection of her poems; instead, she sent him a copy of "No Brigadier throughout the Year," for which he seems to have thanked her, remarking that he liked it better than the first two she had sent.

815

To Maria Whitney   *spring 1883*

Dear Friend,

The guilt of having sent the note had so much oppressed me that I hardly dared to read the reply, and delayed my heart almost to its stifling, sure you would never receive us again. To come unto our own and our own fail to receive us, is a sere response.

I hope you may forgive us.

All is faint indeed without our vanished mother, who achieved in sweetness what she lost in strength, though grief of wonder at her fate made the winter short, and each night I reach finds my lungs more breathless, seeking what it means.

> To the bright east she flies
> Brothers of Paradise
> Remit her home,
> Without a change of wings,
> Or Love's convenient things,
> Enticed to come.
>
> Fashioning what she is,
> Fathoming what she was,
> We deem we dream —
> And that dissolves the days
> Through which existence strays
> Homeless at home.

The sunshine almost speaks, this morning, redoubling the division, and Paul's remark grows graphic, "the *weight* of glory."

I am glad you have an hour for books, those enthralling friends, the immortalities, perhaps, each may pre-receive. "And I saw the Heavens opened."

[288]

I hope that nothing pains you except the pang of life, sweeter to bear than to omit.

With love and wonder,

Emily.

MANUSCRIPT: missing.
PUBLICATION: *L* (1894) 340–341; *LL* 349–350; *L* (1931) 329–330.

Sometime during the early spring Maria Whitney had called at the Dickinson house, and ED had sent word to her saying that she could not receive her. This letter replies to the letter that Maria Whitney subsequently wrote. The first quotation is from 2 Corinthians 4.17: "For our light affliction, which is but for a moment, worketh for us a far more exceeding and eternal weight of glory." The second is from Revelation 19.11.

826

To Charles H. Clark   *early June 1883*

I had, dear friend, the deep hope that I might see your Brother before he passed from Life, or rather Life we know, and can scarcely express the pang I feel at it's last denial.

His rare and hallowed kindness had strangely endeared him, and I cannot be comforted not to thank him before he went so far. I never had met your Brother but once.

An unforgotten once. To have seen him but once more, would have been almost like an interview with my "Heavenly Father," whom he loved and knew. I hope he was able to speak with you in his closing moment. One accent of courage as he took his flight would assist your Heart. I am eager to know all you may tell me of those final Days. We asked for him every Morning, in Heart, but feared to disturb you by inquiry aloud. I hope you are not too far exausted from your "loved employ."

To know of you, when possible, would console us much, and every circumstance of him we had hoped to see. My Sister gives her love with mine.

Though Strangers, please accept us for the two great sakes.

E. D.

MANUSCRIPT: AC. Pencil. Envelope addressed by Lavinia.

PUBLICATION: L (1894) 359; L (1931) 351.
James D. Clark died, 2 June 1883. Charles Clark dated this letter, 6 June.

829

To Edward (Ned) Dickinson   *19 June 1883*

Stay with us one more Birthday, Ned –
"Yesterday, Today, and Forever," then we will let you go.

Aunt Emily.

MANUSCRIPT: HCL (B 120). Pencil.
PUBLICATION: FF 255.
Ned's birthday was on 19 June. During the summer of 1883 Ned suffered from acute rheumatic fever. The quotation is from Hebrews 13.8: "Jesus Christ the same yesterday, and today, and forever."

830

To Maria Whitney   *late June 1883*

Dear Friend,

You are like God. We pray to Him, and He answers "No." Then we pray to Him to rescind the "no," and He don't answer at all, yet "Seek and ye shall find" is the boon of faith.

You failed to keep your appointment with the apple-blossoms – the japonica, even, bore an apple to elicit you, but that must be a silver bell which calls the human heart.

I still hope that you live, and in lands of consciousness.

It is Commencement now. Pathos is very busy.

The past is not a package one can lay away. I see my father's eyes, and those of Mr. Bowles – those isolated comets. If the future is mighty as the past, what may vista be?

With my foot in a sling from a vicious sprain, and reminded of you almost to tears by the week and its witness, I send this sombre word.

The vane defines the wind.

Where we thought you were, Austin says you are not. How strange to change one's sky, unless one's star go with it, but yours has left an astral wake.

Vinnie gives her hand.

Always with love,

Emily.

MANUSCRIPT: missing.
PUBLICATION: *L* (1894) 342–343; *LL* 351–352; *L* (1931) 331–332.
Commencement took place on 27 June.

838

To Mrs. J. Howard Sweetser   *summer 1883*

Dear Nellie,

To have woven Wine so delightfully, one must almost have been a Drunkard one's-self – but that is the stealthy franchise of the demurest Lips. Drunkards of Summer are quite as frequent as Drunkards of Wine, and the Bee that comes Home sober is the Butt of the Clover.

Emily.

MANUSCRIPT: Rosenbach 1170/18 (16). Pencil. Unpublished.

842

To Otis P. Lord   *about 1883*

The withdrawal of the Fuel of Rapture does not withdraw the Rapture itself.

Like Powder in a Drawer, we pass it with a Prayer, it's Thunders only dormant.

MANUSCRIPT: AC. Pencil. Fragment fair copy.
PUBLICATION: *Revelation* 84–85.
The date of this fragment is conjectured from the handwriting.

To Susan Gilbert Dickinson   *about 1883*

Dear Susan,

An untimely knock necessitating my flight from the Kettle, the Berries were overdone – I almost fear to send them, though hope they may have a worthless worth to those for whom they were –

Emily –

MANUSCRIPT: HCL (B 146). Pencil.
PUBLICATION: *FF* 246.

865

To Samuel Bowles the younger?   *about 1883*

To ask of each that gathered Life, Oh, where did it grow, is intuitive.

That you have answered this Prince Question to your own delight, is joy to us all.

> Lad of Athens, faithful be
> To Thyself,
> And Mystery –
> All the rest is Perjury –

Please say with my tenderness to your Mother, I shall soon write her.

E. Dickinson —

MANUSCRIPT: AC. Pencil.
PUBLICATION: *L* (1931) 415.

The recipient of this letter is not known. The handwriting is almost certainly late 1883. No other relationship of son and mother, in ED's associations, suggests itself except that with Bowles. Her signature here is that she used to him. The tone of the message is one she adopted for those about to be married.

To Mrs. J. Howard Sweetser   *early October 1883*

Thank you, Dear, for the loveliness. It is very sweet to know you are near. We are so much grieved for the little Boy –

Emily –

MANUSCRIPT: Pohl. Pencil. Unpublished.

The handwriting is unmistakably late 1883. Very early in October, Gilbert Dickinson was stricken with typhoid fever, and died after a few days' illness, on 5 October. No death during ED's lifetime more deeply shocked and grieved her. This letter was probably written during Gilbert's illness, but before he died.

868

To Susan Gilbert Dickinson   *early October 1883*

Dear Sue –

The Vision of Immortal Life has been fulfilled –

How simply at the last the Fathom comes! The Passenger and not the Sea, we find surprises us –

Gilbert rejoiced in Secrets –

His Life was panting with them – With what menace of Light he cried "Dont tell, Aunt Emily"! Now my ascended Playmate must instruct *me*. Show us, prattling Preceptor, but the way to thee!

He knew no niggard moment – His Life was full of Boon – The Playthings of the Dervish were not so wild as his –

No crescent was this Creature – He traveled from the Full –

Such soar, but never set –

I see him in the Star, and meet his sweet velocity in everything that flies – His Life was like the Bugle, which winds itself away, his Elegy an echo – his Requiem ecstasy –

Dawn and Meridian in one.

Wherefore would he wait, wronged only of Night, which he left for us –

Without a speculation, our little Ajax spans the whole –

> Pass to thy Rendezvous of Light,
> Pangless except for us –
> Who slowly ford the Mystery
> Which thou hast leaped across!

Emily.

MANUSCRIPT: HCL (B 79). Pencil.
PUBLICATION: AM CXV (1915) 42; LL 85.

This most moving Emily Dickinson letter was written after her eight-year-old nephew died of typhoid fever.

873

To Mrs. J. G. Holland *late 1883*

Sweet Sister.

Was that what I used to call you?

I hardly recollèct, all seems so different –

I hesitate which word to take, as I can take but few and each must be the chiefest, but recall that Earth's most graphic transaction is placed within a syllable, nay, even a gaze –

The Physician says I have "Nervous prostration."

Possibly I have – I do not know the Names of Sickness. The Crisis of the sorrow of so many years is all that tires me – As Emily Bronte to her Maker, I write to my Lost "Every Existence would exist in thee –"

The tender consternation for you was much eased by the little Card, which spoke *"better"* as loud as a human Voice –

Please, Sister, to wait –

"Open the Door, open the Door, they are waiting for me," was Gilbert's sweet command in delirium. *Who* were waiting for him, all we possess we would give to know – Anguish at last opened it, and he ran to the little Grave at his Grandparents' feet – All this and more, though *is* there more? More than Love and Death? Then tell me it's name!

Love for the sweet Catharines, Rose and Bud in one, and the Gentleman with the vast Name, and Annie and Ted, and if the softest for yourself, would they ever know, or knowing, covet?

How lovely that you went to "Church"!

May I go with you to the "Church of the first born?"

Emily –

MANUSCRIPT: HCL (H 83). Pencil.

PUBLICATION: LH 182–183.

Gilbert's last words are quoted also, somewhat differently, in letter no. 1020.

The quoted line of poetry is from Emily Brontë's "Last Lines." Higginson read the poem at ED's funeral. The final quotation is from Hebrews 12.23.

876

To Kendall Emerson   *Christmas 1883*

Dear Kendall –

Christmas in Bethlehem means most of all, this Year, but Santa Claus still asks the way to Gilbert's little friends – Is Heaven an unfamiliar Road?

Come sometime with your Sled and tell Gilbert's

Aunt Emily.

MANUSCRIPT: AC. Pencil.

PUBLICATION: *Amherst Alumni News* IV (July 1951) 14.

ED's special feeling for Gilbert's playmate stemmed from the fact that both children had been playing in the same mud hole when Gilbert contracted the typhoid fever from which he died. She continued annually to remember Kendall with a Christmas note (see letters no. 956 and 1027).

877

To Mrs. Henry Hills   *Christmas 1883*

Santa Claus comes with a Smile and a Tear. Santa Claus has been robbed, not by Burglars but Angels. The Children will pray for Santa Claus?

MANUSCRIPT: missing. Unpublished. The text is from a transcript made by George Frisbie Whicher of the autograph when it was still in the possession of Mrs. Hills's daughter, Mrs. Susan H. Skillings. He thought it might have been written in 1872. It is in ink, on paper watermarked 1862.

XII

1884–1886

". . . A Letter is a joy of Earth –
it is denied the Gods."

The elegiac tone of Emily Dickinson's letters, evident after Gilbert's death, becomes insistent after the death of Judge Lord in March 1884. In June she suffered a nervous breakdown and, though she kept up her correspondence, her strength was ebbing and she never fully regained her health. But she continued to read and to correspond about books. Indeed, the long-awaited publication of the first volume of Cross's biography of George Eliot, in 1885, was an event that raised her spirit.

The unexpected passing of Helen Jackson in August 1885, occurred about the time her own final illness was upon her, and after November she was confined for long periods to her room and bed. Yet her pencil was always beside her, and the final messages appropriately were sent to Mrs. Holland, to Colonel Higginson, and to the Norcross cousins.

Perhaps no sentence that she wrote more aptly epitomizes her relationship with people than this, written to James Clark in 1882: "A Letter always seemed to me like Immortality, for is it not the Mind alone, without corporeal friend?" They are the words she had used in writing Higginson in 1869, when for the most part prose rather than poetry had become the mode of her expression.

To Charles H. Clark   *early January 1884*

Dear friend –

I have been very ill since early October, and unable to thank you for the sacred kindness, but treasured it each Day and hasten with my first steps, and my fullest gratitude. Returning from the dying Child, waiting till he left us, I found it on my Desk, and it seemed an appropriate Message – I never can thank you as I feel –

That would be impossible.

The effort ends in tears.

You seem by some deep Accident, to be the only tie between the Heaven that evanesced, and the Heaven that stays.

I hope the winged Days that bear you to your Brother, are not too destitute of Song, and wish that we might speak with you of him and of yourself, and of the third Member of that sundered Trio. Perhaps another spring would call you to Northampton, and Memory might invite you here.

My Sister asks a warm remembrance, and trusts that you are well. With a deep New Year,

Your friend,

E. Dickinson.

MANUSCRIPT: AC. Pencil. Envelope addressed by Lavinia Dickinson: C. H. Clark/361 Degraw St./Brooklyn/L.I. Postmarked: Jan 4 1884.

PUBLICATION: L (1894) 361–362, in part; LL 360, in part; L (1931) 353, entire.

The "third Member" was probably Wadsworth.

886

To Susan Gilbert Dickinson   *February 1884*

Dear Sue –

I was surprised, but Why? Is she not of the lineage of the Spirit?

I knew she was beautiful – I knew she was royal, but that she was hallowed, how could I surmise, who had scarcely seen her since her deep Eyes were brought in your Arms to her Grandfather's – Thanksgiving? She is a strange trust – I hope she may be saved – Redemption Mental precedes Redemption Spiritual. The Madonna and Child descend from the Picture – while Creation is kneeling before the Frame – I shall keep the secret.

Emily.

MANUSCRIPT: HCL (B 102). Pencil.
PUBLICATION: *LL* 54, in part; *FF* 171, in part.

Although the allusion to the Madonna and child is obscure, the picture referred to has been tentatively identified with a photograph of Martha Dickinson (HCL) by Lovell, Amherst, inscribed on the back: With dearest love of/Your Valentine/February the 14th 1884. Since this letter is to Susan, not to Martha, one infers that Susan lent ED the photograph which Martha gave to her mother. It is probable that ED actually saw little of Martha at this time.

888

To Mrs. J. G. Holland   *early 1884*

The Organ is moaning – the Bells are bowing, I ask Vinnie what time it is, and she says it is Sunday, so I tell my Pencil to make no noise, and we will go to the House of a Friend "Weeks off," as Dombey said –

Your reunion with Vinnie was amusing and affecting too, and Vinnie still rehearses it to admiring throngs of which Stephen and I are the thrilled components – I think Vinnie has grown since the interview, certainly intellectually, which is the only Bone whose Expanse we woo –

Your flight from the "Sewer" reminded me of the "Mill on the Floss," though "Maggie Tulliver" was missing, and had she been there, her Destiny could not have been packed in the "Bath Tub," though Baby's may be as darkly sweet in the Future running to meet her –

How quickly a House can be deserted, and your infinite inference that the "Soul's poor Cottage" may lose it's Tenant so, was vaster than

[300]

you thought, and still overtakes me —

How few suggestions germinate!

I shall make Wine Jelly Tonight and send you a Tumbler in the Letter, if the Letter consents, a Fabric sometimes obdurate —

It is warm you are better, and was very cold all the while you were ill —

Baby's flight will embellish History with Gilpin's and Revere's — With love untold,

Your Emily —

MANUSCRIPT: HCL (H 85). Pencil.
PUBLICATION: LH 185–186.

Mrs. Holland had been visiting in Northampton and Vinnie had called on her. Stephen Sullivan was the stableman (see Appendix). The Van Wagenens, with whom Mrs. Holland now lived, were driven out of their house one night that winter by a clogged sewer which flooded the cellar, and had transported the baby's clothes to a nearby hotel in a small tin bathtub. The quoted words in the fourth paragraph reflect a line by Edmund Waller: "The soul's dark cottage, batter'd and decayed."

889

To Maria Whitney   *March 1884?*

Dear Friend,

The little package of Ceylon arrived in fragrant safety, and Caliban's "clust'ring filberds" were not so luscious nor so brown.

Honey in March is blissful as inopportune, and to caress the bee a severe temptation, but was not temptation the first zest?

We shall seek to be frugal with our sweet possessions, though their enticingness quite leads us astray, and shall endow Austin, as we often do, after a parched day.

For how much we thank you.

Dear arrears of tenderness we can never repay till the will's great ores are finally sifted; but bullion is better than minted things, for it has no alloy.

Thinking of you with fresher love, as the Bible boyishly says, "New every morning and fresh every evening."

Emily.

MANUSCRIPT: missing.

PUBLICATION: *L* (1894) 346; *L* (1931) 334–335. Mrs. Todd dated the letter: "Probably 1884."

It is Caliban speaking to Trinculo who says (*Tempest*, II, ii, 170–171): "I'll bring thee/To clustering filberds." The scripture quotation is from Lamentations 3.22–23: "It is of the Lord's mercies that we are not consumed, because his compassions fail not. They are new every morning: great is thy faithfulness."

890

To Mrs. J. G. Holland   *March 1884*

When I tell my sweet Mrs Holland that I have lost another friend, she will not wonder I do not write, but that I raise my Heart to a drooping syllable – Dear Mr Lord has left us – After a brief unconsciousness, a Sleep that ended with a smile, so his Nieces tell us, he hastened away, "seen," we trust, "of Angels" – "Who knows that secret deep" – "Alas, not I –"

Forgive the Tears that fell for few, but that few too many, for was not each a World?

Your last dear words seemed stronger, and smiling in the feeling that you were to be, this latest sorrow came – I hope your own are with you, and may not be taken – I hope there is no Dart advancing or in store –

> Quite empty, quite at rest,
> The Robin locks her Nest, and tries her Wings.
> She does not know a Route
> But puts her Craft about
> For *rumored* Springs –
> She does not ask for Noon –
> She does not ask for Boon,
> Crumbless and homeless, of but one request –
> The Birds she lost –

Do you remember writing to us you should "write with the Robins?" They are writing *now*, their Desk in every passing Tree, but the Magic of Mates that cannot hear them, makes their Letters dim –

[302]

Later –

Vinnie described it all – The going up to take Medicine and forgetting to return – How many times I have taken that very Medicine myself, with lasting benefit! The Jelly and the pink Cheek, the little clutchings at her frame, to make the grace secure, that had too many Wings – Vinnie omitted nothing, and I followed her around, never hearing enough of that mysterious interview, for was it not a lisp from the irrevocable?

> Within that little Hive
> Such Hints of Honey lay
> As made Reality a Dream
> And Dreams, Reality –

Emily

MANUSCRIPT: HCL (H 86). Pencil.
PUBLICATION: *LH* 186–188.

Judge Lord died, 13 March 1884. The quotation "seen of Angels" is from 1 Timothy 3.16. "Who knows that secret deep" may attempt to recall *Paradist Lost*, XII, 575–578: "This having learned, thou hast attained the sum/Of wisdom/. . . All secrets of the deep. . ."

Mrs. Holland had evidently written to ask whether Vinnie had given details of the encounter referred to in letter no. 888, so that here ED adds a postcript assuring Mrs. Holland that Vinnie had indeed omitted no detail.

891

To Louise and Frances Norcross   *late March 1884*

Thank you, dears, for the sympathy. I hardly dare to know that I have lost another friend, but anguish finds it out.

> Each that we lose takes part of us;
> A crescent still abides,
> Which like the moon, some turbid night,
> Is summoned by the tides.

. . . I work to drive the awe away, yet awe impels the work.

I almost picked the crocuses, you told them so sincerely. Spring's first conviction is a wealth beyond its whole experience.

The sweetest way I think of you is when the day is done, and Loo sets the "sunset tree" for the little sisters. Dear Fanny has had many stormy mornings; . . . I hope they have not chilled her feet, nor dampened her heart. I am glad the little visit rested you. Rest and water are most we want.

I know each moment of Miss W[hitney] is a gleam of boundlessness. "Miles and miles away," said Browning, "there's a girl"; but "the colored end of evening smiles" on but few so rare.

Thank you once more for being sorry. Till the first friend dies, we think ecstasy impersonal, but then discover that he was the cup from which we drank it, itself as yet unknown. Sweetest love for each, and a kiss besides for Miss W[hitney]'s cheek, should you again meet her.

Emily.

MANUSCRIPT: destroyed.
PUBLICATION: L (1894) 296–297; LL 345–346; L (1931) 267–268.
This letter responds to a note of sympathy after the death of Judge Lord. The Norcross sisters were especially fond of Maria Whitney. Fanny Norcross was now working as librarian at the Harvard Divinity School, and commuting daily between Concord and Cambridge. ED tries in this letter to recall lines from Browning's "Love Among the Ruins," which opens with the lines: "Where the quiet-coloured end of evening smiles/ Miles and miles." Stanzas 9 and 10 contain the lines: "And I know, while thus the quiet-coloured eve/Smiles to leave . . . That a girl with eager eyes and yellow hair/Waits me there."

898

To Daniel Chester French *April 1884*

Dear Mr. French: –

We learn with delight of the recent acquisition to your fame, and hasten to congratulate you on an honor so reverently won.

Success is dust, but an aim forever touched with dew.

God keep you fundamental!

> Circumference, thou bride
> Of awe, – possessing, thou
> Shalt be possessed by

[304]

Every hallowed knight
That dares to covet thee.

> Yours faithfully,
> Emily Dickinson

MANUSCRIPT: missing.
PUBLICATION: *FF* 58, in part; *Poems* (1955) 1112.

The text is from a transcript supplied the editor by French's daughter, Mrs. William Penn Cresson. The John Harvard statue was unveiled in the Harvard Yard in April 1884. ED probably did not know him well, though he had lived as a boy in Amherst; but Susan Dickinson did, and he was a friend of the Norcross cousins.

899

To Martha Gilbert Smith   *about 1884*

Dear Mattie –

Your "our own" was sweet – Thank you for your constancy –

Icebergs italicize the Sea – they do not intercept it, and "Deep calls to the Deep" in the old way –

To attempt to speak of what has been, would be impossible. Abyss has no Biographer –

Had it, it would not be Abyss – Love for your Little Girl – tho' *is* it now a "Little Girl," Time makes such hallowed strides? The Little Boy was taken –

Ineffable Avarice of Jesus, who reminds a perhaps encroaching Father, "All these are mine."

> Emily –

MANUSCRIPT: HCL (L 29). Pencil.
PUBLICATION: *FF* 252.
This was written while grief for Gilbert's death was still poignant.

901

To Mrs. J. G. Holland   *early June 1884*

Sweet friend.

I hope you brought your open Fire with you, else your confiding

Nose has ere this been nipped –

Three dazzling Winter Nights have wrecked the budding Gardens, and the Bobolinks stand as still in the Meadow as if they had never danced –

I hope your Heart has kept you warm – Should I say your Hearts, for you are yet a Banker –

Death cannot plunder half so fast as Fervor can re-earn –

We had one more, "Memorial Day," to whom to carry Blossoms –

Gilbert had Lilies of the Valley, and Father and Mother, Damson-Hawthorn –

When it shall come my turn, I want a Buttercup – Doubtless the Grass will give me one, for does she not revere the Whims of her flitting Children?

I was with you in all the loneliness, when you took your flight, for every jostling of the Spirit barbs the Loss afresh – even the coming out of the Sun after an Hour's Rain, intensifies their Absence –

Ask some kind Voice to read to you Mark Antony's Oration over his Playmate Caesar –

I never knew a broken Heart to break itself so sweet –

I am glad if Theodore balked the Professors – Most such are Manikins, and a warm blow from a brave Anatomy, hurls them into Wherefores –

MANUSCRIPT: HCL (H 87). Pencil.
PUBLICATION: *LH* 188–189.
Theodore Holland graduated from Columbia Law School in June 1884. The allusion is probably to an oral examination. Mrs. Holland had left New York for her summer home. Amherst weather records indicate that there were freezing temperatures on three successive nights, 29–31 May 1884.

907

To Louise and Frances Norcross   *early August 1884*

Dear Cousins,

I hope you heard Mr. Sanborn's lecture. My *Republican* was borrowed before I waked, to read till my own dawn, which is rather tardy, for I have been quite sick, and could claim the immortal reprimand, "Mr. Lamb, you come down very late in the morning." Eight Saturday noons ago, I was making a loaf of cake with Maggie, when I saw a great darkness coming and knew no more until late at night. I woke to find Austin and Vinnie and a strange physician bending over me, and supposed I was dying, or had died, all was so kind and hallowed. I had fainted and lain unconscious for the first time in my life. Then I grew very sick and gave the others much alarm, but am now staying. The doctor calls it "revenge of the nerves"; but who but Death had wronged them? Fanny's dear note has lain unanswered for this long season, though its "Good-night, my dear," warmed me to the core. I have all to say, but little strength to say it; so we must talk by degrees. I do want to know about Loo, what pleases her most, book or tune or friend.

I am glad the housekeeping is kinder; it is a prickly art. Maggie is with us still, warm and wild and mighty, and we have a gracious boy at the barn. We remember you always, and one or the other often comes down with a "we dreamed of Fanny and Loo last night"; then that day we think we shall hear from you, for dreams are couriers.

The little boy we laid away never fluctuates, and his dim society is companion still. But it is growing damp and I must go in. Memory's fog is rising.

> The going from a world we know
> To one a wonder still
> Is like the child's adversity
> Whose vista is a hill,
> Behind the hill is sorcery
> And everything unknown,
> But will the secret compensate
> For climbing it alone?

Vinnie's love and Maggie's, and mine is presupposed.

Emily.

MANUSCRIPT: destroyed.
PUBLICATION: L (1894) 297–298; LL 367–368; L (1931) 268–269.
ED's illness occurred Saturday, 14 June, and she was attended by Dr. D. B. N. Fish. Frank Sanborn's lecture, given before the Concord School

of Philosophy on Monday, 28 July, was reported in the Tuesday *Springfield Republican*. The "gracious boy at the barn" was Stephen Sullivan.

908

To Susan Gilbert Dickinson   *about 1884*

I felt it no betrayal, Dear – Go to my Mine as to your own, only more unsparingly –

I can scarcely believe that the Wondrous Book is at last to be written, and it seems like a Memoir of the Sun, when the Noon is gone –

You remember his swift way of wringing and flinging away a Theme, and others picking it up and gazing bewildered after him, and the prance that crossed his Eye at such times was unrepeatable –

> Though the Great Waters sleep,
> That they are still the Deep,
> We cannot doubt –
> No Vacillating God
> Ignited this Abode
> To put it out –

I wish I could find the Warrington Words, but during my weeks of faintness, my Treasures were misplaced, and I cannot find them – I think Mr Robinson had been left alone, and felt the opinion while the others were gone –

Remember, Dear, an unfaltering *Yes* is my only reply to your utmost question –

> With constancy –
> Emily –

MANUSCRIPT: HCL (B 158). Pencil.
PUBLICATION: LL 82, four lines; FF 266, in part.

George S. Merriam, *The Life and Times of Samuel Bowles* (New York, 1885, 2 vols.), is the book referred to. In preparing it, Merriam had asked Susan Dickinson for access to Bowles's letters in her possession (his request is in HCL). William S. Robinson ("Warrington") was the Boston correspondent for the *Springfield Republican*. He died in 1876, several months before Bowles. A collection of his writings, *Pen-Portraits. . .* (Boston, 1877), was issued by his wife. He had become serenely sure of immortality in his last years, and expressed his beliefs, as set forth in the memoirs. ED's letter seems to answer a request, as though Sue knew that ED had the book, or had saved certain clippings over the years. This passage from the book (page 162) very aptly explains ED's remark: "This life is so good, that it seems impossible for it to be wholly interrupted by death."

921

To Theodore Holland   *summer 1884*

Dear Sir.

Your request to "remain sincerely" mine demands investigation, and if after synopsis of your career all should seem correct, I am tersely your's –

I shall try to wear the unmerited honor with becoming volume –

Commend me to your Kindred, for whom although a Stranger, I entertain esteem –

I approve the Paint – a study of the Soudan, I take it, but the Scripture assures us our Hearts are all Dongola.

E. Dickinson –

"Cousin Vinnie's" smile.

MANUSCRIPT: HCL (H 88). Pencil.
PUBLICATION: *LH* 190–191.

The sketch which ED received must have been intended to amuse, for it is here acknowledged with mock formality. During the summer of 1884 the fate of General Gordon, sent to relieve the British garrison at Khartoum, was in doubt. Gordon's headquarters was in Dongola.

922

To Forrest F. Emerson   *summer 1884?*

Dear Friend,

I step from my pillow to your hand to thank its sacred contents, to hoard, not to partake, for I am still weak.

[309]

The little package has lain by my side, not daring to venture, or Vinnie daring to have me – a hallowed denial I shall not forget.

I fear you may need the papers, and ask you to claim them immediately, would you desire them.

I trust you are sharing this most sweet climate with Mrs. Emerson and yourself, than which remembrance only is more Arabian.

Vinnie brings her love, and her sister what gratitude.

Emily.

MANUSCRIPT: missing.
PUBLICATION: L (1894) 404–405; L (1931) 393–394.
The Emersons had left Amherst in February 1883. Without the autograph, it is impossible to place this letter accurately. Clearly Emerson has sent ED reading matter, perhaps clippings. There were two periods in the last years when she was too sick to read or write. On 7 June 1884 she became acutely ill, confined to her bed for several weeks. From late November 1885 until her death in May 1886 she mustered strength only intermittently. If Emerson's package was clippings about Helen Jackson's death (August 1885), then this letter was written early in 1886. (See letter no. 1018.)

937

To Helen Hunt Jackson   *September 1884*

Dear friend –

I infer from your Note you have "taken Captivity Captive," and rejoice that that martial Verse has been verified. He who is "slain and smiles, steals something from the" Sword, but you have stolen the Sword itself, which is far better – I hope you may be harmed no more – I shall watch your passage from Crutch to Cane with jealous affection. From there to your Wings is but a stride – as was said of the convalescing Bird,

> And then he lifted up his Throat
> And squandered such a Note –
> A Universe that overheard
> Is stricken by it yet –

I, too, took my summer in a Chair, though from "Nervous prostra-

[310]

tion," not fracture, but take my Nerve by the Bridle now, and am again abroad – Thank you for the wish –

The Summer has been wide and deep, and a deeper Autumn is but the Gleam concomitant of that waylaying Light –

> Pursuing you in your transitions,
> In other Motes –
> Of other Myths
> Your requisition be.
> The Prism never held the Hues,
> It only heard them play –

Loyally,
E. Dickinson –

MANUSCRIPT: BPL (Higg 112). Pencil.

PUBLICATION: L (1931) 318–319, among the letters to Higginson, but with a footnote: "Though included among the letters to Colonel Higginson, this letter was probably written to 'H. H.'"

Helen Jackson sent this letter to Higginson, who kept it. It is a reply to the letter which follows, from Helen Jackson, dated: Colorado Springs/ Sept 5./1884.

937a

My dear friend,

Thanks for your note of sympathy.

It was not quite a "massacre," only a break of one leg: but it was a very bad break — two inches of the big bone smashed in — & the little one snapped: as compound a fracture as is often compounded! –

But I am thankful to say that it has joined & healed – well. I am on crutches now — & am promised to walk with a cane in a few weeks: — a most remarkable success for an old woman past fifty & weighing 170. –

I fell from the top to the bottom of my stairs — & the only wonder was I did not break my neck. – For the first week I wished I had! Since then I have not suffered at all — but have been exceedingly comfortable — ten weeks tomorrow since it happened — the last six I have spent in a wheeled chair on my verandah: — an involuntary "rest cure," for which I dare say, I shall be better all my life. –

[311]

I trust you are well — and that life is going pleasantly with you. — What portfolios of verses you must have. —

It is a cruel wrong to your "day & generation" that you will not give them light. — If such a thing should happen as that I should out-live you, I wish you would make me your literary legatee & executor. Surely, after you are what is called "dead," you will be willing that the poor ghosts you have left behind, should be cheered and pleased by your verses, will you not? — You ought to be. — I do not think we have a right to with hold from the world a word or a thought any more than a *deed*, which might help a single soul.

Do you remember Hannah Dorrance? She came to see me the other day! A Mrs. Somebody, from Chicago. I forget her name. She has grandchildren. I felt like Methuselah, when I realized that it was forty years since I had seen her. Her eyes are as black as ever. —

I am always glad to get a word from you —

Truly yours
Helen Jackson.

MANUSCRIPT: HCL (Dickinson collection).

PUBLICATION: The paragraph touching upon the literary executorship is published in the preface to *Poems by Emily Dickinson*, Second Series (1891), edited by Mabel Loomis Todd. Mrs. Todd must have seen the letter when it was in the possession of Lavinia Dickinson.

ED had read of the accident, and had written a note of condolence to which this is the reply. Hannah Dorrance, daughter of Dr. Gardner Dor-rance of Amherst, had moved to Attica, New York, after her marriage. Presumably she later moved to Chicago. ED's reply to this letter pointedly ignores the request to be made literary executor.

951

To Mrs. J. Howard Sweetser   *late autumn 1884*

Dear Nellie,

I hardly dare tell you how beautiful your Home is, lest it dissuade you from the more mortal Homestead in which you now dwell – Each Tree a Scene from India, and Everglades of Rugs.

Is not "Lead us not into Temptation" an involuntary plea under circumstances so gorgeous? Your little Note dropped in upon us as softly as the flake of Snow that followed it, as spacious and as stainless, a paragraph from Every Where – to which we never go – We miss you more this time, I think, than all the times before –

An enlarged ability for missing is perhaps a part of our better growth, as the strange Membranes of the Tree broaden out of sight.

I hope the Owl remembers me, and the Owl's fair Keeper, indeed the remembrance of each of you, were a gallant boon – I still recall your Son's singing, and when the "Choir invisible" assemble in your Trees, shall reverently compare them – Thank you for all the Acts of Light which beautified a Summer now past to it's reward.

Love for your Exile, when you write her, as for Love's Aborigines – Our Coral Roof, though unbeheld, it's foliage softly adds –

Emily, with Love.

MANUSCRIPT: Rosenbach 1170/18 (8). Pencil. Unpublished.

The date is conjectured from the handwriting. The Sweetsers had moved into their new home during the previous year, and in this letter ED is describing their Amherst house. One of the Sweetser children evidently had a pet owl. George Eliot's "The Choir Invisible" is in *The Legend of Jubal and Other Poems* (1874); for a later reference to it, see letter no. 1042. ED speaks here again of Howard Sweetser's singing.

953

To Mr. and Mrs. E. J. Loomis   *19 November 1884*

Dear friends –

The atmospheric acquaintance so recently and delightfully made, is not, I trust, ephemeral, but absolute as Ether, as the delicate emblem just received tenderly implies.

Thank you for the Beauty – Thank you too for Boundlessness – that rarely given, but choicest Gift.

To "know in whom" we "have believed," is Immortality.

Oh what a Grace is this,
What Majesties of Peace,
That having breathed

The fine – ensuing Right
Without Diminuet Proceed!

With trust,
E. Dickinson –

MANUSCRIPT: AC. Pencil. Envelope addressed by Lavinia, and letter received in Washington 20 November.
PUBLICATION: *L* (1931) 425.
This note acknowledges some small gift, and with it is a note from Lavinia. The scripture reference may be to 2 Timothy 1.12: ". . . for I know whom I have believed, and am persuaded that he is able to keep that which I have committed unto him against that day."

956

To Kendall Emerson   *Christmas 1884*

Missing my own Boy, I knock at other Trundle-Beds, and trust the Curls are in –

Little Gilbert's Aunt –

MANUSCRIPT: AC. Pencil.
PUBLICATION: *Amherst Alumni News* IV (July 1951) 14.
This is the second of three Christmas messages ED sent to Kendall in memory of Gilbert (see letter no. 876).

962

To Louise and Frances Norcross   *14 January 1885*

Had we less to say to those we love, perhaps we should say it of-tener, but the attempt comes, then the inundation, then it is all over, as is said of the dead.

Vinnie dreamed about Fanny last night, and designing for days to write dear Loo, – dear, both of you, – indeed with the astounding nearness which a dream brings, I must speak this morning. I do hope you are well, and that the last enchanting days have refreshed your spirits, and I hope the poor little girl is better, and the sorrow at least adjourned.

[314]

Loo asked "what books" we were wooing now – watching like a vulture for Walter Cross's life of his wife. A friend sent me *Called Back*. It is a haunting story, and as loved Mr. Bowles used to say, "greatly impressive to me." Do you remember the little picture with his deep face in the centre, and Governor Bross on one side, and Colfax on the other? The third of the group died yesterday, so somewhere they are again together.

Moving to Cambridge seems to me like moving to Westminster Abbey, as hallowed and as unbelieved, or moving to Ephesus with Paul for a next-door neighbor.

Holmes's *Life of Emerson* is sweetly commended, but you, I know, have tasted that. . . . But the whistle calls me – I have not begun – so with a moan, and a kiss, and a promise of more, and love from Vinnie and Maggie, and the half-blown carnation, and the western sky, I stop.

That we are permanent temporarily, it is warm to know, though we know no more.

Emily.

MANUSCRIPT: destroyed.
PUBLICATION: L (1894) 298–299; LL 368–369; L (1931) 269–270.

The death of Schuyler Colfax, on 13 January 1885, fixes the date of this letter. The photograph to which ED refers (HCL – Dickinson collection) was one taken in San Francisco in 1865. The three others (not two) in the group were Bowles's companions on the trip: Colfax, then Speaker of the House of Representatives (and later Vice President); William Bross, Lieutenant Governor of Illinois; and Albert D. Richardson, Civil War correspondent and staff member of the *New York Tribune*.

The Norcross sisters moved to Cambridge during 1884, so that Fanny would be nearer to the Divinity School library. *Called Back* (1883), by the British novelist Frederick John Fargus ("Hugh Conway"), was widely popular in its day (see letter no. 1046). Holmes's *Ralph Waldo Emerson* was published in 1885.

963

To Charles H. Clark   *January 1885*

Dear friend –

Though no New Year be old – to wish yourself and your honored

[315]

Father a new and happy one is involuntary and I am sure we are both reminded of that sacred Past which has forever hallowed us.

I trust the Years which they behold are also new and happy, or is it a joyous expanse of Year, without bisecting Months, untiring Anno Domini? Had we but one assenting word, but a Letter is a joy of Earth – it is denied the Gods.

Vivid in our immortal Group we still behold your Brother, and never hear Northampton Bells without saluting him.

Should you have any Picture of any Child of my friend, while we are both below, I hope you may lend it to me for his great sake, as any circumstance of him is forever precious.

Have you Blossoms and Books, those solaces of sorrow? That, I would also love to know, and receive for yourself and your Father, the forgetless sympathy of

Your Friend

E. Dickinson.

MANUSCRIPT: AC. Pencil. Envelope addressed by ED in ink: C. H. Clark./361. Degraw St./Brooklyn./Long Island. Postmarked: Jan 19. Clark endorsed the letter: Jan 18/85.

PUBLICATION: *L* (1894) 364–365; *L* (1931) 356.

In the fourth paragraph ED requests a photograph of Wadsworth's children.

967

To Benjamin Kimball   *February 1885*

Dear friend –

To take the hand of my friend's friend, even apparitionally, is a hallowed pleasure.

I think you told me you were his kinsman.

I was only his friend – and cannot yet believe that

> "his part in all the pomp that fills
> The circuit of the Southern Hills,
> Is that his Grave is green."

His last words in his last Note were "A Caller comes." I infer it to be Eternity, as he never returned.

Your task must be a fervent one – often one of pain.

To fulfill the will of a powerless friend supersedes the Grave.

Oh, Death, where is thy Chancellor? On my way to my sleep, last night, I paused at the Portrait. Had I not loved it, I had feared it, the Face had such ascension.

> Go thy great way!
> The Stars thou meetst
> Are even as Thyself –
> For what are Stars but Asterisks
> To point a human Life?

Thank you for the nobleness, and for the earnest Note – but *all* are friends, upon a Spar.

Gratefully,
E. Dickinson –

MANUSCRIPT: NYPL (Berg collection). Pencil.
PUBLICATION: *Revelation* 68.
Kimball was executor of Judge Lord's estate. Perhaps Lord bequeathed something to ED. (He did not return the letters she had written to him.) This and the letter which follows are in the same collection. With them is an envelope addressed in ink by ED: Benjamin Kimball./8. Congress St./ Boston./Mass. Postmarked: Palmer Mass Feb 20 85. The quoted lines are from Bryant's *June*:

> Whose part, in all the pomp that fills
> The circuit of the summer hills,
> Is that his grave is green.

968

To Benjamin Kimball 1885

Dear friend –

Had I known I asked the impossible, should I perhaps have asked it, but Abyss is it's own Apology.

I once asked him what I should do for him when he was not here, referring half unconsciously to the great Expanse – In a tone italic of both Worlds "Remember Me," he said. I have kept his Command-

[317]

ment. But you are a Psychologist, I, only a Scholar who has lost her Preceptor.

For the great kindness of your opinion, I am far indebted.

Perhaps to solidify his faith was for him impossible, and if for him, how more, for us! Your noble and tender words of him were exceedingly precious – I shall cherish them.

He did not tell me he "sang" to you, though to sing in his presence was involuntary, thronged only with Music, like the Decks of Birds.

Abstinence from Melody was what made him die. Calvary and May wrestled in his Nature.

Neither fearing Extinction, nor prizing Redemption, he believed alone. Victory was his Rendezvous –

I hope it took him home.

But I fear I detain you.

I try to thank you and fail.

Perhaps the confiding effort you would not disdain?

> Sacredly,
> E. Dickinson.

MANUSCRIPT: NYPL (Berg collection). Pencil.
PUBLICATION: *Revelation* 69.

This letter responds to one Kimball had written at ED's request, telling her what he could about Lord as he had known him.

972

To T. W. Higginson   *February 1885*

Dear friend –

It is long since I asked and received your consent to accept the Book, should it be, and the ratification at last comes, a pleasure I feared to hope –

Biography first convinces us of the fleeing of the Biographied –

> Pass to thy Rendezvous of Light,
> Pangless except for us –
> Who slowly ford the Mystery
> Which thou hast leaped across!

> Your Scholar –

Manuscript: BPL (Higg 115). Pencil.
Publication: L (1931) 319–320.

In HCL is J. W. Cross, *The Life of George Eliot*, inscribed by Higginson: "T. W. Higginson from Emily Dickinson, 1885." The first volume was published in February 1885; the third, in 1887. The poem is also in letter no. 868.

974

To Maria Whitney   *spring 1885*

Dear friend

I was much quickened toward you and all Celestial things to read (see) that the Life of our loved Mr Bowles would be with us in Autumn, and how fitting (sweet) that his and George Eliots should be given so near – (should be chosen so near And how strong that his and George Eliots are in the same year)

On his last arriving from California he told us the Highwayman did not say your money or your life, but have you read Daniel Deronda – That wise and tender Book I hope you have seen – It is full of sad (high) nourishment –

Manuscript: AC. Pencil. It is an unfinished rough draft, jotted on a discarded concert program which can be dated 23 March 1885. The fair copy of the draft presumably was sent to Maria Whitney.
Publication: NEQ XXVIII (1955) 305.

The *Springfield Republican* on 7 March 1885 carried the following announcement:

> The Century company of New York will publish next
> autumn a biography of the late editor of The Republican,
> under the title, "The Life and Times of Samuel Bowles."

The first volume of Cross's *Life* [of George Eliot] appeared in February 1885 (see letter no. 972); Merriam's biography of Bowles was published late in the year (see letter no. 908). ED had been enthusiastic about *Daniel Deronda* when she followed its serial publication in *Scribner's Monthly* in 1876 (see letter no. 457), but she may have been wrong about Bowles's last trip to California, which seems to have occurred in 1873. After the publication of *Daniel Deronda* his only known trip was to Virginia, Kentucky, and Chicago, in the spring of 1877.

[319]

To Mabel Loomis Todd   *May 1885*

To the Bugle every color is Red —

MANUSCRIPT: AC. Pencil.
PUBLICATION: L (1931) 421.
Mrs. Todd's diary for 6 May 1885 says that she painted a scarlet lily
which Lavinia had asked her to come to see. This note, in the handwriting
of that time, may have been written to Mrs. Todd after ED had seen the
painting.

To Austin Dickinson and family   *about 1885*

Brother, Sister, Ned.

Enclosed please find the Birds which do not go South.

Emily —

MANUSCRIPT: HCL (B 46). Pencil.
PUBLICATION: FF 232.
The date is conjectured from the handwriting. A note in FF says that
this message accompanied roasting chickens.

To Edward (Ned) Dickinson   *August 1885*

Dear Boy.

I dared not trust my own Voice among your speechless Mountains,
and so I took your Mother's, which mars no Majesty — So you find no
treason in Earth or Heaven.

You never will, My Ned —

That is a personal refraction — shall I question you, or let your
Story tell itself? "Day unto Day uttereth Speech" if you do not teaze
him —

I was stricken with laughter by your Dr Irish – The search for the Syphon is unremitting.

How favorable that something is missing besides Sir John Franklin! Interrogation must be fed –

Your intimacy with the Mountains I heartily endorse – Ties more Eleusinian I must leave to you – Deity will guide you – I do not mean Jehovah – The little God with Epaulettes I spell it in French to conceal it's temerity

What made you quote that sweetest Verse I never heard from Lips but scarcely wake or sleep without re-loving it?

Love for Maria Pearl – and a ruddy remembrance to my Neighbors. Vinnie is still subsoiling, but lays down her Spade to caress you. And ever be sure of me, Lad –

Fondly,
Aunt Emily.

Latest from the Dam –
Telegraphed Torricelli to bring a Vacuum, but his Father wrote that he was'nt at Home.

MANUSCRIPT: HCL (B 183). Pencil.
PUBLICATION: FF 261–262.

"Maria Pearl" was a nickname for Maria Whitney, who had her own cottage at Lake Placid. The reference to the siphon and the dam has to do with some accident in the town waterworks, of which Ned's father was president. The allusion to Evangelista Torricelli (1608–1647), celebrated physicist and mathematician, was probably clear to Ned, who may have mentioned to his aunt that he had become acquainted with the "Torricellian vacuum," or barometer, in a college science course.

1007

To T. W. Higginson   *6 August 1885*

Dear friend.

I was unspeakably shocked to see this in the Morning Paper –

She wrote me in Spring that she could not walk, but not that she would die – I was sure you would know. Please say it is not so.

What a Hazard a Letter is!

When I think of the Hearts it has scuttled and sunk, I almost fear to lift my Hand to so much as a Superscription.

Trusting that all is peace in your loved Abode,

With alarm,

Your Scholar –

MANUSCRIPT: BPL (Higg 116). Pencil. Envelope addressed by ED in ink: Col. T. W. Higginson./Cambridge./Mass. Postmarked: Palmer Aug 6 1885.

PUBLICATION: *L* (1931) 320.

Accompanying the letter is a clipping from the *Springfield Republican* of 6 August, beginning: "Mrs. Helen Hunt Jackson is reported at the point of death in San Francisco, where she has been steadily declining for the past four months." Mrs. Jackson died, 12 August.

A rough draft of two of the sentences (AC – pencil) reads thus:

> What a Hazard a Letter is – When I think of the Hearts
> it has Cleft or healed I almost wince to lift my Hand
> to so much as a superscription but then we always
> except ourselves –

It is published in *NEQ* XXVIII (1955) 305. (See also letter no. 1011.)

1009

To William S. Jackson   *mid-August 1885*

I take the Hand of Mr Bowles to express my sympathy for my grieved Friend, and to ask him when sorrow will allow, if he will tell me a very little of her Life's close? She said in a Note of a few months since, "I am absolutely well."

I next knew of her death. Excuse me for disturbing you in so deep an hour.

Bereavement is my only plea.

Sorrowfully,
E. Dickinson.

MANUSCRIPT: Jackson. Pencil. Envelope addressed by Bowles: Wm S. Jackson Esq./Colorado Springs/Col. Envelope endorsed by Jackson: E Dickenson/Aug 13th 85. Postmarked: Springfield Mass 1885 Aug 20.

1.30 AM. Unpublished. With it ED enclosed a cut envelope showing her name and address.

Immediately after Helen Jackson's death, ED wrote to her publisher Thomas Niles. The letter is missing, but its contents can be inferred by this reply from Niles, dated: Boston, Augt 19 1885. (HCL)

1009a

Dear Miss Dickinson

I have yours asking about Mrs Jackson. A year since, she broke her leg & in the autumn she managed to get down to Los Angeles where she passed the winter leaving there in Mch for home but got no farther than San Francisco where she was taken down with what she called Malarial fever. Judging by her continued letters the doctors did not know what her real trouble was. Most likely they did however, but kept it from her. We only know here what has been telegraphed that she died of Cancer in the stomach.

In her last letter to me, recd. since the news of her death, she says she "has but a few days to live and shall be thankful to be released" and she closes thus:

"I shall look in on your new rooms some day, be sure — but you won't see me — Good bye — Affy. forever, H.J."

And by this you will know that *she* thinks it is the "beginning."

I will send you a photograph of her in a day or two

Yrs truly

T. Niles

1010

To Sara Colton (Gillett)   *late summer 1885*

Mattie will hide this little flower in her friend's Hand. Should she ask who sent it, tell her as Desdemona did when they asked who slew her, "Nobody— I myself."

MANUSCRIPT: Holcombe. Pencil.

PUBLICATION: *Amherst Monthly*, May 1910: "The Poetry of Emily Dickinson," by F. J. Pohl, Jr.; LL 61; *Hartford Daily Times* 7 March 1936. See the note to the following letter.

[323]

To Sara Colton (Gillett)?   *late summer 1885*

What a hazard an Accent is! When I think of the Hearts it has scuttled or sunk, I hardly dare to raise my voice to so much as a Salutation.

E. Dickinson.

MANUSCRIPT: Holcombe. Pencil.

PUBLICATION: *Hartford Daily Times* 7 March 1936, in part reproduced in facsimile.

The same phraseology ED used in writing Higginson just before Mrs. Jackson's death (no. 1007). Among ED's papers at the time of her death was another draft (AC – pencil):

What a Hazard an Accent is! When I think of the
Hearts it has scuttled or sunk, I almost fear to lift my
Hand to so much as a punctuation.

Sara Colton was a friend of Martha Dickinson, whom she visited in the summer of 1885. She later married the Reverend Arthur L. Gillett, a professor in the Hartford Theological Seminary. The *Hartford Times* article was written from material which Mrs. Gillett supplied, which states "that they [this and the preceding note] were written to Mrs. Gillett when she was a girl. . ."

Sara Colton did not know and never saw ED. The preceding letter (no. 1010) is precisely the kind that ED often wrote and sent across the hedge to friends of her niece and nephews. The tone of this one, the signature, the concern with rhetorical effect, make one seriously doubt that it was in fact sent to Sara Colton. Nor was it sent to Susan Dickinson, for ED never signed notes to Sue thus. Whoever received it perhaps presented it to Sara Colton as a memento, maybe at the same time she received the other note.

1013

To Samuel Bowles the younger   *August 1885*

Dawn and Dew my Bearers be –
Ever,
Butterfly.

MANUSCRIPT: Bowles. Pencil. Addressed by ED in ink: Mr and Mrs/ Samuel Bowles.

PUBLICATION: L (1894) 351; L (1931) 340.

It is said to be a note accompanying sweet peas sent by early train to Springfield.

1015

To William S. Jackson?   *late summer 1885*

Helen of Troy will die, but Helen of Colorado, never. Dear friend, can you walk, were the last words that I wrote her. Dear friend, I can fly – her immortal (soaring) reply. I never saw Mrs Jackson but twice, but those twice are indelible, and one Day more I am deified, was the only impression she ever left on any Heart (House) she entered –

MANUSCRIPT: AC. Rough penciled draft.

PUBLICATION: The first two sentences are in L (1894) 426; LL 373; L (1931) 414. The remainder is in a footnote in AB 84.

This rough draft, from which the published texts derive, is written on two sheets of paper. One conjectures that Mr. Jackson replied to the letter ED wrote him in August (no. 1009), and that this is the draft of her projected answer. The phrase "one Day more I am deified" recalls a line from Browning's "The Last Ride Together."

1018

To Forrest F. Emerson   *late September 1885*

Dear Clergyman

In a note which you sent my brother soon after the dying of our child, was a passage, our only spar at the time, and solemnly remembered.

We would gladly possess it more accurately, if convenient to you. "And I can but believe that in such a mysterious providence as the dying of little Gilbert, there is a purpose of benevolence which does not include our present happiness." Vinnie hoped, too, to speak with you of Helen of Colorado, whom she understood you to have a friend, a friend also of hers.

[325]

Should she know any circumstances of her life's close, would she perhaps lend it to you, that you might lend it to me? Oh had that Keats a Severn!

But I trespass upon your thronged time.

With affection for Mrs Emerson, and my sister's love.

Earnestly,

E. Dickinson.

MANUSCRIPT: missing. The text derives from a transcript (AC) made by Mrs. Todd.

PUBLICATION: L (1931) 394.

The Emersons were in Amherst during the week of 20 September 1885, as guests of President and Mrs. Seelye. Mr. Emerson preached at the First Church on Sunday the twentieth. The Emersons were now living in Newport, Rhode Island, where Mr. Emerson occupied a pulpit.

In referring to Helen Jackson, ED alludes to the deathbed moment of Keats, whose friend Joseph Severn was with him and reported Keats's last words: "Severn, lift me up, for I am dying. I shall die easy. Don't be frightened. Thank God it has come."

1020

To Mrs. Edward Tuckerman   *October 1885*

Dear friend.

I thought of you on your lonely journey, certain the hallowed Heroine was gratified, though mute – I trust you return in safety and with closer clutch for that which remains, for Dying whets the grasp.

October is a mighty Month, for in it Little Gilbert died. "Open the Door" was his last Cry – "the Boys are waiting for me!"

Quite used to his Commandment, his little Aunt obeyed, and still two years and many Days, and he does not return.

Where makes my Lark his Nest?

But Corinthians' Bugle obliterates the Birds, so covering your loved Heart to keep it from another shot,

Tenderly,
Emily.

MANUSCRIPT: AC. Pencil.

PUBLICATION: L (1894) 390–391; LL 376; L (1931) 380.

Except for her sister, Mrs. William Esty, living in Amherst, Mrs. Tuckerman at this time had no surviving close relatives. The journey must have been to the funeral of a more distant relative or a friend. For Gilbert's last words, see letter no. 873. "Corinthians' Bugle" may allude to 1 Corinthians 15.52: ". . . for the trumpet shall sound, and the dead shall be raised incorruptible, and we shall all be changed."

1023

To Edward (Ned) Dickinson　　　　　　　　　*early November 1885*

Dear Ned –

Burglaries have become so frequent, is it quite safe to leave the Golden Rule out over night?

With sorrow for his illness,

Aunt Emily –

MANUSCRIPT: HCL (B 58). Pencil. Addressed: Ned –
PUBLICATION: FF 248.
On 5 November 1885 the Austin Dickinson house was robbed while the family were eating supper.

1027

To Kendall Emerson　　　　　　　　　*Christmas 1885*

Dear Kendall.

I send you a Blossom with my love – Spend it as you will –
The Woods are too deep for your little Feet to grope for Evergreen –

Your friend
Emily —

MANUSCRIPT: AC. Pencil.
PUBLICATION: *Amherst Alumni News* IV (July 1951) 14.
This is the third and last of the Christmas notes ED sent to Gilbert's friend (see letters no. 876 and 956).

1034

To Louise and Frances Norcross　　　　　　　　　*about March 1886*

I scarcely know where to begin, but love is always a safe place. I

[327]

have twice been very sick, dears, with a little recess of convalescence, then to be more sick, and have lain in my bed since November, many years, for me, stirring as the arbutus does, a pink and russet hope; but that we will leave with our pillow. When your dear hearts are quite convenient, tell us of their contents, the fabric cared for most, not a fondness wanting.

Do you keep musk, as you used to, like Mrs. Morene of Mexico? Or cassia carnations so big they split their fringes of berry? Was your winter a tender shelter — perhaps like Keats's bird, "and hops and hops in little journeys"?

Are you reading and well, and the W[hitney]s near and warm? When you see Mrs. French and Dan give them a tear from us.

Vinnie would have written, but could not leave my side. Maggie gives her love. Mine more sweetly still.

Emily.

MANUSCRIPT: destroyed.
PUBLICATION: L (1894) 435; LL 378; L (1931) 427–428.
The quotation is from Keats's *Endymion*, and used by Higginson in his essay "The Life of Birds." The Norcrosses were good friends of Daniel Chester French and his mother, as they were of Maria Whitney, who lived with her brother in Cambridge.

1038

To Mrs. J. G. Holland   *early spring 1886*

Concerning the little sister, not to assault, not to adjure, but to obtain those constancies which exalt friends, we followed her to St. Augustine, since which the trail was lost, or says George Stearns of his alligator, "there was no such aspect."

The beautiful blossoms waned at last, the charm of all who knew them, resisting the effort of earth or air to persuade them to root, as the great florist says, "The flower that never will in other climate grow."

To thank you for its fragrance would be impossible, but then its other blissful traits are more than can be numbered. And the beloved Christmas, too, for which I never thanked you. I hope the little heart is well, – *big* would have been the width, – and the health solaced; any news of her as sweet as the first arbutus.

Emily and Vinnie give the love greater every hour.

Manuscript: missing.
Publication: L (1894) 187–188; L (1931) 179–180; LH 200.

Mrs. Holland first went to Florida to escape attacks of rheumatism during the winter of 1885–1886. She may have known more about ED's illness than this letter of thanks would imply. It is the last letter that ED is known to have written her, and probably the final one. George Stearns of Chicopee, a well-known lawyer and humorist, was a contributor to the *Springfield Republican*. The quotation has not been identified, but may be part of a story told to the Hollands and Dickinsons after Stearns (who described it in the *Republican*) had returned from an alligator hunt. The second quotation is from *Paradise Lost*, II, 272–273: "O flowers/That never will in other climate grow . . ."

1042

To T. W. Higginson   *spring 1886*

"Mars the sacred Loneliness"! What an Elegy! "From Mount Zion below to Mount Zion above"! said President Humphrey of her Father –Gabriel's Oration would adorn his Child–

When she came the last time she had in her Hand as I entered, the "Choir invisible."

"Superb," she said as she shut the Book, stooping to receive me, but fervor suffocates me. Thank you for "the Sonnet" – I have lain it at her loved feet.

> Not knowing when Herself may come
> I open every Door,
> Or has she Feathers, like a Bird,
> Or Billows, like a Shore –

I think she would rather have stayed with us, but perhaps she will learn the Customs of Heaven, as the Prisoner of Chillon of Captivity.

You asked had I read "the Notices."

I have been very ill, Dear friend, since November, bereft of Book and Thought, by the Doctor's reproof, but begin to roam in my Room now –

I think of you with absent Affection, and the Wife and Child I never have seen, Legend and Love in one –

Audacity of Bliss, said Jacob to the Angel "I will not let thee go except I bless thee" – Pugilist and Poet, Jacob was correct –

Your Scholar –

MANUSCRIPT: BPL (Higg 101). Pencil.
PUBLICATION: L (1931) 320–321.

Sometime during the winter Higginson had written, inquiring whether ED had read the notices about the death of Helen Jackson. ED replied as soon as she felt able to do so. The opening of the letter attempts to quote from Higginson's "Decoration" (1874): "And no stone, with feign'd distress,/Mocks the sacred loneliness." Helen Jackson's father, Professor Nathan Fiske, had died while on a trip to the Holy Land. On 30 March 1848, the Reverend Heman Humphrey published *A Tribute to the Memory of Rev. Nathan W. Fiske* . . . : "In Jerusalem he died; on Mount Zion, and near the tomb of David was he buried . . . Who at death would not love to go up from Jerusalem below, to Jerusalem above . . . ?" (For an earlier reference to George Eliot's "The Choir Invisible," see letter no. 951.) Higginson's sonnet "To the Memory of H. H." was published in the May issue of the *Century Magazine*. This letter suggests that she had received a transcript of Higginson's sonnet in advance of publication. The scripture allusion at the end of the first paragraph is to Luke 1.28. The final quotation recalls Jacob, who, wrestling with the angel, said (Genesis 32.26): "I will not let thee go, except thou bless me."

1046

To Louise and Frances Norcross   *May 1886*

    Little Cousins,
        Called back.
          Emily.

MANUSCRIPT: destroyed.
PUBLICATION: L (1894) 438; LL 381; L (1931) 430.

It was in a letter written to the Norcrosses in January 1885 (no. 962) that ED spoke of having read Hugh Conway's *Called Back*. During the second week in May she probably came to know that she had but a short time to live. This letter was evidently her last. On the thirteenth she went into a coma. Vinnie sent for Austin and for Dr. Bigelow, who remained with her much of the day. She never regained consciousness, and died about six in the evening, Saturday, 15 May 1886.

APPENDIX
INDEX

BIOGRAPHICAL SKETCHES OF RECIPIENTS OF LETTERS
AND OF PERSONS MENTIONED IN THEM

Persons mentioned casually, who were never significant to ED herself, are briefly identified in the notes to the letters. The names of recipients are starred (*). Localities referred to in the sketches are in Massachusetts unless specified as being elsewhere.

ADAMS, Elizabeth C. (1810–1873), "our dear teacher," taught at Amherst Academy in the early 1840's. After an absence, she returned in 1846, for another term as preceptress, until her marriage to Albert Clark of Conway, 7 April 1847.

ADAMS, John Sydney, a school friend of ED and of Jane Humphrey, was later proprietor of the local bookstore and drugstore.

*ANTHON, Catherine (Scott) Turner (1831–1917) was the daughter of Henry Scott of Cooperstown, New York. Her acquaintance with Susan Dickinson began in 1848, when they both attended Utica Female Seminary. In 1855 Kate Scott married Campbell Ladd Turner, who died two years later. She visited Sue in 1859, at which time ED met her, and the acquaintance was continued when Kate Turner made subsequent visits to Amherst during the sixties. She married John Anthon in 1866. There is no record that her friendship with ED was pursued after that date. ED is known to have written five letters to her between 1859 and 1866, and to have sent her a few poems.

BELDEN, Pomeroy (1811–1849), a graduate of Amherst College (1833), was pastor of the Second Congregational Church ("East Parish") in Amherst from 1842 until his death.

BLISS, Daniel (1823–1916), a graduate of Amherst College (1852), was ordained in the College Church, Amherst, 17 October 1855, upon graduation from Andover Theological Seminary. In the month following, on 23 November, he married Abby Maria Wood (q.v.), one of ED's close childhood friends. He was a leading figure in the founding and development of American Foreign Missions.

*BOLTWOOD, Lucius (1792–1872), a graduate of Williams College (1814), studied law with Samuel Fowler Dickinson and became his law partner in 1817. He married Fanny H. Shepard (1824), a first cousin of R. W. Emerson. From 1828 to 1864 he was Secretary of the Board of Trustees of Amherst College. The Boltwood sons, George and Henry, graduated from Amherst Academy in ED's class of 1847. Though the family was of importance, and the community and college ties of the Boltwoods and Dickinsons were close, one gathers that there was no personal tie between ED and any member of the Boltwood family.

*BOWDOIN, Elbridge Gridley (1820–1893), after graduation from Amherst College (1840), was admitted to the bar in 1847, and practiced law for eight years with ED's father (1847–1855). He then removed to Rockford, Iowa, and set himself up in business. He never married. During the years 1849–1852 ED is known to have sent him two brief notes and a valentine in verse.

*BOWLES, Samuel (1826–1878), was the son of the founder of the *Springfield Daily Republican*, and succeeded his father as editor in 1851. During his lifetime this family paper became one of the most influential in the country, and an organ of liberal Republicanism. A man of wide interests and exhaustless energy, Bowles traveled extensively. His letters were published in the *Republican*, and many of his observations were later collected in books. Greatly admired by all the Dickinsons, with whom he and his family were on intimate terms, he was especially esteemed by Emily. Throughout her lifetime, after 1858, she was steadily in correspondence with him and his wife Mary. She often sent them copies of her poems, and there still survive some fifty letters which she wrote them.

*BOWLES, Samuel the younger (b. 1851), succeeded his father as editor of the *Republican*. After his father's death, ED kept the family tie by communicating with him on special occasions. In May 1884 ED sent regrets to an invitation to his wedding; his marriage to Elizabeth Hoar took place on 12 June.

BULLARD, Asa (1804–1888), a graduate of Amherst College (1828), was ordained in 1832, and in the same year, on 16 May, married ED's aunt Lucretia Gunn Dickinson (1806–1885), her father's eldest sister. They lived at 24 Center Street, Cambridge. For forty years (1834–1874) he was general agent for the Congregational Sunday School and Publishing Society. He was author and editor of various religious publications, such as *Sabbath School Chestnuts*.

CHICKERING, Joseph Knowlton (1846–1899), was a graduate of Amherst College (1869), where he taught English from 1873 until 1885, in which latter year he accepted a call to the University of Vermont. At the time of the death of ED's mother (14 November 1882) he was especially thoughtful of the bereaved sisters.

CHURCH, Horace, an Amherst farmer and sexton of the First Church, was responsible for the upkeep of the Dickinson garden and grounds. Mentioned as early as 1854, he remained in the family's employ until his death in 1881.

CLARK, Mrs. Albert. *See* Elizabeth C. Adams.

*CLARK, Charles H., was the younger brother of James D. Clark (*q.v.*). He did not, like his brother, attend college. At his death he was the second oldest member of the New York Stock Exchange. ED's correspondence with Charles Clark she initiated during James Clark's fatal illness. All the correspondence with the brothers (a total of some twenty letters) focused upon the memory of Charles Wadsworth.

*CLARK, James D. (1828–1883) was the eldest son of Charles and Temperance Clark of Northampton. After graduation from Williams College (1848), he practiced law, taught school, engaged in business, and retired from active affairs in 1875. ED was introduced to him by her father sometime during the decade of the sixties. He was a lifelong friend of Charles Wadsworth (*q.v.*), and he initiated correspondence with ED after Wadsworth's death.

CLARK, William Smith (1826–1886), a graduate of Amherst College (1848), was a professor of chemistry, botany, and zoology at Amherst, 1852–1867. He served as president of Massachusetts Agricultural College from 1867 until 1878. He married the adopted daughter of Samuel Williston (*q.v.*) on 25 May 1853. They had eleven children.

COLEMAN, Lyman (1796–1882), a graduate of Yale College (1817), was principal of Amherst Academy (1844–1846) during the years that ED and her sister attended it. He taught at the Presbyterian Academy in Philadelphia from 1849 to 1858, and at Lafayette College from 1861 until his death. He married Maria Flynt (1801–1871) of Monson, a first cousin of ED's mother. Their children Olivia (1827–1847) and Eliza (1832–1871) were friends of the Dickinson girls. Eliza married John Dudley (*q.v.*).

COLTON, Aaron Merrick (1809–1895), a graduate of Yale College (1835), was pastor of the First Church in Amherst from 10 June 1840 until 4 January 1853, when he went to Easthampton.

*COLTON, Sara Philips, of Brooklyn, N. Y., was a lifelong friend of Martha Dickinson Bianchi. In 1911 she married Arthur L. Gillett (AC 1880), throughout his life a professor in the Hartford Theological Seminary.

*COWAN, Perez Dickinson (1843–1923), ED's favorite "Cousin Peter," was graduated from Amherst College (1866) and Union Theological Seminary. Ordained in 1869, he married Margaret Elizabeth Rhea in the following year. He occupied pulpits in his native Tennessee until 1877, and later in New York and New Jersey. ED had known him as an undergraduate and regarded him with especial warmth. His mother was daughter of a brother of Samuel Fowler Dickinson.

*CROWELL, Mary (Warner) (1830–1903), was the daughter of Aaron Warner, professor of Rhetoric and Oratory, and English Literature in Amherst College (1844–1853), and a girlhood friend of ED. In 1861 she married Edward Payson Crowell (Amherst 1853), professor of Latin at Amherst from 1864 until 1908.

*CURRIER, Elizabeth Dickinson (1823–1886), ED's aunt, was the youngest sister of Edward Dickinson. At forty-three she married Augustus Nelson Currier (1820–1896), a widower, on 10 October 1866. They resided in Worcester, where Currier was engaged in the insurance business.

*CUTLER, George, was a brother of William Cutler, the husband of Harriet Cutler (q.v.). The brothers, leading merchants in Amherst, were proprietors of a general store.

CUTLER, Harriet Gilbert (1820–1865), was an older sister of Susan Gilbert Dickinson (q.v.). She married William Cutler (1811–1870) of Amherst, 22 June 1842. He and his brother George (q.v.) were partners in merchandising business with Luke Sweetser (q.v.) until 1854, when they bought Sweetser out. Harriet Cutler died, 18 March 1865.

DICKINSON, Austin. See William Austin Dickinson.

DICKINSON, Catharine. See Catharine Dickinson Sweetser.

DICKINSON, Edward (1803–1874), ED's father, was the eldest child of Samuel Fowler Dickinson and Lucretia Gunn Dickinson. He prepared for college at Amherst Academy, attended Amherst College for one year — the year of its founding — then transferred to Yale College where he was graduated in 1823 at the head of his class. After reading law in his father's office, and further study in the Northampton Law School, he was admitted to the Hampshire County Bar in 1826. He was a lifelong resident of Amherst, where he engaged in the practice of law for forty-eight years. He became treasurer of Amherst College in 1835, and served in that capacity until his resignation in 1872. On 6 May 1828 he married Emily Norcross, daughter of Joel Norcross of Monson. They had three children: William Austin Dickinson, Emily Elizabeth Dickinson, and Lavinia Norcross Dickinson.

Edward Dickinson was a representative in the General Court of Massachusetts in 1838 and 1839, and a delegate to the National Whig Convention in Baltimore, 16 June 1852. He was elected as a representative to the Thirty-third Congress, 1853–1855. In 1874 he again represented his district in the General Court of Massachusetts, and died of apoplexy 16 June 1874 in Boston while attending the legislative session.

*DICKINSON, Edward ("Ned") (1861–1898), ED's nephew, was eldest of the three children of Austin and Susan Dickinson. He was prevented by illness from graduating with his Amherst College class (1884). ED was warmly attached to him. At the time of his death he was assistant librarian of the college library.

DICKINSON, Elizabeth. *See* Elizabeth Dickinson Currier.

DICKINSON, Emily Norcross (1804–1882), ED's mother, was a daughter of Joel and Betsy Fay Norcross of Monson. She attended a boarding school in New Haven, Connecticut, 1822–1823, and married Edward Dickinson, 6 May 1828. Domestic by nature, she seldom left home except for brief visits to relatives in Monson or Boston. On 15 June 1875 she suffered a paralytic stroke, and until her death, 14 November 1882, the care of the helpless invalid was largely assumed by Emily.

DICKINSON, Gilbert (1875–1883), ED's nephew, was the youngest of the three children of Austin and Susan Dickinson. Though named Thomas Gilbert, he was always called Gilbert or "Gib." His sudden and unexpected death from typhoid fever, 5 October 1883, was a blow from which neither his father nor his Aunt Emily fully recovered.

*DICKINSON, Lavinia Norcross (1833–1899), ED's sister, attended Amherst Academy, and Wheaton Female Seminary in Ipswich. Though she visited friends and relatives more frequently than her mother or sister, she remained for the most part at home. After their mother's paralytic stroke, the sisters assumed the burden of caring for the invalid. With the aid of a family retainer, the sisters continued to live at the homestead after their mother's death. The last twelve years of her life she lived alone. It was through her insistent endeavor that the first volume (1890) of ED's poems was published.

DICKINSON, Lucretia Gunn. *See* Asa Bullard.

DICKINSON, Martha (1866–1943), ED's niece, was the only daughter of Austin and Susan Dickinson. In 1903 she married Alexander E. Bianchi. Her editing of ED's poems began in 1914, with publication of *The Single Hound*.

DICKINSON, Mary. *See* Mark Haskell Newman.

DICKINSON, Samuel Fowler (1775–1838), ED's grandfather, was born in Amherst. Upon graduation from Dartmouth College (1795) he studied law and practiced for many years in Amherst. In 1802 he married Lucretia Gunn (1775–1840) of Montague. Edward Dickinson was the eldest of their nine children. The Squire was instrumental in the founding of Amherst Academy (1814) and Amherst College (1821). He frequently served as representative of the General Court of Massachusetts from 1803 to 1827, and was a member of the state senate in 1828. His support of Amherst College and the cause of education generally brought him acute financial trouble. The homestead he had built in 1813 he was forced to sell twenty years later. He then moved to Cincinnati, and later to

Hudson, Ohio, where he continued to further educational causes, and where he died, 22 April 1838.

*DICKINSON, Susan Gilbert (1830–1913), was the youngest daughter of Thomas and Harriet Arms Gilbert. He was a tavern proprietor severally in Amherst, Deerfield (where Susan was born), and Greenfield. Her mother died in 1837, and she was orphaned by the death of her father in 1841. Reared by an aunt in Geneva, New York, she attended Utica Female Academy. Her older sister Harriet had married William Cutler of Amherst and with them (*q.v.*) she came to live about 1850. ED thus came to know her, and during the decade no other friendship came to mean so much to ED. Susan taught school in Baltimore in 1851–1852. She became engaged to ED's brother Austin in November 1853. They were married 1 July 1856, and moved into a house which his father built for them next to the homestead. Emily and Susan thus remained permanently associated.

DICKINSON, (Thomas) Gilbert. *See* Gilbert Dickinson.

DICKINSON, William (1804–1887), ED's uncle, was the second child of S. F. Dickinson, and therefore nearest Edward Dickinson in age. Born in Amherst, he attended Amherst Academy but did not go to college. Instead, he served a ten-year apprenticeship in paper factories, then settled in 1829 in Worcester where he remained, becoming one of the most prominent and successful businessmen in the city. He married Eliza Hawley of Andover in 1831. She died 31 July 1851, and on 23 October 1852 he married again: Mary Whittier, also of Andover. By his first marriage he was father of William Hawley Dickinson (*q.v.*); by his second, of two sons and one daughter. The brothers Edward and William, though temperamentally different, shared a mutual respect. There was no close bond between ED and her Worcester uncle.

*DICKINSON, William Austin (1829–1895), ED's brother, was in her early years especially close to her. After graduation from Amherst College (1850), he prepared for his profession in the Harvard Law School and his father's office, and was admitted to the bar in 1854. He married Susan Huntington Gilbert (Dickinson) (*q.v.*), 1 July 1856. He practiced law in Amherst throughout his life, succeeding his father as Treasurer of Amherst College in 1873. He was a prominent citizen of the town, especially active in church affairs and village improvements.

*DICKINSON, William Cowper (1827–1899), valedictorian of his Amherst College class (1848), was a tutor at Amherst (1851–1852) before his ordination in 1854. He was a brother of Harriet Austin Dickinson (*q.v.*), and son of the Reverend Baxter Dickinson (1795–1875), a clergyman who taught in several theological schools. The family was distantly related to

[338]

Edward Dickinson, having a common ancestor four generations back.

DICKINSON, William Hawley (1832–1883), ED's favorite "cousin Willie," was graduated from Brown University in 1852, and for many years practiced law in New York City. He died, 15 May 1883. No letters which ED wrote to him survive, though at the time of his death there must have been many. A letter from his widow in 1894, in response to a query from Mrs. Todd, revises her original estimate of "a hundred," but states that it was "a considerable number, all of which after my Husband's death I destroyed" (Millicent Todd Bingham, *Ancestors' Brocades,* New York, 1945, 263).

DUDLEY, John L. (1812–1894), a graduate of Amherst College (1844), married 16 June 1861, one of ED's close friends, Eliza M. Coleman, daughter of Lyman Coleman (*q.v.*). They settled in Middletown, Connecticut, where Dudley had been pastor of the Congregational Church since 1849. They remained there until 1868, when Dudley accepted a call to the Plymouth Congregational Church in Milwaukee, Wisconsin, where he served until 1875. Eliza died 3 June 1871. Dudley married, second, Marion Churchill of Lake Mills, Wisconsin, 23 October 1872.

Eliza's mother, Maria (Flynt) Coleman, was a first cousin of ED's mother. Her youngest brother William Flynt married Eudocia Carter Converse, whose diaries are a repository of much family data.

DWIGHT, Edward Strong (1820–1890), a graduate of Yale College (1838), was installed as pastor of the First Church in Amherst, 19 June 1854, where he served until 28 August 1860, the illness of his wife Lucy Waterman Dwight compelling his departure from Amherst. She died 11 September 1861. They had two children: Annie Waterman Dwight (b. 4 April 1851) and Edward Huntington Dwight (b. 13 July 1856). Dwight served as a trustee of Amherst College from 1855 until his death.

EASTMAN, Charlotte Sewall, was the wife of Benjamin C. Eastman, a Congressman from Wisconsin during the term of office of Edward Dickinson, in 1853–1855. Mrs. Eastman must have met the Dickinson girls at the time, or soon after, for the friendship with the Dickinson family was shortly well established. After the death of her husband in 1856 she lived in Boston. She visited the Dickinsons, and her name together with theirs is on the register at Mount Holyoke, 20 August 1859. A presentation copy of *Jane Eyre* survives, inscribed: "Emily with the love of Mrs. Eastman. Sept. 20th 1865." In 1872 she wrote from Venice urging the girls to join her in Europe. No letters from ED to Mrs. Eastman are known to exist.

EDWARDS, Henry Luther (1822–1903), was graduated from Amherst College in 1847. He served as tutor in the college, 1849–1852, and after theological studies was ordained in 1857.

*EMERSON, Forrest F., served briefly as pastor of the First Church at Amherst from 12 June 1879 until 21 February 1883. Some eight notes which ED wrote him and his wife are known, but they are brief and suggest that the acquaintance was slight.

EMERSON, John Milton (1826–1869) was graduated from Amherst College as valedictorian in the class of 1849, and later served as tutor (1851–1853). He studied law in the office of Edward Dickinson and practiced briefly at Amherst (1854–1856). From 1856 until his death he practiced law in New York City.

*EMERSON, (Benjamin) Kendall, born in Amherst, was graduated from Amherst College (1897), studied medicine and became an orthopedic surgeon, in active practice until 1928, and as consultant subsequently. ED knew him as a youthful friend of her nephew Gilbert Dickinson, and wrote him Christmas notes thrice annually after Gilbert's death in 1883.

*EMMONS, Henry Vaughan (1832–1912), a graduate of Amherst College (1854) and of Bangor Theological Seminary (1859), was ordained as an evangelist in 1860, and occupied pulpits in various New England churches from 1865 until 1902. His friendship with ED's cousin, John Graves (q.v.), during their undergraduate days at Amherst, brought him often to the Dickinson home, and extended to a like friendship with ED, cordial during his undergraduate years, though it lapsed after his departure from Amherst.

ESTY, William Cole (1838–1916), a graduate of Amherst College (1860), was a professor of mathematics and astronomy there from 1865 until 1905. In 1867 he married Martha A. Cushing, a sister of Mrs. Edward Tuckerman (q.v.).

*FARLEY, Abbie C. (1846–1932), was a niece of Judge Otis P. Lord (q.v.). The daughter of Mrs. Lord's sister, after the death of Mrs. Lord in 1877 she and her mother kept home for the Judge until his death in 1884. She later married William C. West. She was a close friend of Susan Dickinson, and strongly opposed the attachment of Judge Lord and Emily Dickinson. She was the chief beneficiary of the Judge's will.

FISKE, Rebecca W., was a daughter of Deacon David Fiske of Shelburne. She was graduated from Mount Holyoke in 1846, and taught there for three years, until her marriage (1849) to the Reverend Burdett Hart. Samuel Fiske (AC 1848) was her brother.

FISKE, Samuel (1827–1864), was graduated from Amherst College (1848) and taught there for three years (1852–1855). He then studied for the ministry and was later ordained.

*FORD, Emily Ellsworth Fowler (1826–1893), was the daughter of William Chauncey Fowler, professor of Rhetoric and Oratory, and English

Literature at Amherst College (1838–1843), and a granddaughter of Noah Webster. She attended Amherst Academy with ED in the early forties. She left Amherst, 16 December 1853, when she married Gordon Lester Ford, a promising lawyer and (later) successful business executive. They made their home in Brooklyn, New York. Herself an author of poems, stories, and essays, she was the mother of two well-known writers, Paul Leicester and Worthington Chauncey Ford.

*FRENCH, Daniel Chester (1850–1931), American sculptor, was the son of Henry Flagg French, who served briefly as first president (1864–1866) of Massachusetts Agricultural College. ED had known him briefly as a boy during the few years his family lived in Amherst.

GILBERT, Harriet Murray. *See* Harriet Gilbert Cutler.

GILBERT, Martha Isabella. *See* Martha Gilbert Smith.

GILBERT, Susan Huntington. *See* Susan Gilbert Dickinson.

GILBERT, Thomas Dwight (1815–1894), eldest of the Gilbert children (see above), was a prosperous lumber dealer in Grand Rapids, Michigan. Before Susan's marriage he contributed liberally to her support, as well as to that of his other sisters, orphaned by the death of their father in 1841 (*see* Susan Gilbert Dickinson). Next to him in age was a brother, Francis Backus Gilbert (1818–1885). The association of the brothers and sisters was close, and remained so throughout their lives.

*GLADDEN, Washington (1836–1918), a graduate of Williams College (1859), was a Congregational clergyman widely known for his lectures and articles popularizing the results of biblical criticism and modern theological views. He was editor of *The Independent* from 1871 to 1875, in which year he resigned his editorship to become pastor of a church in Springfield, where he was residing when ED wrote him in 1882. Shortly thereafter he removed to Columbus, Ohio.

*GOULD, George Henry (1827–1899), who graduated from Amherst College (1850), was a classmate and close friend of Austin Dickinson. After occupying various pulpits, he settled at Worcester in 1872. A "cherished batch" of letters he received from ED was never found (*AB* 254).

*GRAVES, John Long (1831–1915), of Sunderland, was graduated from Amherst College (1855), and ordained in the Congregational ministry in 1860. A few years later he resigned from his calling to go into business, residing in Boston. A cousin of ED, he was always welcome in the Dickinson home during his undergraduate years, as a family member, and this cordiality never abated, although no exchange of letters is known after 1856.

GRIDLEY, Jane L. (b. 1829), was the daughter of Dr. Timothy Gridley. On 17 September 1849 she married Dr. George S. Woodman.

*HALE, Edward Everett (1822–1909), well-known Unitarian clergyman and writer, was pastor of the Church of the Unity in Worcester when ED wrote to him in January 1854 (see letter no. 153).

HASKELL, Abby Ann (1833–1851), was a schoolmate and friend of ED and Jane Humphrey (*q.v.*). She died 19 April 1851, at the age of nineteen.

HAVEN, Joseph (1816–1874), a graduate of Amherst College (1835), became professor of philosophy at Amherst (1851–1858), and of systematic theology at the Chicago Theological Seminary (1858–1870). ED is known to have written his wife, *Mary Emerson Haven, three letters.

*HIGGINSON, Thomas Wentworth (1823–1911), youngest of the ten children of Stephen and Louisa Storrow Higginson, was graduated from Harvard College in 1841. After taking his degree from Harvard Divinity School (1847), he married his cousin, Mary Elizabeth Channing. He became pastor of the First Religious Society (Unitarian) at Newburyport (1847–1852) and of the Free Church at Worcester (1852–1861). Resigning from the ministry, he served in the Union Army (1862–1864) as colonel of the First South Carolina Volunteers. He lived at Newport, Rhode Island (1864–1877), until the death of his wife. In February 1879 he married, second, Mary Potter Thacher. Throughout his life he was a crusader for liberal causes and a prolific writer. The correspondence that ED initiated with him in April 1862 is of first importance in the history of American literature.

*HILLS, Henry F. (1833–1896), entered his father's business in Amherst in 1852, as a manufacturer of straw hats: L. M. Hills & Sons. Leonard Hills, father of Henry, died 8 February 1872. Mr. and Mrs. Henry Hills were neighbors of the Dickinsons.

HITCHCOCK, Catharine (1826–1895), was the eldest daughter of President Edward Hitchcock. Kate Hitchcock married Henry M. Storrs. Her younger sister Jane married Granville B. Putnam (AC 1861) on 31 August 1864.

HITCHCOCK, Edward (1793–1864), after graduation from Yale College (1818), became the first professor of chemistry at Amherst College in 1825. He served as president of the college from 14 April 1845 until 22 November 1854. In 1821 he married Orra White of Amherst, who died on 26 May 1863. As administrator he served the college ably during its most crucial years. As a geologist he won an international reputation.

*HOLLAND, Josiah Gilbert (1819–1881), married Elizabeth Luna Chapin (1823–1896) in 1845. In 1849 he began his long association with Samuel Bowles on the *Springfield Daily Republican*. In 1870 he founded *Scribner's Monthly*, and remained its editor until his death. His many books enjoyed considerable popularity in their day. He was known by the title "Doctor" throughout his life, for as a young man he had qualified as a physician, though he soon abandoned the practice of medicine. Dr. and Mrs. Holland were among ED's closest friends, and Mrs. Holland, with whom she exchanged frequent letters all her life, she often designated "Sister." For ED no other friendship was more enduring. Both were vivacious, candid, and perceptive.

HOLT, Jacob, of Amherst, attended Amherst Academy and studied dentistry in Boston. He returned to Amherst in 1845, and died of consumption 12 May 1848. While a student at the Academy, he published some verses in the *Northampton Courier*: the issues of 29 August 1843, and 25 June 1844. There seems to have been some kinship between ED and him, presumably engendered by their commonly shared interest in poetry.

HOWE, Sabra, a classmate of ED's at Amherst Academy, was the daughter of A. P. Howe, landlord of the Amherst House.

HOWLAND, William (1822–1880) was graduated from Amherst College (1846), where he served briefly as a tutor (1849–1851). He attended Yale Law School and studied law in the office of Edward Dickinson. From 1852 until his death he practiced law in Lynn. He married in 1860.

HUMPHREY, Helen (1822–1866), a sister of Jane Humphrey (*q.v.*), was one of ED's teachers at Amherst Academy (1841–1842). She married Albert H. Palmer, a lawyer in Racine, Wisconsin, on 27 August 1845. He died 12 September 1846. She married (second) William H. Stoddard of Northampton, 1 January 1852.

HUMPHREY, Heman, a graduate of Yale College (1805), was president of Amherst College from 1823 until 1845.

*HUMPHREY, Jane T. (1829–1908), was the daughter of Dr. Levi W. Humphrey of Southwick. After graduation from Mount Holyoke Female Seminary (1848) she became preceptress of Amherst Academy (1848–1849). She gave up teaching in 1858, and on 26 August of that year married William H. Wilkinson. They resided in Southwick. ED's correspondence with her during the early 1850's was singularly warmhearted, but it was abruptly terminated by Jane's marriage.

*JACKSON, Helen Fiske Hunt (1830–1885), was the daughter of Nathan Welby Fiske, professor of moral philosophy and metaphysics in Amherst College, and Deborah Vinal Fiske. Her mother died in 1844, and she was orphaned by the death of her father three years later. She married Edward Bissell Hunt, an army engineer, in 1852. Their first son lived eleven months. In 1863 Major Hunt was accidentally killed in line of duty. Another son Warren ("Rennie") died, aged nine, in 1865. Mrs. Hunt turned to writing and lived for a time in Newport, Rhode Island, where she became acquainted with T. W. Higginson. Though she had attended school briefly with ED in their childhood, she came to know her only in the seventies, by which time "H. H." was acclaimed a leading poet and story writer. In 1875 she married William S. Jackson, and made her home at Colorado Springs. She had seen a few of ED's poems, and was the only contemporary who believed that ED was an authentic poet. Shortly before Helen Jackson's death the acquaintanceship ripened into a friendship of special importance to ED, who probably was deeply touched that Mrs. Jackson had asked to be her literary executor.

JAMESON, John, was the postmaster at Amherst from 20 December 1876 to 30 March 1885. The Jamesons were neighbors of the Dickinsons, and ED knew and wrote occasional notes to two of their children, Annie and Arthur. The eldest son, John Franklin Jameson (AC 1879), became a well-known historian.

*JENKINS, Jonathan Leavitt (1830–1913), was graduated from Yale College (1851) and Yale Divinity School. In 1862 he married Sarah Maria Eaton. Installed as pastor of the First Church at Amherst in December 1866, he remained until 1877, when he accepted a call to Pittsfield. The Jenkinses were especially admired and loved by all members of the Dickinson family, and their removal to Pittsfield did not break the ties. Together with the incumbent pastor of the Amherst church in 1886, the Reverend Mr. George S. Dickerman, Mr. Jenkins officiated at the funeral of Emily Dickinson.

JEWETT, George Baker (1818–1886), a graduate of Amherst College (1840), was a professor of Latin and modern languages there from 1850 until 1854. He was ordained in 1855.

JONES, Thomas (1787–1853), was a manufacturer of cotton and woolen goods in Amherst.

KARR, William S. (1829–1888), was the commencement orator for his Amherst College class of 1851.

KELLOGG, Emeline (1828–1900), was the daughter of James Kellogg, a prominent Amherst manufacturer. Until 1855 the Kelloggs were next door neighbors of the Dickinsons. On 9 October 1855 Emeline married Henry C. Nash (q.v.).

*KIMBALL, Benjamin, was the son of Otis Kimball, of Ipswich, and Lucy Sarah Farley Kimball. At the age of thirty, in 1880, he married Helen Manning Simmons. Throughout his life he practiced law in Boston. He was known to ED because he was a cousin of Judge Otis P. Lord (q.v.), and, after Lord's death, Kimball was entrusted with settling the Judge's estate.

KINGMAN, Martha (1832–1851) and Ellen Mary (1838–1851), school friends of ED, were daughters of Cyrus Kingman (1794–1854), who moved from Pelham to Amherst in April 1850. He was paralyzed 9 November 1852. His eldest and only surviving daughter, Jane Juliette, died 26 May 1854. Martha and Ellen died within the space of two weeks. The father died 29 December 1854.

LINNELL, Tempe S. (1831–1881), a school friend of ED and Jane Humphrey (q.v.), came to Amherst in 1839 with her two brothers and widowed mother, who wished to provide an education for her sons. Tempe never married, and spent her life caring for her mother who died, aged 85, on 11 February 1879. She ran a popular boarding house for students, and died, aged 50, on 6 November 1881.

*LOOMIS, Eben Jenks (1828–1912), and his wife Mary Wilder Loomis were the parents of Mabel Loomis Todd. He was an astronomer, for fifty years assistant in Nautical Almanac (senior assistant 1859–1900) in the Naval Observatory in Washington. The Loomises visited their daughter in Amherst in the autumn of 1884.

*LORD, Otis Phillips (1812–1884), the son of the Hon. Nathaniel and Eunice Kimball Lord, was born at Ipswich. Graduated from Amherst College in 1832, he studied law and was admitted to the bar in 1835, first in Ipswich, then in 1844 in Salem, where thereafter he resided. In 1843 he married Elizabeth Wise, daughter of Captain Joseph Farley of Ipswich. She died 10 December 1877. During the forties and fifties, Lord served in the Massachusetts legislature and State Senate. With the establishment of the Superior Court in 1859 he was appointed an associate justice, in which capacity he served until his elevation to the state Supreme Court in 1875. Ill health compelled his resignation from the bench in 1882. He died on 13 March 1884. Judge Lord was one of Edward Dickinson's closest friends, and the Lords were frequent guests in the Dickinson home. He continued to visit, for a week or so at a time, during the early eighties, staying with his nieces at the Amherst House. The surviving letters and drafts of letters which ED wrote him about this time indicate that she was very much in love with the Judge. The attachment seems to have been mutual.

MACK, David, Jr. (1778–1854), the son of Colonel David Mack of Middlefield, served as a major in the War of 1812, and was promoted to brigadier general of militia in 1821. Known generally as Deacon Mack, he was a successful Amherst businessman, and a trustee of Amherst College (1836–1854). He purchased the Dickinson homestead on 22 May 1833, and lived there until his death on 6 September 1854. His first wife, Independence Pease Mack, died in 1809. They had a son, David (1804–1878), who was graduated from Yale College in Edward Dickinson's class of 1823, and a daughter Julia (born in 1806). He married, second, Mary Ely (1787–1842) in 1812. They had one surviving son when they moved to Amherst, Samuel Ely Mack, born in 1815. Mary Ely Mack died 15 December 1842, and Deacon Mack married, third, on 16 May 1844, Harriet Parsons Washburn (1793–1874), daughter of the Reverend Dr. David Parsons of the First Church in Amherst, and widow of Royal W. Washburn, who had been pastor of the same church (1826–1833).

Edward Dickinson and his family occupied the east part of the homestead until April 1840, when they moved to a frame house on North Pleasant Street. This was ED's home until 1855, at which time Edward Dickinson purchased the homestead on Main Street from Samuel E. Mack and his wife Rebecca Robins Mack, of Cincinnati, and moved his family back to it.

MACK, Mrs., who worked for the Dickinsons in the 1850's as a laundress, was sometimes referred to as "Emerald" Mack to distinguish her from members of the family of Deacon David Mack.

MAHER, Margaret (Maggie), who had emigrated from Ireland, began domestic service with the Dickinsons in March 1869 and worked for them until Lavinia's death in 1899, becoming a part of the family life.

MARCH, Francis A. (1825–1911), a graduate of Amherst College (1845), was a tutor at the college, 1847–1849. He became a distinguished Shakespearean scholar.

MATTHEWS, Richard (Dick), the Dickinson stableman, who had emigrated from England, lived with his wife Ann in back of the Dickinson place on North Pleasant Street; of their sixteen children, nine died young.

MERRILL, Calvin, married on 9 September 1851 Fanny D. Benjamin. It was the third marriage for both. He was fifty-four years old, and she forty-six.

MERRILL, Harriet, a daughter of Calvin Merrill, was a classmate of ED at Amherst Academy. She taught school first at Amherst Academy and later at Pittsfield.

*MONTAGUE, George (1804–1893), an older brother of Harriet and Zebina Montague was a first cousin of ED's grandfather Samuel Fowler Dickinson, and a son of Luke and Irene Dickinson Montague. Educated at Amherst Academy, he was in business for thirty years in various cities in the South and West. He returned to Amherst in 1866, and served as treasurer of Massachusetts Agricultural College until his retirement in 1884. He married, first, in Columbus, Georgia, Mary A. Parsons; they had two sons and a daughter, the latter being the mother of Eugenia

[346]

Hall. Three years after the death of his wife Mary, in 1853, he married Sarah M. Seelye of New York. She was still living at the time of ED's death.

NASH, Henry Clark (1829–1900), a graduate of Amherst College (1851), succeeded his father as principal of Mount Pleasant Institute (1854–1877) in Amherst. On 9 October 1855 he married Emeline Kellogg (*q.v.*).

*NEWMAN, Clarissa (Clara) Badger (1844–1920), sister of Anna (*q.v.*), married, 14 October 1869, Sidney Turner of Norwich, Connecticut. Both Anna and Clara, together with their older sisters Catherine and Sara became wards of their uncle Edward Dickinson, in the charge of their aunt Hannah Haskell Newman (Mrs. Samuel A. Fay) when they were orphaned by the death of their parents in 1852. In October 1858 Clara and Anna (aged respectively 14 and 12) lived with Austin and Susan Dickinson until Clara's marriage in 1869.

NEWMAN, Mark Haskell (1806–1852), a graduate of Bowdoin College (1825), became a publisher of school books in New York City. He married, on 2 October 1828, Mary Dickinson (1809–1852), a daughter of Samuel Fowler Dickinson, and aunt of ED. Of their five children who lived to maturity, the two that ED knew best are described above.

NEWTON, Benjamin Franklin (1821–1853), who did not attend college, studied law in the office of ED's father (1847–1849) and was admitted to the bar in 1850, at Worcester. He was appointed state's attorney for Worcester County in 1852. He married Sarah Warner Rugg on 4 June 1851. He died of consumption on 24 March 1853. His widow survived until 1899. There is every reason to believe that ED corresponded with him after he left Amherst; he had guided her early interest in literature, and his death was for her poignantly distressing. But none of the letters survive, nor could Mrs. Todd trace any even before Mrs. Newton's death.

*NILES, Thomas (1825–1894), was a Boston publisher. Starting his career with the firm of Ticknor, he later became editor of Roberts Brothers. The correspondence between Niles and ED began soon after the publication of *A Masque of Poets*, in 1878, in which her poem "Success" first appeared.

NIMS, Seth (1798–1877), was the postmaster at Amherst from 1845 until 1849, and again from 1853 until 1861.

NORCROSS, Emily Lavinia (1828–1852) was the daughter of Hiram Norcross (1800–1829), the eldest brother of ED's mother. After the early death of Hiram Norcross, his widow married Charles Stearns of Springfield, but died a few years later. Brought up in Monson, Emily Norcross attended Mount Holyoke Seminary where ED was her roommate during the one year that ED attended. She died, 2 July 1852, and an only brother, William Henry Norcross, died two years later.

*NORCROSS, Joel Warren (1821–1900), was the youngest brother of ED's mother. He married Lamira H. Jones of Chicago, 17 January 1854, after having established himself as a Boston importer, residing at 31 Milk Street. During the year that Austin Dickinson taught school in Boston (1851–1852) his family addressed all letters to him in care of Joel Norcross. Lamira Norcross died, 3 May 1862, and Joel married, second, Maggie P. Gunnison of Roxbury, 24 April 1866. There were two children by the first marriage, and one by the second.

NORCROSS, Loring (1808–1863), a dry goods commission merchant of Boston, married his cousin Lavinia Norcross (1812–1860), a favorite sister of ED's mother. He served as secretary of the Massachusetts Temperance Union and as member of the Boston School Board. She died 17 April 1860, aged 47. He died 17 January 1863, aged 55. Their eldest daughter, Lavinia, died 19 May 1842, aged four. For their other daughters, Louise and Frances, see below.

*NORCROSS, Louise (1842–1919) and Frances Lavinia (1847–1896), daughters of Loring and Lavinia Norcross (*q.v.*), were ED's "Little Cousins." The girls were orphaned when Louise was twenty-one. As children, Loo and Fanny had always been welcome at the Dickinson home, and it was with them that ED stayed when her eye trouble compelled her to sojourn in Cambridge for several months in 1864 and 1865 to be under the care of a Boston physician. The sisters lived together until Fanny's death, occupied with what genteel employment occasion offered. ED constantly exchanged letters with them, and on a domestic level had an especial affection for them. All the letters, destroyed after Fanny's death, derive from transcripts supplied to Mrs. Todd before 1894.

The spelling of Louise's name is given as *Louisa* in the manuscript Norcross genealogy (New England Historical and Genealogical Society Library) compiled by Joel Warren Norcross of Lynn. But in the Concord death records and in the records of the Old Ladies' Home at Concord, where she died, it is given as *Louise*. A letter from her, among family papers in Monson, is signed *Louise*.

NORCROSS, Sarah Vaill (1788–1854), was the second wife of Joel Norcross of Monson, ED's grandfather. They were married in 1831. He died 5 May 1846; she died 25 April 1854.

O'BRIEN (O'Bryan), Margaret, worked as a domestic for the Dickinsons, probably after their return to the old family home in 1855. She remained with the family until her marriage to Stephen Lawler in 1865.

PALMER, Helen. *See* Helen Humphrey (Mrs. Albert Palmer).

PHELPS, Susan Davis, was engaged to Henry Vaughan Emmons. The engagement was broken in May 1860. She died, 2 December 1865.

READ, Eliza M. Kellogg, married Hanson L. Read on 25 November 1851. ED attended the wedding. He was engaged in business in Amherst and served there as superintendent of schools, 1868–1871 and 1885–1887. On 26 December 1873 the two Read sons, both in their teens, were drowned while skating on Adams Pond.

*ROOT, Abiah Palmer (b. 1830), was the daughter of Deacon Harvey Root of West Springfield (Feeding Hills). She attended Amherst Academy for one year (1843–1844), and then transferred to Miss Margaret Campbell's school in Springfield. The early friendship with ED was warm-hearted, but it seems to have been dropped after Abiah's marriage to the Reverend Samuel W. Strong of Westfield in 1854.

ROOT, Henry Dwight (1832–1855), of Greenfield, was graduated from Amherst College (1852) and attended Harvard Law School. He was a friend of Austin's. He died, 3 September 1855.

*SANBORN, Franklin Benjamin (1831–1917), a graduate of Harvard College (1855), lived in Concord where, after a vigorous participation in the abolition movement, he became editor (1863–1867) of the *Boston Commonwealth*. He served as resident editor (1868–1872) of the *Springfield Republican*, of which he had been corresponding editor since 1856. In 1873 he returned to Concord, acting as special correspondent. He was intimately acquainted with the Concord writers, and in later years devoted his time to editing their literary remains.

SANFORD, John Elliot (1830–1907), was graduated as valedictorian of his Amherst College class (1851), and served as tutor for one year (1853–1854). After studying law in the office of Edward Dickinson he settled in the practice of his profession at Taunton. He was a trustee of Amherst College from 1874 until his death, in later years as president of the board. During his senior year in college he was a frequent caller in the Dickinson home.

SCANNELL, Dennis, whose family (called also Scanlon, Scanlan, Scanlin, and Scanelly) served the Dickinsons for many years, worked for them in the 1870's and was a pallbearer at ED's funeral. His son Jerry, a boy of fourteen, was the runaway mentioned in letter no. 685. The coachman Tim, mentioned in letter no. 337, may also have been a member of the family.

SEELYE, Julius Hawley (1824–1895), a graduate of Amherst College (1849), was ordained in 1853. A professor in the college (1858–1890), he served as President from 1876 until 1890. He was pastor of the College Church, 1877–1892.

SMITH, Henry Boynton (1815–1877), was professor of moral philosophy and metaphysics from 1847 until 1850, when he joined the faculty of Union Theological Seminary, where he remained until his death.

*SMITH, Martha Gilbert (1829–1895), was an older sister of Susan Gilbert Dickinson (q.v.). On 20 October 1857 she married John Williams Smith (1822–1878), a dry goods merchant of Geneva, New York. An infant son, Frank, died, 14 June 1861, and a daughter, Susan, died, 3 November 1865, aged two. Their daughter Elizabeth Throop Smith was born, 30 June 1868.

STEARNS, William Augustus (1805–1876), was a graduate of Harvard College (1827) and Andover Theological Seminary (1831). He was pastor of a church in Cambridgeport, Vermont, when he accepted the presidency of Amherst College in 1854, in which position he served until his death.

*STEARNS, William F., the son of William A. Stearns (q.v.), entered business in India, where he died. His widow returned to Amherst where she kept a girls' school. A daughter Ethel died at Amherst, 15 October 1882.

STEBBINS, Milan C. (1828–1889), was salutatorian of the Amherst College class of 1851. On 24 November 1853 he married Sophia Pitts. He was successively a minister, teacher, and merchant.

STODDARD, Mrs. William H. *See* Helen Humphrey.

STRONG, Mrs. Samuel W. *See* Abiah Root.

SULLIVAN, Stephen, was the Dickinson stableman in later years. He was married in 1887, at the age of twenty-three.

*SWEETSER, Catharine Dickinson (1814–1895), ED's favorite aunt Katie, was a sister of Edward Dickinson. She married Joseph A. Sweetser of New York in 1835. He was a brother of Luke Sweetser (q.v.). On 21 January 1874 he left their apartment at the Fifth Avenue Hotel to attend a committee meeting at the Madison Square Presbyterian Church, across the street. He was never subsequently heard from or traced.

SWEETSER, Charles Humphreys (1841–1871), was an orphaned nephew of Luke Sweetser. He came to live with the Luke Sweetsers in 1847, and was graduated from Amherst College in 1862. After an apprenticeship on the *Springfield Daily Republican* in 1863, he established with his cousin Henry E. Sweetser a weekly paper, *The Round Table*, in New York. He married his cousin Mary Newman Sweetser, daughter of Catharine and Joseph Sweetser (qq.v.), and died of consumption, 1 January 1871.

*SWEETSER, John Howard (1835–1904), was the only child of Luke Sweetser (q.v.). He left Amherst College in his junior year to go into business with his uncle Joseph in New York. He received his Bachelor of Arts degree in 1871. On 2 February 1860 he married Cornelia Peck, the "Mrs.

Nellie" to whom ED often wrote in her later years. Their three children were Alice Munsell Sweetser (Mrs. Henry C. Hall), Howard Sweetser, and "Nettie."

SWEETSER, Luke (1800–1882), born in Athol, came to Amherst in 1824 and became a leading merchant of the town. In 1833 he married Abby Tyler Munsell. In 1834 Abby Wood (q.v.), his three-year-old niece, came to live with them. The Sweetsers had one son, John Howard Sweetser (q.v.). He died on 27 July 1882, and his wife on 19 October of the same year. The Sweetsers were lifelong neighbors of the Dickinsons.

TAYLOR, Jeremiah (1817–1898), a graduate of Amherst College (1843), was principal of Amherst Academy, 1843–1844. He was subsequently ordained and occupied various New England pulpits.

THOMPSON, John H. (1827–1891), a classmate of Austin Dickinson (AC 1850) and an especially close undergraduate friend, settled as a lawyer in Chicago.

THURSTON, Benjamin Easton (1827–1870), after graduation from Amherst College (1852) went into business.

*TODD, Mabel Loomis (1856–1932), daughter of Eben Jenks Loomis (q.v.), married David Peck Todd (1855–1939), in 1879. A graduate of Amherst College (1875), he returned there as Director of the Observatory (1881–1920) and as professor of Astronomy and Navigation (1892–1920). The account of Mrs. Todd's part in editing the poems and letters of ED is set forth at length in Millicent Todd Bingham's *Ancestors' Brocades* (1945).

TRACY, Sarah, was one of the "circle of five" who made up ED's intimate Amherst Academy friends. Very little is known about her. She was a boarder, and the last reference to her is of a visit she made in Amherst in August 1851. In the Academy group, ED was "Socrates," Abiah Root was "Plato," and Sarah was "Virgil."

*TUCKERMAN, Edward (1817–1886), was professor of Botany in Amherst College from 1858 until his death, and an international authority on lichens. It was for him that Tuckerman's Ravine in the White Mountains was named. In 1854 he married Sarah Eliza Sigourney Cushing, who survived him by twenty-nine years. They had no children, but Mrs. Tuckerman was always held in loving memory by four orphaned nephews whom she reared, children of her sister, Mrs. William Cole Esty. The warm attachment ED felt for her is attested by the quality of the many notes she wrote her.

*TURNER, Mrs. Sidney. *See* Clara Newman.

TYLER, William Seymour (1810–1897), a graduate of Amherst College (1830), was a professor of Latin and Greek there throughout his life.

VAILL, Joseph (1790–1869), after his graduation from Yale College (1811) was ordained and continued in the ministry all his life. He was a trustee of Amherst College from the date of its founding until his death. After 1854 he lived at Palmer.

VANDERBILT, Gertrude Lefferts (ca. 1824–1896), was the wife of Judge John Vanderbilt of King's County, New York. She was a close friend of Catherine Anthon (q.v.). It was through Kate Anthon that Mrs. Vanderbilt knew the Dickinsons.

WADSWORTH, Charles (1814–1882), after graduation from Union College (1837), was ordained and became one of the leading pulpit orators of his day. He was pastor of the Arch Street Presbyterian Church in Philadelphia from 1850 until April 1862, when he went to Calvary Church in San Francisco. He returned to Philadelphia in 1870, where he remained until his death. ED probably met him in Philadelphia in 1855. She corresponded with him, and he is known to have called upon her twice, once in 1860, and again in the summer of 1880. She seems to have turned to him for spiritual consolation, but none of her letters to him survive.

WARD, Pat, one of the "faithful workmen" who helped carry the bier at ED's funeral, is identified with "little Pat," who came in the spring of 1854 to take care of the Dickinson's horse, and whose continuing connection with the family is recorded in ED's later correspondence.

WHITMAN, Mary C., was graduated from Mount Holyoke in 1839. She served as assistant principal in 1842, and after Miss Lyon's death acted for one year as principal of the institution. In 1851 she married Morton Eddy.

*WHITNEY, Maria (1830–1910), was the daughter of Josiah Dwight Whitney, a Northampton banker. Through the Dwights she was related to Mrs. Samuel Bowles. She spent much time with members of the Bowles family in their home and on their travels, especially during the sixties and seventies. Like the Bowleses she saw a good deal of Austin and Susan Dickinson, and thus knew ED. From 1875 until 1880 she was Teacher of French and German in Smith College. She was a sister of the Yale philologist William Dwight Whitney; of the Harvard geologist Josiah Dwight Whitney; and of James Lyman Whitney, director of the Boston Public Library.

WILKINSON, Mrs. W. H. See Jane Humphrey.

WILLISTON, Lyman Richards (1830–1897), the adopted son of Samuel Williston (q.v.), was graduated from Amherst College (1850) and served there for a year as professor of Latin and modern languages (1856–1857).

WILLISTON, Samuel (1795–1874), of Easthampton, founded Williston Seminary in 1841. A well-to-do manufacturer, he was a trustee of Amherst College, 1841–1874, and one of its benefactors.

WOOD, Abby Maria (1830–1915), was a daughter of Joel and Abby Moore Sweetser Wood of Westminster. After her father's death in 1833 and the marriage of her uncle Luke Sweetser (*q.v.*) in December 1833, Abby lived with the Sweetsers. On 23 November 1855 she married the Reverend Daniel Bliss (*q.v.*). She was a girlhood friend of ED.

WOODMAN, George S. (1823–1906), a graduate of Amherst College (1846), married Jane Gridley (*q.v.*) on 17 September 1849. He practiced medicine in Amherst from 1851 until 1858.

INDEX

Adams, Elizabeth C. (Mrs. Albert Clark), 7, 9, 333
Adams, John Sydney, 63, 67, 333
"Alabaster" poem, 161–163
Alcott, Amos Bronson, 208
Allen, Charles, 150
American Association for the Advancement of Science, 152
Ames, Mrs. Silas, born Mary Humphrey, 5–6
Amherst Academy, 2, 5–6, 7, 109, 117
Amherst and Belchertown Railroad, 75, 76
Amherst College, 119, 192
Amherst Collegiate Magazine, 121
Amherst Record, 239, 260, 263, 271
Anthon, Mrs. John H., born Catherine Scott (Turner), 333; see letters no. 208, 209, 222
Arabian Nights, 22
Archer, Robert, 62
Atlantic Almanac (1870), 201
Atlantic Monthly, 172, 173, 182, 196, 211, 252, 272

Bacon, Francis, 274
Baker, Alfred, 6–7
Baker, Osmyn, 6–7
Banfield, Mrs. Everett Colby, 208–209
Banks, Miss (seamstress), 92
Barbauld, Anna Letitia, "How blest the righteous when he dies," 110
Baxter, Richard, 101
Beecher, Henry Ward, 57, 59
Belden, Pomeroy, 23–24, 333
Bell and Everett Party, 158
Benjamin, Theodore H., 93
Bentham, Jeremy, 97, 99
Beston, John, 102–103
Bianchi, Mrs. Alexander. *See* Dickinson, Martha
Bible (Old Testament): *I Kings*, 196;

Psalms, 267; *Ecclesiastes*, 9, 11; *Isaiah*, 247; *Lamentations*, 301–302
Bible (New Testament): *Matthew*, 58–59, 107–108, 224, 238–239, 270–271; *Luke*, 107–108, 136–137; *John*, 56, 59; *I Corinthians*, 56, 59, 142–143, 217, 218, 326–327; *II Corinthians*, 288–289; *I Timothy*, 302–303; *II Timothy*, 261–262, 276, 313–314; *Hebrews*, 215–216, 290; *Revelation*, 136–137, 172, 233–234, 242, 252–253, 288–289
Bigelow, Dr. O. F., 330
Bismarck, Otto von, 212
Blind, Mathilde, *Life of George Eliot*, 286–287
Bliss, Daniel, 333
Bliss, Mrs. Daniel, born Abby Maria Wood, 9, 16–17, 19, 22–23, 39, 72, 83, 85, 92, 126, 132, 353
Boltwood, Lucius, 47, 333–334
Boltwood, Mrs. Lucius, 333–334; see letter no. 629
Boston, ED's visits to, 7–11, 59–62, 184–186
Boston Sunday Globe, 240
Bowdoin, Elbridge Gridley, 48–49, 53, 60–62, 65, 93, 100, 334; see letter no. 41
Bowles, Charles, 154
Bowles, Mary D. (later Mrs. W. H. King), 144–145
Bowles, Samuel, 226, 233, 240–243, 248, 252, 262–263, 290, 308–309, 315, 334; see letters no. 189, 193, 205, 219, 223, 249, 250, 251, 277, 415, 438, 465, 466, 489, 515
Bowles, Mrs. Samuel, born Mary Schermerhorn, 144–145, 150, 248, 262, 292, 334; see letters no. 189, 196, 216, 532, 536, 724
Bowles, Samuel (the younger), 144–